W9-CMK-424

3 3015 00120 3206

The Annual Journal of the Costume Society of America

DRESS

R
391
D81c
2000
v27

Volume 27, 2000

– FOCUS ON HATS –

Editor:
Linda Welters
University of Rhode Island
Kingston, Rhode Island

Managing Editor:
Patricia Cunningham
Ohio State University
Columbus, Ohio

Associate Editors:
Linda Baumgarten
Patricia Campbell Warner

Editorial Assistant:
Kate Irvin

Reviewers for this issue:
Christina Bates
Linda Baumgarten
Catherine Cerny
Beverly Chico
Nancy Page Fernandez
Charlotte Jirousek
Mary Littrell
Kimberly Miller
Jo Anne Olian
Alexandra Palmer
Rachel Pannabecker
Jo Paoletti
Phyllis Tortora
Patricia Campbell Warner
Laurel Wilson
Geitel Winakor

Design:
UniGraphics
Bowling Green State University
Bowling Green, Ohio

Printer:
Post Printing
Minster, Ohio

ISSN 0361-2112

Front cover: *L'atelier de couture*, ca. 1785. Antoine Raspal. Collection Musée Réattu, Arles. Photograph courtesy of Musées d'Arles.

Contents

Sophie White

The Shape of French Costume Studies: Focus on the Eighteenth Century

Sophie White is an independent scholar. She received her Ph.D. in the history of dress from the Courtauld Institute of Art, working on French Colonial Louisiana.

In many respects, the field of eighteenth-century French costume studies encapsulates the divisions apparent in the scholarship on all periods of French dress history. Indeed, a number of methodologies have made their mark on the subject, whether they are steeped in art history, economic history or object-based connoisseurship, and this diversity emerges in the writings devoted to the eighteenth century as well. The range of approaches is as much a reflection of the current state of scholarship in Western dress history as it is a consequence of those aspects of dress that are unique to France. This latter feature has influenced some of the precise questions asked about the experience of dress in France. For instance, not only have scholars seen clothing as an incarnation of national values, but they also have begun to evaluate dress as an expression of local character, differing from region to region. While scholarship on eighteenth-century dress parallels that on other periods, this review essay focuses on the eighteenth century and makes the case that this area is one of the most dynamic and varied areas of scholarly research on French dress history.

At the international level, the work that propelled the eighteenth century to the forefront of French costume studies was Daniel Roche's ambitious account of the character of clothing consumption in eighteenth-century Paris. In terms of its value in providing a theoretical framework for the study of dress, Roche's *The Culture of Clothing: Dress and Fashion in the "Ancien Regime"* shares the stage with two influential but uneven works on dress in France, the historian Philippe Perrot's *Fashioning the Bourgeoisie: A History of Clothing in the Nineteenth Century* and the philosopher Gilles Lipovetsky's *The Empire of Fashion: Dressing Modern Democracy*.[1] Translated into English in 1994, Roche's *The Culture of Clothing* delivered one of the most complex visions of dress of any period and context and made the compelling argument that the study of dress should be a matter for mainstream historians rather than treated as a marginal discipline, a position upheld in Roche's newest book, *A History of Everyday Things*. *The Culture of Clothing* is built around Roche's analysis of the wardrobe contents of Parisians at two points in time, 1700 and 1789. For a book as rich and detailed as this one, a valuable advantage of the English translation over the French original lies in the inclusion of clothing terms in the index. Using a large sample of probate inventories, Roche charts the shifts in clothing practices over the period among the various social classes, noting the increase in wardrobe holdings and the "invention of underwear" among the most momentous (revolutionary, according to Roche) and lasting changes. Roche supports his research with selective evidence from a rich body of contemporary sources, though few visual sources are discussed, and references to surviving dress are non-existent. Though its core is based on Roche's own research, this book is a vast work of synthesis – one of its greatest strengths – which draws heavily on the findings from master's theses and doctoral dissertations undertaken under the direction of Roche himself at the Université de Paris and his colleagues elsewhere in France. Like Roche's analysis, those studies are grounded in the social sciences and primarily adopt a quantitative approach. The theses testify to the rich materials available for the study of French dress in the eighteenth century, but they remain for the most part unpublished and are hard to obtain. That this is the case points to a fundamental shortcoming of the field of French costume studies. Only recently has there been a surge in the number of

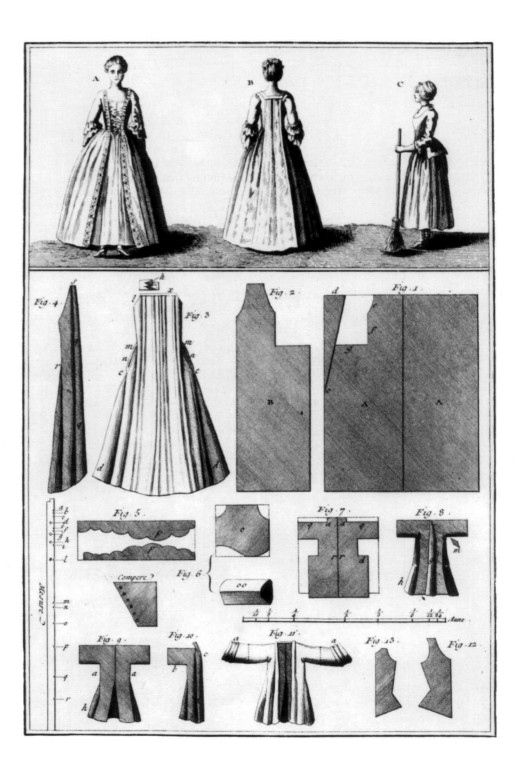

Figure 1. Anonymous, Couturiere, *1777. Engraving, France. Plate 117 in* Suite de recueil de planches, sur les sciences, les arts libéraux et les arts méchaniques avec leur explication. *Colonial Williamsburg Foundation, Williamsburg, Va.*

published scholarly secondary sources on the subject, and there remains no academic journal dedicated to the study of dress.

The interest in the rise of consumerism in pre-industrial France has proven to be a particularly fertile area of recent research. While lagging behind studies of Britain's more pronounced consumer revolution,[2] innovative work is being carried out by economic historians, textile historians and material culture specialists that directly addresses the impact of fashion on the French textile industry and attributes a wider societal role to the clothing and textile industries. The proceedings from two conferences provide a vital introduction to these recent developments in the field of French textile and clothing consumption. Jacques Bottin and Nicole Pellegrin edited a special issue of the journal *Revue du Nord* devoted to the proceedings from one conference: *Échanges et cultures textiles dans l'Europe pré-industrielle.* Robert Fox and Anthony Turner edited the proceedings from another conference, *Luxury Trades and Consumerism in Ancien Regime Paris: Studies in the History of the Skilled Workforce.*[3] The two books include essays in both French and English, with English-language summaries in the former volume. As indicated by their titles, neither book is dedicated *per se* to dress and textiles, nor to France alone. However, the bulk of the essays directly concern either the manufacture and marketing of new and used goods within France, or they address foreign consumption of key French textiles and apparel (Figure 1). What is clear from both volumes, and readily acknowledged by the editors, is that these are not exhaustive surveys, but rather compilations of work in progress in an area of research that has hitherto been downplayed by historians. Indeed, the very existence of a "consumer revolution" in France (as opposed to Britain for example) is a concept that has not always been acknowledged, and essays by Michael Sonenscher and Daniel Roche in the Fox-Turner volume touch on this question in different ways. Less questionable was the international reputation of French fashion and French goods in this period. Of particular note for historians of American dress are two essays, one by André Lespagnol and the other by Jean Tanguy, on the importance to colonial markets of two types of linens, *bretagnes* and *crées*. Both essays argue that the popularity of these textiles lay in the fact that they had become brand products, or *produits-phares* in the phrase coined by Bottin and Pellegrin to describe a generic class of goods instantly recognizable as a leading product on the national and international markets for dress. Also in the Bottin-Pellegrin volume, Robert S. DuPlessis's account of the flow of textiles (and with it the exchange of values) between France and New France, like Eddy Stols's discussion of the sartorial culture of eighteenth-century Brazil, makes significant contributions to the social history of dress in specific arenas of colonial America.

Some crossover between the two volumes of essays is seen in the work of Carolyn Sargentson and Lesley Miller on the design and marketing of luxury silks. The Fox-Turner edition includes separate but complementary essays by these two authors, whose subsequent collaboration resulted in the co-authored essay published in the Bottin-Pellegrin volume: "Paris-Lyon:

Patterns of Distribution of Luxury Silk Fabrics in the 18th Century." This is a groundbreaking analysis of the Lyon silk industry from the contrasting perspectives of designers and manufacturers in Lyon on the one hand, and of silk merchants in Paris on the other (see Figure 2). Perhaps the most striking aspect of their research is the finding that silk designs underwent mostly minor alterations (modifications to existing patterns) from season to

season rather than major stylistic changes, a reassessment that has implications for our reading of the pace and scope of changes in French fashions during the eighteenth century.

The wider context of the Parisian mercers' role in manufacturing, marketing, and distributing high fashion (whether apparel, or household goods such as furniture and porcelain) is addressed by Sargentson in her book *Merchants and Luxury Markets: The Marchands Merciers of Eighteenth-Century Paris*. Profusely illustrated, this work allies careful analysis of surviving artifacts with knowledge of documentary evidence to provide a reinterpretation of the growing importance of the *marchands merciers* in influencing Parisian taste.

Sargentson's work eloquently makes the case that economic histories of consumerism can be enriched by the object-based research more usually associated with museum exhibitions. Exhibition catalogues have typically been the backbone of French dress history, with regular offerings at the Musée de la Mode et du Costume, Palais Galliera, in Paris. Few exhibitions have focused on the eighteenth century (as did the 1989 exhibition *Modes & révolutions, 1780-1804*), though many have incorporated material on the period (the catalogue for the exhibition *Histoires du jeans de 1750 à 1994*, on which French and American scholars collaborated, is a good example).

Exhibitions at the Palais Galliera have tended to present mainstream dress history. However, an increasingly prominent characteristic of exhibitions

Figure 2. Man's suit, *ca. 1760. Silk; velours miniature (produced in Lyon). Rhode Island School of Design, Museum of Art. Gift of the Museum Associates in honor of Eleanor Fayerweather. (82.287.2a-c).*

Figure 3. *L'atelier de couture, ca. 1785. Antoine Raspal. Collection Musée Réattu, Arles. Photograph courtesy of Musées d'Arles.*

of dress and textiles in France is their regional focus. This emphasis on regional particularities can be considered one of the more significant developments in the field, and in her 1989 book, *Les Vêtements de la liberté: Abécédaire des pratiques vestimentaires en France de 1780 à 1800*, the historian Nicole Pellegrin made the case that sartorial regionalism was a key feature of the experience of dress in eighteenth-century France. This area of research has endured as the domain of museum curators, folklorists, ethnologists, and private collectors, and

much of their work remains little known outside of France. In 1986 Marguerite Bruneau published her two-volume study of costume in Normandy, *Histoire du costume populaire en Normandie*, and in 1987 the Grand Palais in Paris held an important exhibition of surviving costume and related artifacts that placed regional diversity in its historical context, *Costume – Coutume*. A 1998 exhibition at the Museon Arlaten, *Façon arlésienne: Étoffes et costumes au XVIIIe siècle*, marked a new era in the presentation of exhibits of regional dress by bringing together

art historians, dress historians, archivists and museum curators to address the subject of provincial dress. The resulting in-depth essays explore the ways in which dress in one eighteenth-century locality, the town of Arles, evolved its own very distinctive character by assimilating external influences (whether the vogue for cotton goods, many of which were manufactured in the area, or new fashions harking from Paris) while remaining grounded in local sartorial traditions (Figure 3). Even an exhibition of seventeenth- and eighteenth-century liturgical vestments from Toulouse, *Soieries en sacristie: Fastes liturgiques, XVIIe-XVIIIe siècles*, at the Musée Paul Dupuy, becomes a richly detailed consideration of local practices. In the accompanying catalogue, Christine Aribaud discusses the embroidery that was applied by local craftsmen to ecclesiastical vestments, many of which had originated as gifts of secular clothing that needed to be transformed for religious use. Beyond documenting the embroidery skills practiced locally, which stood in contrast technically and stylistically to the better known skills of Parisian *brodeurs*, Aribaud also describes how the rural economy of the area around Toulouse dictated local practices, emphasizing the need for cost and time-saving measures (e.g., repeatedly dyeing, refurbishing, repairing).

Not all published studies of regional dress have resulted from exhibitions. Nonetheless, surviving artifacts have provided the basis for the majority of such works. The collector Michel Biehn's authoritative study of the dress of Provence, *En jupon piqué et robe d'indienne: Costumes provençaux*, and Gilberte Vrignaud's careful analysis of dress in Lorraine, *Vêture et parure en France au dix-huitième siècle*, which is based on her examination of surviving textile samples found attached to mercantile records, are two such examples which deserve wider recognition.

Much of the impetus toward object-based studies stems from the interest in surviving textiles, with dress as a secondary concern. For example, the surviving textiles rather than dress history stand out as the centerpiece of the works of Aribaud, Vrignaud, and, arguably, of Biehn. The tension between dress and textile history manifests itself also in the volumes of essays edited by the teams of Pellegrin-Bottin and Fox-Turner.

Countering the emphasis on textiles are two recent books that place dress at the forefront of the discussion. It is unfortunate, therefore, that the work whose title holds the most promise, Madeleine Delpierre's *Dress in France in the Eighteenth Century*, is the most disappointing. Delpierre's book, originally published in France in 1996, belongs to the stable of works on dress history presently promoted by Yale University Press. (Princeton University Press, which has also published works on dress as part of its series on *New French Thought*, does not offer any eighteenth-century titles.) Yale offers one other French-language work in English translation, and this is Françoise Piponnier and Perrine Mane's *Dress in the Middle Ages*.[4] Though not without its weaknesses, the latter is a rich work that displays rigorous scholarship and a varied and assured use of primary sources, from visual and documentary material to surviving objects. However, the lack of footnotes detracts from the importance of Piponnier and Mane's scholarship, thereby hindering the cause of dress history as a serious academic subject. Delpierre's book on the eighteenth century includes footnotes, but these are minimal. Indeed, a glaring weakness of this book emerges in Delpierre's frequent assertions that she fails to back up with evidence of any sort, whether material, archival or visual. This lack of substantiation is all the more aggravating as Delpierre's lengthy tenure as curator at the Musée de la Mode et du Costume at Palais Galliera in Paris made her ideally placed to comment on the evidence from surviving dress. She does not discuss any specific examples of surviving dress from French collections in the text. Only five black-and-white plates show reproductions of surviving artifacts, and these were selected to illustrate textiles.

The choice of the works of Delpierre and Perrine and Mane for publication in English seems to have been an expeditious way for Yale University Press to fill a gap in the market. With their small-scale format and lack of color reproductions, these two books stand in contrast to Yale's other two offerings in dress history, both by the same author, Aileen Ribeiro. The first was *The Art of Dress: Fashion in England and France, 1750-1820*.[5] With *Ingres in Fashion: Representations of Dress and Appearance in Ingres's Images of Women*, Ribeiro gives free rein to her preoccupation with the complex relationship between dress and its depiction in art (having honed

Figure 4. Portrait of Madame Charles Hayard. *Jean-Auguste-Dominque Ingres, French, ca. 1812. Drawing. Fogg Art Museum, Harvard University Art Museums. Bequest of Paul J. Sachs, Class of 1900, "a testimonial to my friend Grenville L. Winthrop."*

her expertise in this area with her contributions to numerous exhibition catalogues) by making this subject the focus of an entire book devoted to a single artist (Figure 4). Ribeiro's two books, so obviously grounded in art history, are glossy editions with the lavish use of color reproductions befitting a visual subject. For the study of dress history, which can draw on so many diverse sources and which is relevant to so many disciplines, is ultimately an intrinsically visual matter. This remains the case whether the starting point is an example of surviving costume, a representation of dress, or a desire to understand the visual impact of clothing and consumption on social and economic relations in a given period and place. French dress history is no exception.

[1] See *Dress* 22 (1995): 89-90 for a review of *The Empire of Fashion*.

[2] Daniel Miller, ed., *Acknowledging Consumption: A Review of New Studies* (London: Routledge, 1995).

[3] Technical and industrial aspects of textile production were addressed in a special issue of the *Revue du Nord* published in 1995: *Industrie textile et croissance régionale: Europe du Nord-Ouest et Pologne*, edited by Albert Broder.

[4] Odile Blanc's work on medieval dress does not exist in translation: *Paradis et parures* (Paris: Flammarion, 1997).

[5] See *Dress* 22 (1995): 85-87 for a review of *The Art of Dress: Fashion in England and France, 1750-1820*.

BIBLIOGRAPHY

Aribaud, Christine. *Soieries en sacristie: Fastes liturgiques, XVIIe-XVIIIe siècles.* Toulouse: Musée Paul Dupuy, 1998.

Biehn, Michel. *En jupon piqué et robe d'indienne: Costumes provençaux.* Marseille: Editions Jeanne Lafitte, 1987; reprint 1999.

Bottin, Jacques, and Nicole Pellegrin, eds. *Échanges et cultures textiles dans l'Europe pré-industrielle.* Collection Histoire, no. 12. *Revue du Nord*, special issue (1996).

Bruneau, Marguerite. *Histoire du costume populaire en Normandie, tomes I et II.* Rouen: Le Cercle d'action et d'études normandes, 1986.

Delpierre, Madeleine. *Dress in France in the Eighteenth Century.* Translated by Caroline Beamish. New Haven: Yale University Press, 1997.

_____. *Se vêtir au XVIIIe siècle.* Paris: Société nouvelle Adam Biro, 1996.

Fox, Robert, and Anthony Turner, eds. *Luxury Trades and Consumerism in Ancien Regime Paris: Studies in the History of the Skilled Workforce.* Aldershot: Ashgate Publishing, 1998.

Galeries Nationales du Grand Palais. *Costume – coutume.* Paris: Editions de la réunion des musées nationaux, 1987.

Lipovetsky, Gilles. *The Empire of Fashion: Dressing Modern Democracy.* Translated by Catherine Porter. Princeton, N.J.: Princeton University Press, 1994.

_____. *L'Empire de l'éphémère: La mode et son destin dans les sociétés modernes.* Paris: Editions Gallimard, 1987.

Museon Arlaten. *Façon arlésienne: Étoffes et costumes au XVIIIe siècle.* Arles: Museon Arlaten, 1998.

Palais Galliera. *Histoires du jeans de 1750 à 1994.* Paris: Editions Paris-Musées, 1994.

_____. *Modes & révolutions, 1780-1804.* Paris: Editions Paris-Musées, 1989.

Pellegrin, Nicole. *Les Vêtements de la liberté: Abécédaire des pratiques vestimentaires en France de 1780 à 1800.* Aix-en-Provence: Editions Alinea, 1989.

Perrot, Philippe. *Fashioning the Bourgeoisie: A History of Clothing in the Nineteenth Century.* Translated by Richard Bienvenu. Princeton: Princeton University Press, 1994.

_____. *Les dessus et les dessous de la bourgeoisie: Une histoire du vêtement au XIXe siècle.* Paris: Librairie Arthème Fayard, 1981.

Piponnier, Françoise, and Perrine Mane. *Dress in the Middle Ages.* Translated by Caroline Beamish. New Haven, Conn.: Yale University Press, 1998.

_____. *Se vêtir au Moyen Âge.* Paris: Société nouvelle Adam Biro, 1995.

Ribeiro, Aileen. *The Art of Dress: Fashion in England and France, 1750-1820.* New Haven, Conn.: Yale University Press, 1995.

_____. *Ingres in Fashion: Representations of Dress and Appearance in Ingres's Images of Women.* New Haven, Conn.: Yale University Press, 1999.

Roche, Daniel. *A History of Everyday Things: The Birth of Consumption in France, 1600-1800.* Cambridge: Cambridge University Press, 2000.

_____. *Histoire des choses banales.* Paris: Librairie Arthème Fayard, 1997.

_____. *La Culture des apparences: Une histoire du vêtement, XVIIe-XVIIIe siècles.* Paris: Librairie Arthème Fayard, 1989; reprint, Paris: Le Seuil, 1991.

_____. *The Culture of Clothing: Dress and Fashion in the "Ancien Regime."* Translated by Jean Birrell. Cambridge: Cambridge University Press, 1994.

Sargentson, Carolyn. *Merchants and Luxury Markets: The Marchands Merciers of Eighteenth-Century Paris.* Malibu, Calif.: J. Paul Getty Museum, 1996.

Vrignaud, Gilberte. *Vêture et parure en France au dix-huitième siècle.* Paris: Editions Messene, 1995.

Diane Maglio

Luxuriant Crowns: Victorian Men's Smoking Caps, 1850-1890

Diane Maglio is a menswear historian and adjunct faculty member at the Fashion Institute of Technology, New York City. She is also a merchandiser and designer for the men's apparel industry.

Sublime Tobacco! which from east to west
Cheer's the Tar's labour or the Turkman's rest;
Which on the Moslem's ottoman divides
His hours, and rivals opium and his brides;

. . . .

Like other charmers, wooing the caress
More dazzlingly when daring in full dress;

The Right Hon. Lord Byron[1]

As Byron's words suggest, writers, artists, tourists and affluent men of the Victorian era embraced the culture and color of the Islamic East and, in the process, enjoyed the opiate effects of tobacco.[2] While visiting North Africa, Delacroix produced a collection of paintings, including *Women of Algiers,* that expressed the sensuality of the people he found there, and John Frederick Lewis conveyed visions of harem life to Western eyes. The proliferation of paintings, books, and international exhibitions brought the arts and crafts of the East to the attention of Western manufacture and taste. Six million people attended the 1851 Great Exhibition of All Industries in London, including author Charlotte Brontë, who wrote: "It may be called a bazaar or fair as Eastern genii might have created . . . with such a blaze and contrast of colours and marvellous [sic] power of effect."[3] Brontë's reference to the Moslem jinni underscored the significant impression the Islamic East made in the eyes and minds of Western people. While touring Constantinople, the American writer Herman Melville recorded in his journal on December 9, 1856, this exotic image of the people and lifestyle he found there:

> . . .two "beys effendi" in long furred robes of yellow, looking like Tom Cats. They had their harems with them. . .some very pretty women of the harem. . . .The courts and grounds of Seraglio have a strange, enchanted sort of look.[4]

In the austere world of behavior and dress for the Victorian gentleman of the industrial West, this resplendent vision of a sultry culture stimulated the imagination and intoxicated the senses. Men adopted Orientalist influence in the elaborate robes, slippers and caps of silk, velvet and brocade that they wore in their private rooms and for smoking.[5]

While in public men dressed uniformly in sedate black business clothing, at home they wore tactile and sensuous materials of silk velvet decorated with beads and embroidery. In his book *Fashion: The Power That Influences the World*, published in 1871, George Fox acknowledged the fashion of smoking, which he believed probably originated in the East.[6] While examining twelve smoking caps in the costume collection of the Museum of the City of New York (MCNY), I observed colorful and "noble" materials of silk and velvet ornately embellished with gold and silver embroidery, beading, appliqué, and braiding.[7] The ornamental designs applied to ten of these smoking caps were Western interpretations of the designs found in Islamic art, architecture and textiles of the eastern Mediterranean countries, North Africa and India. The smoking cap usually took the form of a round pillbox with a long tassel attached to the crown in a manner similar to an Eastern fez.[8] It replaced the nightcap when smoking became a popular pastime after the Crimean War of 1853-56. Scholars have conjectured that gentlemen wore these elaborate caps, their personal crowns of luxury, to keep their hair from smelling of smoke.[9] Yet these ornamented caps, often richly embellished, appeared to serve more than a utilitarian function. My research aimed to study the opulent smoking caps worn by Victorian gentlemen not only as a colorful and exotic contrast to somber public dress, but also as a medium to show off the fancywork or decorative needlework of Victorian women.

Smoking caps in the collections of the Victoria and Albert Museum, London, and the Museum of London were also studied. Using the traditional art historical method, I traced the subject through paintings, personal journals, novels, etiquette books and magazines of the period.

Margaret Conkling, in *The American Gentleman's Guide to Politeness and Fashion* (1857) wrote:

> The universal partiality of our countrymen for *black*, as the color of dress clothes [*sic*], at least, . . . has another more important effect, which is to test, in the severest way, the wearer's claims to a *distinguished appearance.*[10]

In the fast-growing industrial and financial communities of the Western world, sobriety in public dress was imperative. Philippe Perrot observed that the successful man of the mid-nineteenth century dressed in black for business, representing a puritanical elegance and the rejection of external pleasure.[11] According to John Harvey, staid black clothing indicated that the Western gentleman "can be relied on . . . for it says he is unseduced by cheap pleasures and temptations. A man in black is a man you can trust [even] with your money."[12] In contrast to the sober black uniform of men's daytime clothing, August Debay observed: "our rich gents compensate for this insipid uniformity by wearing a magnificent indoor costume. . . . His velvet toque, embellished with embroidery and a massive gold tassel [was very expensive]."[13] Evidence of the contrast between sober day dress and luxurious private dress was discovered in a portmanteau of clothing, packed sometime between 1840 and 1859, belonging to J. W. Close, British consul at Tornay Charente, France, now in the collection of the Museum of London. Its contents included a black frock coat for public dress and a black silk smoking cap

Figure 1. Portrait of Amos Lawrence, *ca. 1845. Chester Harding. Oil on canvas. Given in memory of the Rt. Rev. William Lawrence by his children (1994.1.1). Photograph © Board of Trustees, National Gallery of Art, Washington, D.C.*

with gold embroidery for private use. Mr. Close's cap consists of five panels, each embellished with gold braid that was laid and couched in floral and leaf configurations and topped with a long silk tassel. The pattern resembles the style advocated by Mlle. Roche in the November 1860 issue of *Peterson's* magazine for ladies' work. She suggested a five-panel velvet braided lounging cap for the "comfort it bestows on those gentlemen who are compelled by custom to wear a hat the greater portion of the day," referring to the formality of the businessman's dress.[14] By day Mr. Close wore his sedate frock coat, and for his private dress he changed into an elegant gold embroidered cap.

Charles F. Beezley, etiquette writer in 1892, praised the home as a paradise: "And it is at the family fireside where a man's real self is disclosed. There he throws off the little disguises in which he appears before the world and we behold him in his true character."[15] By day the Victorian gentleman wore hard-finished and sturdy woolens such as serge, cheviot, or cassimere.[16] At night, in the privacy of his own rooms, he could emerge in Orientalist dress, enrobing himself in soft, silky fabrics, costumed from head to foot like a Turk. Mr. Amos Lawrence, a New England merchant and philanthropist and the sitter in the painting *Amos Lawrence* by Chester Harding (Figure 1), is depicted in colorful smoking regalia from his cap to his slippers.[17] By donning these exotic clothes, Victorian gentlemen like Mr. Lawrence could dress in an opulent way as a discernible and conspicuous expression of wealth and cosmopolitan taste. In 1896, Dr. Lydstrom described how he felt when he dressed for smoking:

> When I put on my Turkish fez and gown, drunk a glass of that incomparable punch and light my hookah, I . . . am as languorously, dreamily, pensively happy as one could hope to be in this world. All my ways are bliss and all my paths are peace.[18]

Other affluent Western men like Mr. Lawrence and Dr. Lydstrom could have conceivably felt the same way as they donned an exotic ensemble topped with a smoking cap for their intimate hours at home.

Women's publications of the mid-nineteenth century, including *Godey's Lady's Book* and *Peterson's* magazine, offered instructions to make caps in the "Oriental style," meaning the mode of the Mediterranean East. Islamic art and ornament was simplified, modified, and homogenized as it was adapted and published in ladies' periodicals for the fancy needleworkers of America to copy. Mlle. Roche, writing for *Peterson's* magazine, was of the opinion that smoking caps were "a most acceptable present [from a lady to a gentleman], an article of ornament that is really useful."[19] The Victoria and Albert Museum has in its collections a smoking cap from Brazil, South America, with raised curvilinear metallic-thread embroidery design interspersed with embroidered silk floss flowers (acc. no. T230-1931). An inscription in the band reads: "Como linbranca e signal de amizade offerece ao Snr Jose Carlos Alkaini Heleninha Cochrane . . . 1856."[20] The cap was a gift of friendship from a Brazilian woman to a gentleman. Mrs.

Weaver considered smoking caps, tobacco pouches and cigar cases made by ladies also suitable contributions to charity bazaars where "men are expected to purchase largely."[21] Indeed, society embraced smoking and its related paraphernalia so much that one author questioned how the world got on before the year 1550, when Sir Walter Raleigh popularized smoking: "Our mouths were undecorated with cigars. . . . No young ladies, then, embroidered tobacco-pouches, or sold them at fancy fairs for fancy prices."[22]

The businessman who came home from work "so much worried and exhausted that he cannot eat, read, or sleep, [was] recommended to smoke, to strengthen his nerves," advised author John Thompson in 1880.[23] The smoking caps in the MCNY collection, possibly made by fancy needleworkers at home after the instructions given in the ladies' books, include a wine-colored velvet cap with hand-quilted lining (Figure 2). The cap has twisted gold braid hand sewn in an arabesque configuration. *The Dictionary of Needlework* published in the nineteenth century defines arabesque designs as "patterns in the style of the Arabian flat wall decorations which originated in Egypt, . . . [and were] adopted by the French who gave the style the name Arabesque."[24] John Sweetman, author of *The Oriental Obsession*, noted

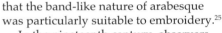

that the band-like nature of arabesque was particularly suitable to embroidery.[25]

In the nineteenth century, observers emphasized the importance of the Islamic influence in the application of art to manufacture. Owen Jones attempted to categorize the numerous designs of ancient and modern cultures, including those attributed to Eastern European, Indian and Asian countries in his *Grammar of Ornament* (1852). He wrote that design had:

> so much skill and judgment in its application, with so much of elegance and refinement in the execution as was observable in all the works . . . of the other Mohammedan contributing countries . . . which excited a degree of attention from artists, manufacturers, and the public, which has not been without its fruits.[26]

A black velvet smoking cap in the collection of the MCNY (acc. no. 32.252) has a curvilinear design with gold thread outlining an interlooped ombre-colored braid laid and couched in an arabesque mode reflecting the Arabic configurations detailed in *The Grammar of Ornament*. This style of design shows the influence of artwork from Mohammedan countries that fancy needleworkers interpreted for smoking caps. Jones noted that designs were often "taken from hookahs, of which there was an immense variety exhibited in 1851," referring to the popularity of smoking paraphernalia.[27] Wallpaper patterns featured in the 1851 Great Exhibition of All Industries in London show styles of curvilinear designs similar to the embroidery on the cap.[28] This luxuriant crown is finished with hand-quilted red silk lining and a black and gold silk tassel.

When visiting Constantinople, Mark Twain recorded in his log on August 17,

Figure 2. Smoking cap, ca. 1850-60. Red velvet, embroidered with gilt tassel; green quilted lining. Gift of Mrs. Grover C. Fritts, Museum of the City of New York (42.213.2).

Figure 3. Smoking cap, *ca. 1860. Purple velvet, embroidered. Gift of Mrs. John T. Philips, Museum of the City of the New York (46.192.17).*

Figure 4. Smoking cap, *ca. 1865. Red velvet skull cap, embroidered in blue silk and pearl beads. Gift of Miss Jane McLean, Museum of the City of New York (43.178.2.).*

Figure 5. Smoking cap, *ca. 1850-60. Red velvet, embroidered with red beads, metallic thread and raw silk; red and metallic tassel. Gift of Miss Harriet McDonald, Museum of the City of New York (38.426.3).*

1867, that he saw "embroidered jackets of gold and purple, blue and crimson—splendid."[29] In their costume worn at home, Western men emulated the colorful clothing that impressed Twain in Constantinople. A purple silk velvet cap in the collection of the MCNY (Figure 3) has green chenille yarn applied to the surface in a free-form design of arabesque inspiration. Threads of chenille are pliable and can be worked quickly, but they are also the most costly material used in embroidery aside from precious metals.[30] The gentleman wearing this cap would appreciate the subtle connotation of the expensive chenille yarn without the added display of beading and tassels. He combined colorful luxury with simplicity in his smoking cap.

Materials suggested by magazine writers for embellishing lavish smoking caps were often expensive and suitable to the upper classes. For an appliquéd lounging or smoking cap, Mrs. Jane Weaver writing in *Peterson's* recommended a pattern of leaves appliquéd in velvet, edged in cord, and ornamented in braid and gold beads.[31] For a cap with fine gold braid, five bunches of jet beads and one skein of black embroidery silk, the

cost of materials came to approximately five dollars.[32] A smoking cap of plain colored plush or velvet with a tassel could be purchased from Bronners and Company for $.98 to $1.25 in 1888. The Lord and Taylor Catalogue of 1881 listed the cost of a man's silk alpaca coat at $4.75. The materials for making a beaded and embroidered cap by a fancy needleworker at home exceeded the price of a purchased ready-to-wear man's coat. When using braid, Mlle. Roche advised: "The braid should be light and fine, which makes the work look to much more advantage." She also recommended sewing "with a very fine silk, matching exactly in color, so as to make it difficult to observe the stitches; when these are seen the beauty of the work is much injured."[33] The passementerie embroidery of the wine-colored velvet cap (Figure 4) consists of gold cord and pearl beads filling the curved areas. The braid appears to be hand stitched and the curves very well defined. An ornamental design of leaves from a mural in the vestibule of Sikandra, the tomb of the Indian emperor Akbar, may have inspired the designs featured at the Great Exhibition that women's magazine writers suggested for the caps.[34]

Although one author of an 1879 etiquette book said that "the home department belongs exclusively to the wife; the province of the husband is to rule the house—hers to regulate its internal movements,"[35] wives were criticized for insisting that their husbands give up smoking at home. Since "everybody smokes, from the potboy to the prince," observed Oida in *A Smoker's Dream,*[36] it was considered "the Correct Thing . . . For the lady of the house to remember the saint who built her husband a smoking room, and do likewise."[37] One wife proudly boasted how much better her husband looked when she thought he gave up the weed, but then "At last a friend led her to the top of the house, and through a glass door she beheld her lord, costumed from head to foot like a Turk, and in beautiful nicotian meditation." She was so enthralled with his appearance that she decided not to insist he give up tobacco, saying: "after all he smokes so *gracefully.*"[38] The husband in exotic Turkish dress was enticing to his wife. One anonymous writer of 1848 believed: "Your true smoker is the true 'model husband.'"[39] The "model husband" in beautiful nicotian meditation may have worn a cap similar to the wine-colored silk velvet embroidered with gold thread and red and gold beads (Figure 5). The irregular outline of the wine-colored, satin-stitched floral buds indicate a freehand embroidery technique. The cap's tassel stands out with its gold beads hanging from the silk fringe. By day a wife could be attractive to her husband in a lavish dress; by night his exotic outfit was equally as opulent.

In contrast to the freehand technique of satin stitch embroidery, the overlaid technique described by Santina Levey involves "metal threads [that] were laid over strips of leather or card to create a flat, sharply delineated effect."[40] An embroidered blue velvet cap in the collection of MCNY has sequins, a thick gold silk tassel, and a smooth, continuous outline of small gold buds in raised relief on the velvet substrate (38.393.94). This cap probably belonged to an affluent man comfortable with displaying his wealth in the privacy of his home while lounging in luxurious clothing. Dr. Lydstrom, like the men who dressed for smoking at home, enjoyed "the double-distilled comfort and perfumed luxury [of] the hookah . . . I wonder those cross-legged Turks ever get their legs untangled. I wouldn't care to straighten them out at all, were I a Turk."[41] The substance smoked in the hookah might have fueled a man's imagination, and the sensuous feeling of luxury fabrics embellished with Islamic designs replicated, if only in the gentleman's mind, the sense of being a sultan. Balzac admitted he felt like a sultan when wearing his *termolama* dressing gown. He wrote:

> Now I must tell you that for me this Persian or Circassian fabric was something fabulous. . . . My *termolama* is black, sprinkled with pressed palmettes surrounded by flowers. . . . I walk about in the glory of my palms like a sultan.[42]

Mrs. Sarah Barclay Johnson, while touring Damascus with her husband in 1858, described the bazaars as incomparable to those in any other oriental city. She thought that although they "had not the least pretensions to taste, [they] often make a great display of richly embroidered goods." She was impressed by "gold and silk braid-caps of scarlet cloth with high raised gold work, and tassels half a yard in length."[43] A brown velvet cap with a long silk tassel has gold cording laid and couched around a floral motif with a raised disk center and cording applied in the shape of leaves (Figure 6). Gold silk cross-stitched embroidery fills the petals of the richly embroidered flowers. Silk velvet pile was difficult to embroider with costly gold and silver threads, making such an ornamented fabric expensive in both Eastern and Western cultures. Because it was precious and laborious to make, it also connoted high social status.[44] The embroidery design of the cap is reminiscent of the *saz* design style of a sixteenth-century Ottoman sultan's weaving studio.[45] Jennifer Wearden described the *saz* style as consisting of curving, serrated leaves and composite flowers. This style is reflected in an Imperial Ottoman silk caftan of the sixteenth century now in the Topkapi Sarayi Museum, Istanbul.[46] Richly ornamented caftans dazzled men and women touring the Islamic countries. Mrs. Johnson, like other affluent Victorian women, was accustomed to dressing in expensive fabrics with lavish embroidery displaying her husband's wealth through clothing. On the other hand, a Victorian husband who dressed in somber black in public would very likely feel comfortable wearing a luxuriant style of ornamentation adapted from Islamic splendor only in private.

Berlin work, or embroidery on canvas substrate, was extremely popular with Victorian women.[47] Nancy Dunlap

Figure 6. Smoking cap, *ca. 1860. Embroidered brown velvet with tassel. Gift of Miss Martia Leonard, Museum of the City of New York (33.372.16).*

Bercaw wrote that "Berlin work offered busy women an alternative to traditional, elaborate embroidery because it was easy to master, quick to execute, and less expensive."[48] *The Art Journal Illustrated Catalogue* for the 1851 Exhibition featured Berlin wool-work of interlaced patterns that were "simple and good in design." The author acknowledged:

> The taste for embroidery has ranked high amongst the elegant arts of refined life in past ages, and modern experience teaches us that it still maintains its position; it well becomes the manufacturer . . . to devote his attention to this widely-spread taste, and endeavor to obviate any tendency to commonplace imbecility of design in its pursuit.[49]

A Berlin wool-work cap in the costume collection of the Museum of London appears to be hand made (acc. no. 81.92). The cap has a black substrate with vivid colors of orange, green, pink and lavender creating an interlaced chain design. Needlework journalist Mlle. Roche advised her readers as to how to finish a smoking cap: "a handsome silk tassel must complete the top."[50] In compliance with Roche's instructions, the maker of this cap chose a bright orange silk tassel to complete the project.

Figure 7. Smoking cap, ca. 1860-70. Purple crocheted cap; metallic and purple tassel; gold and blue border. Gift of Miss Martia Leonard. Museum of the City of New York (33.372.17).

As Owen Jones wrote: "The Exhibition of the Works of Industry of All Nations in 1851 was barely opened to the public ere attention was directed to the gorgeous contribution of India."[51] An unlined crocheted purple wool smoking cap embellished with simplified fragments of Indian *buta* or paisley (Figure 7) was, in contemporary terms, another form of women's handwork made at home. In her novel *Cranford*, Victorian writer Mrs. Gaskell described needleworker Miss Pole as "becoming as much absorbed in crochet as she had been once in knitting." Miss Pole was one of the growing numbers of middle-class ladies practicing the needle arts in good taste. She characterized her social set: "We are none of us what may be called rich, though we all possess a genteel competency, sufficient for tastes that are elegant and refined, and would not, if they could, be vulgarly ostentatious."[52] Lacking any expensive threads or beads, the simple finish of this cap would lead to the speculation that a gentleman of the emerging middle-class wore it and perhaps purchased it at a bazaar for which it was made by a woman such as Miss Pole. Mrs. Weaver, writing for *Peterson's* magazine, gave instructions for a crochet smoking cap made from two ounces of Berlin wool and a half-ounce of blue silk cordon, or packthread. "This cap may be worked in any bright colors, according to taste, and considerably improved by ornamenting it with

cross-stitch or point russe."[53] Another crochet cap featured in an 1867 issue of *Godey's Lady's Book* is made from a "rather thick pursesilk in treble crochet" using a steel needle (Figure 8). The writer notes: "Ladies may object that a certain gentleman does not smoke; but even then he will have no objection to a smoking-cap, which he will use . . . for lounging."[54]

In contrast to the simple stitches of the unlined purple cap, a blue silk crochet cap in the collection of the MCNY (acc. no. 33.109.6) shows fine, regular, neat stitches and has a lining, indicating its probable manufacture by a professional. The lightweight cap lacks any embellishments applied to the surface, but rather has the design crocheted into the form. Where the unlined purple cap has fragments of paisley around the border, the blue cap has a multi-colored border pattern of green, gold, peach and black resembling the Turkish plate XXXVI from Owen Jones's *Grammar of Ornament*. Inside the cap is a two-inch leather band. Mlle. Roche wrote instructions for a braided lounging cap in *Peterson's* in 1860, advising a needleworker to add a strip of leather to the inner band: "this enables it to be taken off the head with greater facility than when lined with the silk alone; it also preserves the cap."[55]

The allure of the East endured throughout the nineteenth century. When American author Mark Twain toured the

Figure 8. Crochet smoking cap. Godey's Magazine and Lady's Book (January 1867). Courtesy of the Fashion Institute of Technology Library.

eastern countries of the Mediterranean and India, he at first thought the appeal of the Eastern cultures and arts were a passing fad which "would all become commonplace in a week; [yet time] only enhanced its fascinations."[56] Victorian men developed an appreciation for the art and exoticism of the Islamic masculine world and symbolized their own wealth and good taste by wearing abundantly rich dress at home. William Makepeace Thackeray wrote that the habit of smoking made the Turks such "well-bred men," and gentlemen concurred by emulating their luxurious costumes and smoking habit.[57] Dressed in the style of the Turk, perhaps even fancying himself a Western effendi, the Victorian man could smoke, relax and meditate. In contrast to his stoic black business attire, the colorful silk velvets and embroidery of the smoking caps satisfied the soft, sensuous and luxurious

Figure 9. Receiving visitors in dressing gown and cap. In Gentleman's Magazine (January 1863). Courtesy of the Fashion Institute of Technology Library.

side of the man. He could receive visitors at home dressed in opulent clothing, as nineteenth-century fashion plates depicted (Figure 9), enhancing his stature through this display of affluence in his private suite. The smoking cap served as a luxuriant crown that complemented the elaborate and expensive clothing the gentleman wore in celebration of his own status, wealth and love of the exotic.

1 The Right Hon. Lord Byron, *The Island: or Christian and His Comrades*, 3rd ed. (London: John Hunt, 1823), 41.

2 For this study, the Victorian period begins around 1841, the birth date of the Prince of Wales, and extends through the 1890s.

3 Charlotte Brontë, "Inside the Crystal Palace: The Great Exhibition, 1851," in *Eyewitness to History*, ed. John Carey (New York: Avon Books, 1987), 324. The jinni, sometimes spelled genie, were one of the supernatural beings in Moslem mythology often at the service of men. *Funk and Wagnalls Standard Desk Dictionary*, vol. I (New York: Funk and Wagnalls, 1979), 350.

4 Jay Leyda, *The Melville Log: A Documentary Life of Herman Melville 1819-1891* (New York: Harcourt, Brace and Company, 1951), 535, 538. The effendi, according to the Reverend H. J. Van Lennep, was the Turkish businessman or landowner who was sufficiently wealthy "to enable [him] to life without labor." *The Oriental Album* (New York: Anson D. F. Randolph, 1862), 11.

5 Richard Martin and Harold Koda, *Orientalism: Visions of the East in Western Dress* (New York: Metropolitan Museum of Art, 1994), 38. Richard Martin and Harold Koda define Orientalism as "the historical term used to describe the West's fascination with and assimilation of the ideas and styles of the East" (7).

6 George P. Fox, *Fashion: The Power That Influences the World: The Philosophy of Ancient and Modern Dress and Fashion* (New York: Sheldon and Co., 1871), 118.

7 Perrot discusses the contrast of somber, neutral colors worn in public with the bright colors hidden as linings or vests, under collars and lapels, and in private life as dressing gowns. Colors appeared in "noble" materials, which included satin, silk, velvet and moiré. Philippe Perrot, *Fashioning the Bourgeoisie: A History of Clothing in the Nineteenth Century* (Princeton, N.J.: Princeton University Press, 1994), 33. Braiding is defined as "A form of ornamental needle-work. . . . The Asiatics, Greeks, Turks, and Indians have always used it largely for decorations. . . . Braids, of what ever kind, can be laid upon velvet, [etc.] and are backstitched to these materials with strong silk thread." S. F. A. Caulfield, ed., *The Dictionary of Needlework: An Encyclopaedia of Artistic, Plain, and Fancy Needlework*, 2nd ed. (London: L. Upcott Gill, n.d.), 39.

8 "A fez is a brimless, tapering felt cap usu. red and having a black tassel . . . after *Fez*, a city in Morocco. Also known as a Tarboosh worn by Moslem men with colored silk tassels." *Funk and Wagnalls Dictionary*, s.v. "fez." A Turkey red wool felt fez with a black silk tassel in the collection of the Costume Institute, Metropolitan Museum of Art, New York (53.11.2), dates to the nineteenth century. Mahmoul II, Sultan of Turkey, made the fez part of the Turkish official dress in the early part of the nineteenth century. It was considered the special badge of a Turkish subject and even if not a Moslem, he was obliged to wear it. Noble Charles C. Riddle, *The History of the Fez*, http://www.pagemaker.ca/~shriners/fez2.html.

9 Penelope Byrd, *The Male Image: Men's Fashion in Britain, 1300-1970* (London: B. T. Batsford, Ltd., 1979), 184. Byrd is also of the opinion that "it may just have been a natural continuation of the old idea of wearing a cap with an informal gown."

10 Margaret Conkling, *The American Gentleman's Guide to Politeness and Fashion* (New York: Derby and Jackson, 1857), 29, 68.

11 Perrot, *Fashioning the Bourgeoisie*, 33.

12 John Harvey, *Men in Black* (Chicago: University of Chicago Press, 1995), 146-47.

13 August Debay, "Hygiène vestimentaire," as quoted in Perrot, *Fashioning the Bourgeoisie*, 113.

14 Mlle. Roche, "Braided Lounging Cap," *Peterson's* (November 1860): 394.

15 Charles F. Beezley, *Our Manners and Social Customs: A Practical Guide to Deportment, Easy Manners, and Social Etiquette* (Chicago: Elliott and Beezley, 1892), 36.

16 *Serge*: Hard or soft finish worsted material, plain colors, excellent wearing, but wears shiny. *Cheviot*: Rough-finished surface. Like serge but heavier. So called from shaggy wool of Cheviot sheep. Wears well. *Cassimere*: Cloth for men's suits made of hard-spun yarns, finished without nap. Ellen Beers McGowan et al. *Textiles and Clothing* (1919; rev. ed., New York: MacMillan Co., 1931), 181, 179.

17 Although attired with a smoking cap, Mr. Lawrence "placed the use of tobacco in the same category with that of strong drink. He regarded it as a filthy practice." William M. Thayer, *The Poor Boy and Merchant Prince* (Boston: Gould and Lincoln, 1857), 63.

18 G. Frank Lydstrom, *Over the Hookah: The Tales of a Talkative Doctor* (Chicago: Fred, Klein Company, 1896), 48.

19 Roche, "Braided Lounging Cap," 394.

20 Translation: As a gift keepsake and sign of friendship to be offered up to Señor Jose Carlos Alkaini Heleninha Cochrane.

21 Mrs. Jane Weaver, "Turkish Tobacco Bag," *Peterson's* (September 1865): 210.

22 *An Armchair in the Smoking-Room: or Fiction, Anecdote, Humour, and Fancy* (London: Stanley Rivers and Co., 1876), 1.

23 John Thompson, *Three Fashionable Luxuries: Namely Smoking, Chewing and Snuffing or Facts About Tobacco* (England: John Thompson, ca. 1880), 23.

24 Caulfield, *Dictionary of Needlework*, 12.

25 John Sweetman, *The Oriental Obsession: Islamic Inspiration in British and American Art and Architecture, 1500-1920* (Cambridge: Cambridge University Press, 1988), 21.

26 Owen Jones, *The Grammar of Ornament* (1856; reprint, New York: Van Nostrand Reinhold Company, 1972), 78.

27 Ibid.

28 *The Art Journal Illustrated Catalogue* (London: George Virtue, 1851): 129.

29 Mark Twain, *Mark Twain's Notebook*, vol. 22, *The Complete Works of Mark Twain*, (1896; reprint, New York: Harper and Brothers, 1935), 76.

30 Georgiana Brown Harbeson, *American Needlework: The History of Decorative Stitchery and Embroidery from the Late 16th to the 20th Century* (New York: Coward-McCann, Inc., 1938), 135.

31 Mrs. Jane Weaver, "Smoking Cap," *Peterson's* (November 1866): 351.

32 Mrs. Jane Weaver, "Smoking Cap in Application," *Peterson's* (June 1863): 468.

33 Roche, "Braided Lounging Cap," 394.

34 Sheila S. Blair and Jonathan M. Bloom, *The Art and Architecture of Islam* (New Haven: Yale University Press, 1994), 276.

35 S. L. Louis, *Decorum: A Practical Treatise on Etiquette and Dress of the Best American Society* (1879; reprint, Tyrone, Penn.: Westvaco, 1979), 218-19.

36 Oida, *A Smoker's Dream* (London: J. & D. A. Darling, 1846), B.

37 Florence Hall, *The Correct Thing in Good Society, by the author of "Social Customs"* (Boston: Estes and Lauriat, 1888), 56.

38 A Veteran of Smokedom, *The Smoker's Guide, Philosopher, and Friend* (London: Houlston and Wright, 1864), 84-85.

39 A Modern Epicurean, *Cigars, Tobacco, Wine, and Women As They Are* (London: Kent and Richards, 1848), 34.

40 Santina Levey, "Embroidery," in *Textiles: 5000 Years*, ed. Jennifer Harris (New York: Harry N. Abrams, Inc., 1993), 212.

41 Lydstrom, *Over the Hookah*, xvii.

42 H. de Balzac, *Correspondance de H. de Balzac, 1819-1850*, vol. II (Paris: Ancienne Maison Michel Lévy Frères, 1876), 418-19. Translated in Perrot, *Fashioning the Bourgeoisie*, 231n.

43 Sarah Barclay Johnson, "Oriental Sketches," *Peterson's* (December 1858): 496.

44 Jennifer Wearden, "Central Asian Textiles," in *Textiles: 5000 Years*, ed. Jennifer Harris (New York: Harry N. Abrams, Inc., 1993), 94, 96.

45 Jennifer Wearden, "The *Saz* Style," *Hali* (April 1986): 25. "The *saz* style, named after the *saz qalami* or reed pen used by artists, . . . is characterized by curling leaves, composite blossoms and lotus-like palmettes. . . . The treatment of the subject can be traced through Persian art to China."

46 Ibid., 25.

47 Erica Wilson, *Erica Wilson's Embroidery Book* (New York: Charles Scribner's Sons, 1973), 127.

48 Nancy Dunlap Bercaw, "Solid Objects, Mutable Meanings: Fancywork and the Construction of a Bourgeois Culture, 1840-1880," *The Winterthur Portfolio* 26, no. 4 (winter 1991): 234.

49 *The Art Journal Illustrated Catalogue*, 92.

50 Roche, "Braided Lounging Cap," 394.

51 Jones, *Grammar of Ornament*, 77.

52 Mrs. Gaskell, *Cranford* (1853; reprint, New York: Grosset and Dunlap, n.d.), 28, 239-40.

53 Mrs. Jane Weaver, "Crochet Cap," *Peterson's* (December 1866): 432.

54 *Godey's Lady's Book and Magazine* (January 1867): 89.

55 Roche, "Braided Lounging Cap," 394.

56 Twain, *Mark Twain's Notebook*, 276.

57 William Makepeace Thackeray, *Comic Tales and Sketches* (London: H. Cunningham, 1841), in *Tobacco: Its History*, vol. IV (New York: The Rosenbach Company, 1953), 269.

BIBLIOGRAPHY

Bercaw, Nancy Dunlap. "Solid Objects, Mutable Meanings: Fancywork and the Construction of a Bourgeois Culture, 1840-1880." *The Winterthur Portfolio* 26, no. 4 (winter 1991): 231-47.

Blair, Sheila S., and Jonathan M. Bloom. *The Art and Architecture of Islam*. New Haven: Yale University Press, 1994.

Brontë, Charlotte. "Inside the Crystal Palace: The Great Exhibition, 1851." In *Eyewitness to History*, edited by John Carey. New York: Avon Books, 1987.

Byrd, Penelope. *The Male Image: Men's Fashion in Britain, 1300-1970*. London: B. T. Batsford, Ltd., 1979.

Harbeson, Georgiana Brown. *American Needlework: The History of Decorative Stitchery and Embroidery from the Late 16th to the 20th Century*. New York: Coward-McCann, Inc., 1938.

Harvey, John. *Men in Black*. Chicago: University of Chicago Press, 1995.

John, Edith. *Creative Stitches*. Boston: Charles T. Branford Company, 1967.

Levey, Santina. "Embroidery." In *Textiles: 5000 Years*, edited by Jennifer Harris. New York: Harry N. Abrams, Inc., 1993.

Leyda, Jay. *The Melville Log: A Documentary Life of Herman Melville, 1819-1891*. New York: Harcourt, Brace and Company, 1951.

Martin, Richard, and Harold Koda. *Orientalism: Visions of the East in Western Dress.* New York: Metropolitan Museum of Art, 1994.

Perrot, Philippe. *Fashioning the Bourgeoisie: A History of Clothing in the Nineteenth Century.* Translated by Richard Bienvenu. Princeton, N.J.: Princeton University Press, 1994.

Sweetman, John. *The Oriental Obsession: Islamic Inspiration in British and American Art and Architecture, 1500-1920.* Cambridge: Cambridge University Press, 1988.

Wearden, Jennifer. "Central Asian Textiles." In *Textiles: 5000 Years*, edited by Jennifer Harris. New York: Harry N. Abrams, Inc., 1993.

_____. "The *Saz* Style." *Hali* (April 1986): 22-29.

Wilson, Erica. *Erica Wilson's Embroidery Book.* New York: Charles Scribner's Sons, 1973.

PRIMARY SOURCES

An Armchair in the Smoking-Room: or Fiction, Anecdote, Humour, and Fancy. London: Stanley Rivers and Co., 1876.

The Art Journal Illustrated Catalogue. London: George Virtue, 1851.

Beezley, Charles F. *Our Manners and Social Customs: A Practical Guide to Deportment, Easy Manners, and Social Etiquette.* Chicago: Elliott and Beezley, 1892.

By a Gentleman. *The Perfect Gentleman or Etiquette and Eloquence.* New York: Dick and Fitzgerald, 1866.

Byron, The Right Hon. Lord. *The Island: or Christian and His Comrades.* 3rd ed. London: John Hunt, 1823.

Caulfield, S. F. A., ed. *The Dictionary of Needlework: An Encyclopædia of Artistic, Plain, and Fancy Needlework*, 2nd ed. London: L. Upcott Gill, n.d.

Conkling, Margaret. *The American Gentleman's Guide to Politeness and Fashion.* New York: Derby and Jackson, 1857.

"Crochet Smoking Cap." *Godey's Lady's Book and Magazine* (January 1867).

Fowler, Harriet P. *Our Smoking Husbands.* New York: The Author's Publishing Co., 1879.

Fox, George P. *Fashion: The Power That Influences the World. The Philosophy of Ancient and Modern Dress and Fashion.* New York: Sheldon and Co., 1871.

Gaskell, Mrs. *Cranford.* 1853. Reprint, New York: Grosset and Dunlap, n.d.

Hall, Florence. *Social Customs.* Boston: Estes and Lauriat, 1887.

_____. *The Correct Thing in Good Society*, by the Author of "Social Customs." Boston: Estes and Lauriat, 1888.

Johnson, Sarah Barclay. "Oriental Sketches." *Peterson's* (December 1858): 496.

Jones, Owen. *The Grammar of Ornament.* 1856. Reprint, New York: Van Nostrand Reinhold Company, 1972.

Logan, Mrs. John A. *The Home Manual: Everybody's Guide in Social, Domestic, and Business Life.* Boston: A. M. Thayer and Company, 1889.

Louis, S. L. *Decorum: A Practical Treatise on Etiquette and Dress of the Best American Society.* 1879. Reprint, Tyrone, Penn.: Westvaco, 1979.

Lydstrom, G. Frank. *Over the Hookah: The Tales of a Talkative Doctor.* Chicago: Fred, Klein Company, 1896.

A Modern Epicurean. *Cigars, Tobacco, Wine, and Women As They Are.* London: Kent and Richards, 1848.

Oida. *A Smoker's Dream.* London: J. & D. A. Darling, 1846.

The Oriental Album. New York: Anson D. F. Randolph, 1862.

Roche, Mlle. "Braided Lounging Cap." *Peterson's* (November 1860).

Thackeray, William Makepeace. "Comic Tales and Sketches." In *Tobacco: Its History.* Originally published by H. Cunningham, London, 1841. vol. IV. New York: The Rosenbach Company, 1953.

Thompson, John. *Three Fashionable Luxuries: Namely Smoking, Chewing, and Snuffing or Facts About Tobacco.* England: John Thompson, ca. 1880.

Twain, Mark. *Mark Twain's Notebook.* Vol. 22. *The Complete Works of Mark Twain*, 1896. Reprint, New York: Harper and Brothers, 1935.

A Veteran of Smokedom. *The Smoker's Guide, Philosopher, and Friend.* London: Houlston and Wright, 1864.

Walker, Isaac. *Dress: As it has been, is and will be.* New York: Isaac Walker, 1885.

Weaver, Jane. "Braided Smoking-Cap Ornamented with Beads." *Peterson's* (January 1864).

_____. "Crochet Cap." *Peterson's* (December 1866).

_____. "Gentleman's Cap in Oriental Appliqué." *Peterson's.* (February 1865).

_____. "Segar-Case in Braiding." *Peterson's* (April 1861).

_____. "Smoking Cap." *Peterson's* (November 1866).

_____. "Smoking Cap in Application." *Peterson's* (June 1863).

Gender Headwear Traditions in Judaism and Islam

Beverly Chico, a specialist in the history of headwear, is Professor of History and Humanities in the School of Professional Studies at Regis University in Denver, Colorado.

From birth to burial and over many centuries, headwear customs within Judaism and Islam have reflected differentiated roles for males and females. Socially, these differences have related to external appearance versus internal seclusion; and religiously, to individual declaration (with the Divine) versus personal modesty or concealment.

In Judaism, for example, the *tallit* (prayer shawl), *tefillin* (ritual paraphernalia for prayer) and *yarmulke* (*kippa*) worn by men relate to God and the Torah; while the *tiechel* (scarf), *shaytl* (wig) and Sabboth veil worn by women reflect ancient traditions associated with women's modesty and place in the home.

Similar ideas developed over generations in Islam as the turban, *kola* (Pakistan pillbox), *taj* (Dervish hat), or *agal* and *ghutra* (cord and scarf, also called *kaffiyeh*) and other headwear became associated with men's status in society and religious affiliation, while *hijāb* ("to conceal"), the practice of wearing head, face and body veils (*burqu'* / India, *chador* / Iran, and others), when applied to women means modesty and seclusion from the public.[1]

While both religions began in the Middle East, as they spread geographically around the world, variations of headwear customs, designs, and fabrication became associated with local ethnic traditions, and occasional changes of headwear usually related to appearance or style. In contrast, the *religious purpose* of covering the head for observant Jewish and Muslim males and females has remained virtually unchanged for centuries. Religious writings and life-cycle rituals document this continuity. In recent years, however, Western democratic ideas of individual rights and freedoms have impacted ancient cultural practices in both religions. Some Jewish women question why they cannot wear the *yarmulke* and pray with the *tallit* and *tefillin* (which

males have done for centuries) as a public religious commitment, while many Muslim women are choosing whether or not to wear the head and face veils instead of merely accepting veiling imperatives that have been passed down through custom and tradition. In both cases, headpieces have become sartorial signs associated with a raised consciousness regarding women's social and legal status emanating from Western influences in contemporary religion.[2]

Religious Writings

These two religions have relied heavily on sacred writings for maintaining religious traditions associated with covering the head. In both cases, headwear has assumed significantly different roles for men and women. While male headwear refers to *Yahweh* or *Allah*, female headcoverings have been largely related to sexual modesty.

Jewish biblical metaphors dealing with hair and headwear, for example, indicate religious dedication by alluding to *male* costume or armor. In Numbers (6:7) it is stated: "Their consecration to God is upon the head,"[3] and in Isaiah (59:17): "He put on righteousness like a breastplate, and a helmet of salvation on his head."[4] The apostle Paul, a Jew, used similar military allusions in his first letter to the Thessalonians by writing: "Let us be sober, and put on the *breastplate* of faith and love, and for a *helmet* the hope of salvation" (1 Thessalonians 5:8).[5]

Islamic *hadith* (oral tradition of Mohammed) and proverbs also refer to a superior leadership role for men using headwear symbolism: "Turbans are the crowns of the Arab;" "To put on the turban means to adopt Islam;" "On the day of judgment a man will receive light for every winding of the turban;" and "The community will never decay as long as they wear turbans over their caps."[6]

In contrast, religious writings referring to women's headcoverings assign different social and religious roles, associated neither with God nor eternity. Biblical references usually refer to women wearing veils or scarves as a sign of humility, modesty and purity in relationship to temporal society and men, but not to God. Moreover, uncovered hair on women has been associated with guilt, sex and sin.[7]

The Book of Isaiah (3:16-24) chastises the women of Jerusalem for their emphasis on worldly beauty:

> The LORD said: Because the daughters of Zion are haughty and walk with outstretched necks, glancing wantonly with their eyes . . . the Lord will afflict with scabs the heads of the daughters of Zion, and the LORD will lay bare their secret parts. In that day the Lord will take away the finery of the anklets, the headbands, and the crescents; the pendants, the bracelets, and the scarfs; the headdresses, the armlets, the sashes, the perfume boxes, and the amulets; the signet rings and nose rings; the festal robes, the mantles, the cloaks, and the handbags; the garments of game, the linen garments, the turbans, and the veils. Instead of perfume there will be a stench; and instead of a sash, a rope; and instead of well-set hair, baldness.[8]

Numbers (5:16-19) describes the judgment of a woman accused of adultery:

> The priest shall set the woman before the LORD, dishevel the woman's hair, and place in her hands the grain offering of remembrance, which is the grain offering of jealousy. . . . Then the priest shall make her take an oath.[9]

The Koran contains similar passages. In Surah XXXIII:59, for example, it is written:

> O Prophet! Tell Thy wives, and daughters, and the believing women that they should cast their outer garments over their persons (when out of doors): that is most convenient, that they should be known (as such) and not molested.[10]

And Surah XXIV:31 states:

> And say to the believing women, that they should lower their gaze and guard their modesty; that they should not display their beauty and ornaments except what (ordinarily) appear thereof; that they should draw their veils over their bosoms and not display their beauty except to their husbands, their fathers, their husbands' fathers, their sons, their husbands' sons, their brothers, or their brothers' sons, or their sisters' sons, or their women, or the slaves whom their right hands possess, or male attendants free of sexual desires, or small children who have no carnal knowledge of women.[11]

(In other words, they can only be seen by their husbands or men ineligible to be their husbands.)

Leaders of both religions reinforced the practice of covering women in later written interpretations. Jewish Aggadic writings continued to associate women's shame with unveiling. In 3 Maccabees 4:6, reference is made to the imprisonment of Alexandrine Jews by decree of Pharaoh Ptolemy IV (222-204 B.C.E.):

> and the young women who had but lately entered the marriage chamber for the society of wedded life, with lamentations instead of joy, and with their perfumed locks covered with dust, were carried away unveiled, sang a dirge in place of the wedding hymn, scarred by the cruel treatment of the heathen; and as prisoners *exposed* to public *gaze* . . . they were dragged along with violence.[12]

The "Susanna and the Elders" story, which was inserted into the Book of Daniel (13:32-33), depicts the righteous heroine who was to be tried for adultery after being unjustly accused by two elderly men: "as she was veiled, the scoundrels ordered her to be unveiled so that they might feast their eyes on her beauty. Those who were with her and all who saw her were weeping."[13]

Turning to Rabbinic material, the Mishnaic Law of Women states that if

a married woman went into the street "with her hair flowing loose," her husband could claim divorce without repaying her dowry (Ketubot 7:6). In contrast, unmarried girls were not bound by this regulation (Ketubot 2:11).[14] Other sources refer to the shame of transgressing Mosaic and Jewish laws regarding veiling as stemming from woman's guilt for Eve's sin as recorded in Genesis. Some rabbis, as documented in *Berakoth*, even claimed women's hair caused sexual excitement, and therefore when exposed it was like women being naked.[15]

Religious leaders in both Judaism and Islam and modern secular scholars have argued for centuries over what exactly these passages really mean. Nevertheless, observing men within Judaism and Islam have worn headpieces since antiquity for different reasons than women.

Jewish Headwear Traditions

Since Talmudic times, some men adopted the tradition of wearing a hat that came to be called *kippa* (meaning "dome" in Hebrew), or *yarmulke* ("awe of God" in Yiddish according to folk etymology). Thus, over centuries, these headpieces have served as constant reminders of men's relationship to God. Variations of design and fabrication depended on local cultural customs.

Eli and Elise Davis in *Hats and Caps of the Jews* have documented numerous variations of *kippot*. They illustrate, from the East, a four-sided peaked Bukharan pillbox decorated with intricate gold-threaded patterns; a Boteh motif, four-sectional folding *kippa* from Soviet Georgia (also found in Uzbekistan); and a seed-pearl, bead-and-gold threaded round *kippa* from India. From Western Europe, black felt skullcaps, berets, and gold-thread patterned velvet caps are shown. Other hats worn by Jewish men in Europe for pious reasons—but also following fashions—include bicornes, tricornes, streimels, spodics, fur hats, toppers and fedoras.[16] In modern Israel, a wide variety of knitted caps are produced and worn, including the *kippa sruga* associated with the popular B'nai Akiva Youth Movement, an arm of the Mizrachi (an organization fostering orthodoxy in religious study and traditions).[17]

In contrast, observant Jewish women have worn different types of headcoverings aimed specifically at covering the hair. In many locations, the three-cornered scarf called *tiechel* (in Yiddish) or *mitpachat* (in Hebrew) is traditional. Both words mean "kerchief" or "scarf," but have no references to God.

During the Middle Ages in Europe, Jews living under Christian rulers were required to wear restrictive or identifying clothing and headwear. Sumptuary laws applied to women, for example, issued by a Commission of Jewish leaders held at Forli, Italy, in 1416 decreed: "No woman shall wear . . . a gold hair-net on her head unless it be concealed except that newly-married brides may wear golden hair-nets unconcealed for thirty days after the wedding; after that time they must wear the veil over the net." [18] In this case, women had to cover not only their hair for modesty, but additionally their ostentatious hairnets so as not to antagonize Christian rulers.

Another anti-Semitic statute was issued during 1690 in Metz (France):

On Saturdays and festive occasions women are allowed to wear only ordinary veils. . . .Veils of gold or silver are expressly forbidden, except on the Saturday preceding a wedding, to the mother of the bride, her mother-in-law, sisters, sisters-in-law, grandmothers and aunts. This privilege lasts for the two days before the wedding and extends to women who conduct the synagogue on the morning of the wedding and those who accompany her under the *chupah*. . . . All coiffures made to imitate non-Jewish fashions like *godrons,* en cheveux, fontanges, are strictly forbidden.[19]

By the nineteenth century, as modern Enlightenment ideas of individual rights and freedoms spread throughout Europe, governments gradually abandoned discriminating clothing requirements. Once Western European Jews were allowed to wear what they could afford, the centuries-old question again arose as to whether there was a *halahic* (i.e. legal) prohibition in Judaism against bareheadedness. There is none, only tradition. Therefore, some male Ashkenazim in places such as France and Germany decided to adopt the position of praying with uncovered heads. Followers of the Hasidic movement continued the ancient custom of covering the head with renewed commitment.[20]

Similarly, Jewish women in modern Western Europe who desired to be more fashionable, yet still observant of ancient practices, began wearing the *shaytl,* or wig, when outside the home. By the 1800s, some Jewish women of prosperous families in Eastern Europe retained the traditional *tiechel* but in a more elaborate and elegantly ornamented style. A decorative headdress, called *stern-tiechel,* became popular in nineteenth-century Poland. For everyday, Jewish women would wear a *shleier* (veil), a simple cotton or wool kerchief tied at the back of the head with extending ends. But for special occasions, many Polish women wore the *stern-tiechel* over the *shleier.* Its base of black silk or velvet formed a crown or coronet divided into two parts, each of which had three semi-circles decorated with pearls and semi-precious stones (imitations for the less wealthy).[21] Such fashion changes in Jewish women's lives have been interpreted as reflecting a change of both the Polish and Russian governments aimed at assimilating Jews into the cultural mainstream. In contrast, Sephardic (Jews of Spanish descent) and Oriental Jewish women living in isolated Middle Eastern and North African areas were subjected to cultural head and face covering restrictions similar to local Islamic women.[22]

Islamic Headwear Customs

The turban (derived from the Persian *dulband,* which became "turband" and then "turban"; *Imāma* in Arabic; *sarik* in Turkish) is the traditional headdress of Muslim males. It consists of a cap covered by a length of cloth, usually rectangular in shape and measuring from several up to fifty yards long, that is wound around it in various ways.

In pre-Islamic Arabia, Bedouins are believed to have worn turbans. No actual records exist regarding the Prophet's adoption of the turban, but over time it has come to be recognized as the "crown of the Arabs," and religious conversion to Islam became associated with the phrase "to put on the turban," thus distinguishing Muslims from unbelievers. Traditionally, devout Muslims wore the turban when entering the mosque, reflecting the ancient belief that "God and the angels bless him who wears a turban on Fridays."

Historically, white is the common color of turbans. Green (associated with Paradise) is the recognized badge of Mohammed's descendants (Abbasids); and even though the Prophet has been depicted (in violation of human imaging) in Persian miniatures as wearing a green turban, there is no written evidence attesting to this case.[23] In some areas of the Sahara Desert, where ancient Islamic customs of desert dress still exist, different styles of white and dark turbans identify tribal affiliation.[24]

As with Jewish ritual practices, such as "laying on of the *tefillin*" (see note 33), Islamic traditions associated with the turban are also ritually prescribed. Muslim boys are given the turban at the time they begin growing a beard (puberty). When putting on his turban, a man should be standing (following the tradition associated with the Prophet) and with his right hand twist the cloth to the right around his head. If possible, a new turban should be worn for the first time on a Friday. Fabric quality and the number of turban cloths owned depends on what one can afford. The turban size should be modest, and turbans should not be decorated with gold and silver ornaments. This last tradition was obviously violated, particularly during the sixteenth-century Ottoman rule, when turbans became ostentatious, sometimes measuring as much as two feet tall or wide over the head.[25]

The turban has also been used as a symbol of investiture in the Islamic state. Mohammed is said to have placed a turban on the head of Ali, his son-in-law, and to have wound turbans on the heads of governors, thereby teaching manners and dignity. Later caliphs, following this example, placed turbans on their viziers.

For Islamic women, cultural variations have always existed for their veiling: from the *hijāb* (meaning "curtain" in Arabic) or head scarf, as is common in contemporary Turkish examples, to the *niqāb* (meaning "to perforate"), identified with the face veil (either pierced with two eyeholes or designed to drape over the face) and exposing only the eyes, which is used in North African countries such as Morocco and Algeria, as well as in Saudi Arabia.[26] The extreme black *abaya*, a large wraparound garment with armholes, is worn throughout the Middle East, particularly in Iraq; and the *chador* (meaning "large cloth or sheet") is used in Iran, Afghanistan, Pakistan and India as the large flat cloth draped around women for outdoorwear. The *burqu'* (a sewn, tent-like enveloping

Figure 1. Chadri *(sometimes referred to as* burqu'*), worn by Muslim women in Afghanistan and in some areas of Pakistan and India. Photograph by Karen Rubin.*

garment covering the entire head, face and body) is also worn in Afghanistan, Pakistan and India, usually with a mesh embroidered area over the eyes that allows vision for the wearer. In Afghanistan it is also known as the *chadri* (Figure 1). The *burqu'* can also be a face veil fastened at the sides of the temple leaving only the wearer's eyes visible.[27]

It becomes obvious that the names and meaning of these headcoverings have nothing to do with Allah, but rather derive from the notion that women should be separated from society and covered when outside the home. Nevertheless, customs are not uniform everywhere. Some exceptions exist in rural and isolated mountainous areas, particularly in Central Asia, as Islamic women wear merely their ethnic headpiece with neither head nor face veil; and if working in the fields, some women may go bareheaded entirely. In Malaysia and Indonesia, Muslim women have never veiled.

Life-Cycle Rituals—Jewish

Different roles for men and women are particularly underscored by hair or headwear worn at life-cycle rituals in both religions. Jewish boys, for example, are circumcised and dedicated to Yahweh eight days after birth at the *brit-milah* (*bris*–Yiddish) ceremony, usually performed by the community *mohel* (specially trained circumciser) assisted by other adult males wearing *kippot*, or black hats in the case of Hasidic Jews. Occasionally, a tiny *kippa* is placed on the child's head as well.[28]

Celebrating the passage from infancy, the hair of Hasidic Jewish boys grows until age three, when they have the traditional ritual hair cut (*opsherenish*), meaning "cutting" in Yiddish. Family friends gather as the boy's locks are snipped, leaving only the *peyot*, or sidelocks, unshorn.[29] Its metaphorical interpretation is associated with nature in the symbol of a fruit tree, which should be allowed to grow three years before any fruit is picked. In the primordial sense, hair is also seen as the collector of spiritual energy (as in the case of the biblical character Samson), and cutting with scissors implies human intervention. There are no corresponding rituals for females—merely a "naming ceremony" in synagogue for infant girls, which in no way carries the importance of circumcision. Nor is there a "hair-cutting" ritual for girls.

For centuries, teenage Orthodox Jewish boys have become members of the community through Torah study and preparation of a dissertation that they deliver at their Bar Mitzvah ceremonies, marking entrance into manhood. They learn to pray with traditional symbolic headpieces: the *tallit* and *tefillin*. The *tallit* is a prayer shawl woven of white wool or silk, usually with blue or black stripes on its borders, worn during daylight prayers by observant Jewish males.[30] Customarily, its size may vary from fifty-four inches to ninety-six inches in length and thirty-six inches to seventy-two inches in width.

To each of the four corners of the *tallit* are attached tassels, or *tsitsith*, consisting of four threads run through an eyelet near the corner and then doubled and knotted in a prescribed manner so that eight long threads hang down. The number of twists and knots has been given symbolic interpretation referring to the one God and the 613 precepts, 248 positive and 365 negative, of the Torah. A white silk ribbon, silver-corded lace or brocade strip (sometimes with embroidery), called *crown* ('*atarah*), is attached on top, thus indicating how the *tallit* should be worn. The word *tsitsith* is derived from the Hebrew *metzitz*, meaning "looking," which implies that God is watching the actions of humans.

Besides praying with the *tallit*, Hasidic and some Orthodox Jews also wear under their upper clothing a

garment with fringes called *tallit katon* ("small *tallit*"), also known as *arba kanfot* ("garment with four fringes"). It consists of a piece of rectangular cloth, usually wool, about three feet long and one foot wide, with tassels fastened to the four corners (Figure 2). This small *tallit* may have originated during persecution times when Jews had to refrain from exhibiting the *tallit* with tassels in public, or when the large *tallit* became too cumbersome for everyday wear. The large *tallit* is thought to have developed from the Roman *pallium*, a shawl that by the third

Figure 2. Hasidic Jewish boy wearing a Bukharan-style kippa (yarmulke) *and small* tallit *under his clothing. Note the* tsitsith *(fringes) hanging down from the waist on each side and the* peyot *(uncut sidelocks of hair). Photograph by Marilyn Kopelman.*

century was used by learned men. The biblical source for the *tallit* is found in Numbers (15:37:39):

> The LORD said to Moses: Speak to the Israelites, and tell them to make fringes on the corners of their garments throughout their generations and to put a blue cord on the fringe so that, when you see it, you will remember all the commandments of the LORD and do them.[31]

The *tefillin* (sometimes called *phylacteries*)[32] are two square boxes bound to the head and left arm with straps according to a prescribed ritual taught to young boys preparing for their Bar Mitzvah.[33] Today they are usually worn only during morning weekday prayers by observant adult male Jews, but in Talmudic times, they were worn all day. In some areas of Morocco, Jewish males wear two pairs of *tefillin* in honor of the great teachers: Rashi (d. 1105 C.E.) and his grandson, Rabbenu Tam (d. 1170 C.E.).[34] Inserted in the boxes are parchment strips with hand-written Hebrew passages from Exodus and Deuteronomy, including references to the Jewish exodus from Egypt. They also state:

> Keep these words that I am commanding you today in your heart. Recite them to your children . . . and talk about them when you are at home and when you are away, when you lie down and when you rise. Bind them as a sign on your hand, fix them as an emblem on your forehead, and write them on the doorposts of your house and on your gates.[35]

The head *tefilla* (singular) symbolizes intellectual loyalty, while the hand *tefilla* reminds the wearer to serve God with all his strength. Jewish boys receive as Bar Mitzvah gifts the entire set of prayer shawl, *tefillin* and special bags. Even though in very recent years a comparable rite of passage called Bat Mitzvah has been introduced for Jewish girls after they participate in extended Torah study, there is no reference to or association with the ancient practice of praying with the holy *tallit* and *tefillin*.

Marriage is the next important transition in a Jewish woman's life, and headwear has always played an important part in matrimonial attire. Jewish wedding costumes usually incorporate ethnic variations, and the ceremonies take place under a canopy, or *chupah*, a tradition that began in the Middle Ages. Alfred Rubens's *A History of Jewish Costume* provides artists' illustrations of Jewish bridal variations in different settings, including one of an Ashkenazi couple wearing what may have been the fashion of Frankfurt, Germany, in the eighteenth century. The groom has on a tricorne, and the bride a white veil, as they are married standing under the *chupah*.[36] Another depicts a nineteenth-century Turkish Sephardic couple under the *chupah* with the groom wearing the traditional *kippa*, similar to the Muslim fez. The bride has on a pasteboard horn adorned with flowers and sprigs of wormwood, paralleling Armenian tradition to insure fertility.[37]

The modern, popular all-white bridal veil was introduced during the nineteenth-century Victorian era in England and France, and later adopted in North America and other European countries. The veil, symbol of virginity, also represents liminality, a formal divider that is swept aside as the bride assumes her new status. Jewish brides as far eastward as Odessa, in the Ukraine, and even to Ahmedabad, India, have adopted the white wedding veil.[38] Contemporary American Orthodox couples wear U.S. fashions, including the bride's romantic white head veil, but still under the *chupah*. In some Sephardic communities, the *tallit* may be used for the *chupah*, either by suspending it from a frame or over the heads and shoulders of

Figure 3. Hasidic bride with face veil (Belzer Wedding, Jerusalem, Israel), late twentieth century. Photograph by Joan Roth.

the bridal couple.[39]

Centuries-old European wedding traditions called for veiling the bride's face as documented in a German engraving of 1705.[40] The Hasidic movement of the eighteenth century revived and continued the tradition of completely covering the bride's face to the present time. (Hasidic Jews today reject modern clothing styles as do some Protestant denominations such as the Amish and Mennonites.) (See Figure 3.)

The veiling ritual commemorates two Biblical couples: Isaac and Rebekah, and Jacob and Rachel, both referred to in Genesis. When Rebekah saw Isaac coming, she covered her face with a veil. After learning from a servant who she was, Isaac took Rebekah into his tent and made her his wife (Genesis 24:65-67). The story of Jacob and Rachel actually has influenced Hasidic rituals. Laban, a kinsman of Jacob, had two daughters: Leah and Rachel. Jacob worked seven years for Laban in order

to win Rachel (whom he loved) as a wife. Unbeknownst to Jacob, Laban substituted the older daughter Leah at the wedding ceremony, and Jacob found himself married to the wrong daughter. So he had to work another seven years for Rachel (Genesis 29:15-28).[41] Because of this duplicity, during Hasidic wedding ceremonies, the groom lifts the bride's veil, just to make sure he is getting the wife he expects.

Due to cultural antiquity dating back some 2,000 years and geographic isolation living under Arab rule for thirteen centuries, the Orthodox Jews in Yemen have maintained ancient customs. The distinctive headpiece worn everyday by women and girls, called the *gargush*, is made of dark cotton or velvet with rows of tiny silver pendants (*agrat*) of minute rings, discs, balls and triangles dangling over the forehead like fringe. The neck fastener must always be attached in public; left open, its wearer could be considered a sexually loose woman[42] (Figure 4).

Bridal *gargushes* are impressively decorated with rows of golden chains, cords, coins and jewelry, and with magnificently crafted silver or gold filigree. These works of art, passed down over generations, obviously reflect a community highly skilled in metal craftsmanship.[43] The *gargush* has undergone modifications, due largely to changes in lifestyle after 1950, when 50,000 surviving Yemenite Jews were airlifted to Israel. Contemporary versions are made of various fabrics and usually lack the exquisite metallic ornamentation of former times. In recent years, the *gargush* generally has been discarded for everyday wear by

Figure 4. Yemenite gargush *(Jewish) of velvet, silver braid, and tiny silver pendants* (agrat) *composed of minute rings, discs, balls, triangles and dangling metallic coins. Photograph by Karen Rubin.*

Figure 5. Hungarian Jewish women with shaved heads. Meah Shearim religious section in Jerusalem. Photograph by Joan Roth.

young Israeli women of Yemenite background and only brought out for weddings and festivals.

Marriage for Jewish women not only provided the community with successive generations via procreation, but it also served as protection for single women against kidnapping and forced conversion throughout the diaspora. To prevent such catastrophes, Jewish women in isolated areas such as Ethiopia and Yemen have been known to shave their heads, thus making themselves less sexually attractive. Another reason for shaving the head has arisen among Hungarian Jewish women in association with the requirements of ritual bathing in the *mikvah.* Jewish law forbids pulling any living thing from its roots on the

Sabbath. If a woman must bathe and completely wash her hair, the combing process inevitably involves tearing hairs from the scalp. Thus, observant Polish women cut their hair short, and some Hungarian women are known to shave their heads entirely to eliminate this problem (Figure 5).

Excluded from praying with the *tallit* and *tefillin*, married Jewish women *are* expected to maintain the Sabbath rituals at home. One major responsibility is the weekly lighting of the Sabbath candles.[44] Some modern women don a special veil for this purpose. In India, Jewish women may wear the traditional sari covering the head. While preparing *challah*, traditional Sabbath bread, observant Israeli wives may also wear a

Figure 6. Women with shawls during blessing of the Kohanim *(Bukhara, Uzbekistan). Photograph by Joan Roth.*

beret as a headcovering.[45] And in very traditional communities, such as in Bukhara (Uzbekistan), some women in their separated synagogue area still cover their heads and faces with shawls during the blessing of the *Kohanim* (Jewish priest of the Levitical tribe) (Figure 6).

Even at the end of life, there are still differences between male and female headcoverings. Jewish burial practices require a ritual cleansing of the deceased, who is then interred in a simple white linen shroud (*tachrichim*). Men may be buried wearing the *kippa*, sometimes with the *tallit* placed over the shoulders with one fringe cut, symbolizing that the man is no longer responsible for carrying out the Commandments, particularly praying to God.[46] In this case the *tallit* is considered *pasul* (ritually unfit). Traditionally, Jews cover the corpse's head, and there is no viewing of the body, nor demonstrations of beauty or wealth.[47] North American versions of the shroud have an accompanying head-covering hood used by observant Jews, but not if the mourning family wishes exposure of the deceased's face in an open coffin. Men's hoods are merely two pieces of cloth sewn along a circular edge.

American women's hoods have two strings. Ancient beliefs derived from the Mystical Teachings of the Kabbalah maintain that the neck, from which the soul emerges, divides the lower, physical body from the upper, spiritual part—the head. The ties on women's hoods (which signify a "connection") are frequently twisted around from the back of the neck and arranged at the forehead hairline in the shape of a *Shin*, a Hebrew letter referring to one of God's names. This ritual is interpreted by some as compensation for the fact that women throughout their lives did not pray with the *tallit*.[48]

Life-Cycle Rituals—Islamic

Less emphasis is given to headwear in Islamic life-cycle rituals. However, a traditional infant "hair shaving" ceremony is usually performed within a month or two after birth. (It is sometimes part of the *Hakika*—when a sacrificial animal is slaughtered and its meat distributed to the poor.) The child's hair is shaved off, weighed and its equivalent weight in silver or gold donated to the poor. The hair is then wrapped and thrown into a river or flowing water. This ceremony is performed for both boys and girls with a double meaning: physically, the new growth of hair will come in stronger; and spiritually, the hair becomes symbolic of the Islamic commitment toward charity.

The Islamic transition from infancy is marked by the *Bismalla* ceremony held at home with a visit by the imam when the child (about three or four years old) begins learning to read the Koran. Thereafter, classes at the mosque include learning prayers and memorizing the Koran. For this important event, boys and girls dress in special clothes, including a cap, scarf or stole. Children are expected to read the entire Koran before leaving elementary school.[49]

Circumcision (*sunna*) is the puberty rite performed on Islamic boys, aged anywhere from five to fifteen. In rural areas, the village barber performs the rite, but today it is frequently carried out in urban hospitals. Turkish boys from five to eight years old dress in a special costume, including a hat (or crown), sash and cape. Hats may be white (symbol of innocence), red (for sacrifice), or blue (royalty).[50] The word MASALLAH, emblazoned on a Turkish boy's sash, means "God created a wonder," alluding to the transition from boyhood to manhood. It is also a prayer: "Praise be to Allah." In Turkish villages, boys are treated like "kings" for several days, usually carried around town with their friends and father on carriages festooned with flowers, lanterns and streamers (Figure 7). In the Sudan, boys wear a gold or gilt crown, often preserved by families and used for circumcisions and weddings.

Circumcision for girls, a controversial custom originally based on social and cultural traditions, is practiced in certain areas, particularly in Africa, and is sometimes associated with Islam. Several types of female circumcision involve no special headwear.[51] In the Sudan, however, a girl may have her mother's wedding shawl tucked around her during the ritual.[52] Reaching puberty for Muslim girls involves protective veiling or covering of the head and face; the girl's parents usually make the decision regarding when to veil.

As in Judaism, Islamic weddings are elaborate, sometimes lasting for days. Brides dress in ornate ethnic costumes and head attire. In a Pakistani version, the young couple sits together during the ceremony. The bride wears the traditional *hijāb*, which may be pulled down covering her face; and the groom also might have an ornate gilded face veil (sometimes made of garlands), called *sahara*, attached over the turban. After exchanging vows, the groom flips the veil back or removes it entirely, with his new status symbolized by the turban (Figure 8). Since some traditional Islamic brides have their faces completely covered during the ceremony, like Hasidic Jews, Muslim grooms need to take precautions to verify the identity of their new wives.

With Muslims continuing to migrate from the Middle East and Asia to Europe and the United States, wedding costumes and customs are becoming a mixture of cultures. In some cases, the Islamic bride

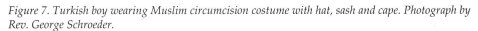

Figure 7. Turkish boy wearing Muslim circumcision costume with hat, sash and cape. Photograph by Rev. George Schroeder.

Figure 8. Pakistani Muslim bride with hijāb, *and groom wearing gilded* sahara *over his turban (side view). Photograph by Kamal Hamid.*

Figure 9. Bridal couple (to right of center) in Western-style clothes during wedding reception at Sheraton Hotel, Cairo, Egypt, 1993. Photograph by Beverly Chico.

retains tradition by wearing her ethnic costume with the *hijāb*, while the groom may wear a Western-style suit. Further penetration of Western influences can be seen in cosmopolitan urban centers of the Middle East, such as Cairo, Egypt, where brides wear long white bridal dresses with Victorian-inspired veils, and the grooms, Western tuxedos (Figure 9). The same is true for Israeli wedding couples, many of whom include in their ceremony a prayer visit to the Western Wall in Jerusalem. Still, in largely Islamic countries, the turban for married men not only associates them with Islam, but also represents male "honor." The worst humiliation for a Muslim would be to have his turban snatched away and thrown on the ground.

As with Judaism, Islamic burial practices also differentiate how male and female bodies are covered. Instructions distributed from the Islamic Center in Washington, D.C., specify the procedure for cleansing of the body and then shrouding it:

Males - The man is to be shrouded in three layers. The first sheet extends from the neck to above the feet. The second extends from the head to the feet. The third is a larger cover than the latter—it exceeds the head and feet, and will be tied above the head and below the feet.

Females - The woman is to be shrouded in five layers. The first is something like a shirt or chemise in very simple form. The second is a short veil to be put on the head and face loosely. The third is a sheet of cloth to be enclosed from the head to the feet. The fourth is a sheet of cloth to be fastened around the abdomen and breast. The fifth is a large cover to hide the entire body.[53]

Even in death, the woman is to be covered with many more layers than the man, especially the head, face and chest. For men, an ancient proverb gives instructions about preparing a male Muslim corpse for burial: "Wash him and wind a turban around his head." The attendant would reply: "Am I both washer and guarantor of entry into heaven?"[54] Another ancient custom persists in some isolated Middle Eastern areas, such as the Sudan, whereby the turban may act as a shroud if death comes unexpectedly to a desert traveler. Islamic burials in urban areas are changing, however, and some Muslims are being buried in Western-style clothes.

Contemporary Changes

Finally, within both religions, Western democratic ideas are currently influencing traditional attitudes and practices, and headwear often symbolizes these changes. Within Judaism, for example, the issue has arisen of women wearing heretofore male headpieces (*kippa, tallit, tefillin*) that have centuries-old relationships to God and prayer as opposed to their traditional headcoverings that signify only sexual or pious modesty. Difficulties posed by the prohibition against cross-dressing, or women wearing men's clothing (Deuteronomy 22:5), must be overcome. In Islamic communities, the issue of veiling becomes even more complex since it relates to personal piety, political consciousness, social status and privacy, as well as to economic factors. (The idea of Muslim women wearing the turban today because of its associations with religious dedication and eternal reward does not exist, although some aristocratic women have worn turbans in the past.)[55] A few examples will demonstrate.

Paralleling the modern women's movement, Jewish women in the U.S. began to enter the rabbinate in the 1970s. Sally Preisand broke 3,000 years of Jewish tradition in 1972 when she was ordained as the first female Jewish rabbi in the Reform Movement at Hebrew Union College, Cincinnati, Ohio. Today

Figure 10. Tallit *of Rabbi Eve Ben-Ora, Congregation Emmanuel, Denver, Colorado, 1995. Photograph by Beverly Chico.*

there are about 400 women rabbis in the U.S., and with this status comes the acceptance of women rabbis wearing the *tallit*. As a result, new styles based on old traditions have emerged. One is a narrow (approximately six inches in width), stole-like *tallit* that rests over the shoulder but does not cover the head. It has an embroidered or brocade *átarah* (or "crown" at the neck) and might be made of wool, silk or synthetic fabric, but never wool and linen together. A prohibition in Leviticus (19:19) and Deuteronomy (22:11) forbids the *shatnez* ("mixing") of these two fibers (Figure 10).[56] Another is a large silk *tallit* with hand-painted (or embroidered) Jewish symbols that, like traditional versions, can envelop head and shoulders. Both have the required *tsitsith*.

There are records of women in history who personally claimed the right to pray with the male holy headpieces. One such unusual example, Chana Rochel, studied Torah, Talmud, other commentaries and

Figure 11. *Preschool girl's personally decorated* kippa *(her name, "Naomi," in Hebrew is painted in gold, pink and green letters). Temple Emmanuel Preschool, Denver, Colorado. Photograph by Beverly Chico.*

even the mystical texts of the Kabbalah in the nineteenth-century Polish town of Ludomir. After her father's death, she converted her home into a small synagogue, prayed with the *tallit* and *tefillin* and counseled village people as any male rabbi would, but without approval of a male rabbinic authority.[57] The daughters of Rashi are said to have worn the *tallit* also.

On another level, contemporary Jewish women, many within Reform and Conservative congregations, no longer cover their hair in the traditional way. Some have created a new custom of wearing a female version of the *kippa*, or *yarmulke*, as a religious statement relating themselves in a more personal and symbolic way to God. Many new styles of women's *kippot* are currently being produced and worn, such as metallic/cotton crocheted versions with ornate hat pins; suede ones with daisy floral decorations; and multi-colored, abstract plastic ones secured with Velcro.[58] Little girls, beginning at age three, are even being encouraged to wear the *kippa*, and some are decorating their own in temple preschool (Figure 11).

Hadassah, the Women's Zionist Organization of America, Inc., which has over 300,000 members, is in the process of publishing a consciousness-raising Jewish woman's educational trilogy for distribution within various Jewish denominations (e.g. Reform, Conservative

and Orthodox). The first volume, *Jewish Women Living the Challenge*, came out in 1997. The second, *Moonbeams*, edited by Carol Diament, appeared in 2000 and contains a course of study for contemporary women's groups in the U.S. who meet on the festival of the new moon (Rosh Hodesh) to pray and explore women's spiritual qualities within Judaism. Chapter Two treats the *kippa, tallit* and *tefillin* by discussing headcoverings in Jewish literature with numerous quotes from the Torah, Mishnah, Babylonian Talmud and noted rabbinic writings. Finally, under "Suggested Activities and Programs," the authors encourage Jewish women to try on the *kippa, tallit* and *tefillin* and reveal their feelings (positive and negative) about the experience, relating these to the religious texts already discussed.[59]

Also, the question of ordaining Orthodox women rabbis has been raised and discussed in contemporary circles. The image of a modern woman wearing a traditional male *tallit* and *tefillin* is undoubtedly controversial, but it may be

Figure 12. *"New Face of Orthodox Rabbis?" (woman wearing* tallit *and* tefillin*). Moment magazine cover, December 1993. Photograph by Jack Silver,* Moment *magazine.*

only a matter of time until this ancient tradition is modified as depicted on a *Moment* magazine cover with related articles (Figure 12). Accompanying this change, other questions may arise as to whether Orthodox women should remain separated from men (*mechitzah*), whether they could be counted in the *minyan* (the quorum of ten men required for communal prayer), and if women rabbis might be obligated to the time-bound *mitzvah* (or obligation) of praying daily at certain times—something men have done for centuries.[60]

In the Islamic world, veiling and unveiling has become a complex of political, religious and social statements, particularly in countries like Egypt. There, unveiling began in 1923, associated with Huda Shaarawi and the founding of the Egyptian Feminist Union, aimed at improving women's educational, legal and political status.[61] The women's movement became part of the nationalist struggle against British colonialism.[62] By the time Egypt achieved independence as a Republic in 1953, many educated urban women had chosen to go in public unveiled and to wear Western-style clothing, while in villages, traditional veiling customs prevailed.[63] Similar trends took place from Morocco to Iran from the 1940s to the late 1970s.

Today, as part of a wave toward Islamic revivalism, in many Middle Eastern countries, activists are seeking to preserve traditional Islamic culture from extensive Western influences. In some cases, women are mandated by governments to veil (Iran and Afghanistan), and in others, such as Egypt and Morocco, young educated women are choosing to veil (Figure 13).[64] Parallel Islamic sartorial commitments are springing up in the U.S. and Europe (France), sometimes creating legal controversies.[65]

The complexity of these changes is embodied in the following nine reasons

Figure 13. Educated professional Muslim woman, resident of Cairo, Egypt, who chose to don the veil after making a Hajj *(pilgrimage) to Mecca, 1993. Photograph by Beverly Chico.*

identified by Yvonne Haddad as to why Islamic women wear and have worn the veil:[66]

(1) **Religious:** as an act of obedience to God's will and religious commitment. Jennifer Scarce (*Women's Costume of the Near and Middle East*) reproduced a Persian print dated 1306 in which the artist depicted veiled women attendants assisting at the birth of Mohammed with head-and-shoulder-covering veils similar to those worn by many contemporary women in Turkey.[67]

(2) **Economic:** as a sign of affluence implying that the wearer is a "lady of leisure." The superbly crafted

nineteenth-century Makkan veil of gold and pearls depicted in *The Kingdom of Saudi Arabia* has to be one of the most exquisite *hiqābs* ever produced.[68]

(3) **Practical:** for the less wealthy. It reduces costs for clothes worn in public. (This aspect would be especially important for rural women migrating to urban areas.)

(4) **Demographic:** as an indicator of urban dwellers. Scarce reinforces this point from studying Persian miniatures,[69] while Haddad shows how veiling has also become a status symbol for the recently urbanized.[70]

(5) **Cultural:** as a public statement and display of commitment to chastity and morality.[71]

(6) **Domestic:** as compliance with the desires of male family members.[72]

(7) **Psychological:** as an affirmation of religious authenticity by returning to cultural roots.[73]

(8) **Political:** as a sign of disagreement with or obedience to the current political power group.[74]

(9) **Revolutionary:** the need for Islamization of society as the only means of salvation.

Reasons (8) and (9) are intertwined and span the long history of Islam, as the following examples attest:

(a) The tradition of Islamic women fighting goes back at least to A'isha, Mohammad's favorite wife who, with two colleagues, led an attack against Caliph Ali at Basra (in Iraq) on December 4, 656 C.E. Historians call this the "Battle of the Camel," referring to the camel carrying A'isha. (*Hijāb*, or separation, was first required of the Prophet's wives, then later of all Muslim women.)

(b) The 1979 Khomeini-led revolution against the Shah's rule in Iran required women to reassume the veil and redefine it as a symbol of their resistance to Western-style modernity

Figure 14. Woman in black chador wearing portraits of Ayatollah Ruhollah Khomeini (right) and President Sayyed Ali Khamenei at Tehran Stadium, December 1986. Photograph courtesy of Associated Press.

(Figure 14).[75]

(c) Likewise, many Algerian Muslim women re-adopted the veil during the 1950s struggle (and again in the 1990s) as a sign of resistance against French domination. Some have been known to use veiling as a subterfuge for smuggling arms.

Some contemporary Jewish women in Jerusalem also engage in public activities challenging government and religious authority. During the 1980s, one group ("Women of the Wall") tried to pray with the *tallit* at the Western Wall, but was eventually prevented by the Ministry of Religious Affairs and the Israeli High Court because they were not "keeping with the custom of the site."[76] Hostility was still evident at the wall in 1997, as documented by an American woman wearing a *kippa*.[77] During May 1994, a right-wing women's group demonstrated against the peace agreement over the Gaza Strip and Jericho by impersonating P.L.O. members in men's headdresses (*kaffiyehs* and *agals*) along with masks of Yassar Arafat and Yitzhak Rabin.[78] Finally, whatever the reasons for choosing to cover or not cover one's head, large numbers of Jewish and Islamic women, because of an increased awareness of their status in modern society, have many more options today than ever existed for earlier generations.

[1] For a lengthy discussion of "veiling" etymology, see Fadwa El Guindi, *Veil: Modesty, Privacy and Resistance* (Oxford and New York: Berg, 1999), 6-9.

[2] This research was originally presented at the conference "Women, Families and Children in Islamic and Judaic Traditions: History and Contemporary Concerns," sponsored by the Institute for Islamic-Judaic Studies at the University of Denver, October 23-25, 1994. Since that time, a number of gender studies on women in changing

Islamic societies have appeared. Most refer peripherally to the practice of female veiling (e.g. Yvonne Yazbeck Haddad and John L. Esposito, eds., *Islam, Gender and Social Change* [New York and Oxford: Oxford University Press, 1998]). Only Fadwa El Guindi focused solely on the veil (*hijāb*). None attempted to demonstrate parallels between headcovering practices in Islam and Judaism, both of which originated in the Middle East and spread to other cultures throughout the globe. For a recent scholarly feminist rebuttal of Jewish customs related to women and haircoverings, see Norma Baumel Joseph, "Hair Distractions: Women and Worship in the Responsa of Rabbi Moshe Feinstein," in *Jewish Legal Writings by Women*, eds. Micah D. Halpern and Chana Safrai (Jerusalem: Urim Publications, 1998), 9-22.

3 *The Holy Bible, Containing the Old and New Testaments*, New Revised Standard Version (Iowa Falls, Iowa: World Bible Publishers, Inc., 1989), 125. Biblical citations not footnoted have been taken from this edition, which includes discoveries and interpretations from Semitic language documents, Dead Sea texts and the *Biblia Hebraica Stuttgartensia* fixed by Jewish scholars ("Masoretes").

4 *Holy Bible*, RSV, 706.

5 *Holy Bible*, RSV (New Testament), 196.

6 W. Björkman, "Turban," in *Encyclopaedia of Islam*, vol. 4 (Leyden: E. J. Brill, 1913): 885. Björkman discusses many variations and interpretations of the turban.

7 In her original archaeological/linguistic studies of prehistoric textiles and clothing, Elizabeth Barber has pointed to the association of women's hair with fertility. She traces the string skirt (apron) as covering female nether anatomy back to Paleolithic "Venus" figures (of Lespugue, France, and Gargarino, Russia, ca. 20,000 B.C.E.) to Neolithic figures from Balkan sites (Vinca culture, ca. 5,000 B.C.E.) and to later historic Slavic cultures when these string items became bridal clothing interpreted as protection against harmful spirits and advocating fertility. The analogy of associating hair on the head with pubic hair (indicative of the ability to bear children) may well be the clue as to why in organized monotheistic religions the mandate was adopted for women to cover their hair. See E.J.W. Barber, "On the Antiquity of East European Bridal Clothing," in *Folk Dress in Europe and Anatolia: Beliefs about Protection and Fertility*, ed. Linda Welters (Oxford and New York: Berg, 1999), 29-30.

8 *Holy Bible*, RSV, 646-47. In Jewish tradition, the LORD is usually referred to as *Adonai* ("the/my Lord") or *Ha-shem* ("the Name").

9 *Holy Bible*, RSV, 124-25.

10 *The Holy Koran*, revised and edited by the Presidency of Islamic Researches (IFTA, Kingdom of Saudi Arabia, H. 1413), 1264-65.

11 *Holy Koran*, 1012-13.

12 R. H. Charles, ed., *The Apocrypha and Pseudepigrapha of the Old Testament* (Oxford, England: Oxford at the Clarendon Press, 1913), 168.

13 Wayne A. Meeks, ed., *The HarperCollins Study Bible*. New Revised Standard Version with the Apocryphal/ Deuterocanonical Books (New York: HarperCollins, 1993), 1639.

14 Jacob Neusner, *A History of the Mishnaic Law of Women, Part II: Ketubot* (Leiden: E. J. Brill, 1980), 79-80.

15 Rabbi Dr. I. Epstein, ed., *The Babylonian Talmud, Berakoth* (London: Soncino Press, 1936), 24a. See also Samuel Krauss, "The Jewish Rite of Covering the Head," in *Beauty in Holiness: Studies in Jewish Customs and Ceremonial Art*, ed., Joseph Gutman (New York: KTAV Publishing House, 1970), 420-67.

16 Eli Davis and Elise Davis, *Hats and Caps of the Jews* (Israel: Massada Ltd., 1983), 1-60.

17 Suzanne Baizerman, "The Jewish *Kippa Sruga* and the Social Construction of Gender in Israel," in *Dress and Gender: Making and Meaning in Cultural Contexts*, eds. Ruth Barnes and Joanne B. Eicher (Providence and Oxford: Berg, 1992), 92-105. Baizerman elaborates on how traditional Israeli women have made the special *kippa sruga* to identify a political subculture of the popular B'nai Akiva Youth Movement (part of the Mizrachi—an organization that promotes immigration to Israel for the purpose of combining strict orthodoxy with religious study).

18 Alfred Rubens, *A History of Jewish Costume* (New York: Crown Publishers, 1973), 184.

19 Ibid., 186. For coiffures denied to seventeenth-century Jewish women, see Mary Trasko, *Daring Do's: A History of Extraordinary Hair* (Paris and New York: Flammarion, 1994), 43-45.

20 For a recent discussion that originated from the 1987 U.S. Congress legislation regarding military wearing the *yarmulke*, see Harry Steinhauer, "Holy Headgear," *The Antioch Review* 48, no. 1 (winter 1990), 4-25. The term Ashkenazim is generally used as a designation for Jews who originally settled along the Rhine River areas in Germany during the early medieval period; it also includes their descendants living in Europe and throughout the world. Hasidism, a movement combining elements of Kabbalistic mysticism, messianism and popular piety, emerged in the Ukraine during the eighteenth century, an era of political upheaval and profound religious questioning. It spread to Poland, Galicia and White Russia, and eventually to Israel and America.

21 Giza Frankel, "Notes on the Costume

of the Jewish Woman in Eastern Europe," *Journal of Jewish Art* 7 (1980): 52.

22 See Joan Roth, *Jewish Women: A World of Tradition and Change* (New York: Jolen Press, 1995), 55, for a contemporary illustration of a woman in Yemen wearing a black *lithma* (material draped around the head and covering all the face except the eyes).

23 Yanni Petsopoulos, *Tulips, Arabesques and Turbans: Decorative Arts from the Ottoman Empire* (New York: Abbeville Press, 1982), 200. Figure 198, a miniature from a seventeenth-century Ottoman genealogy tracing lineage back to Adam and Eve via the Prophet, depicts several rulers with green turbans. Figures 199 and 200 portray Sultans Mehmed II and Suleyman I wearing white turbans over green caps (from a copy of Lokman's *Physiognomy of the Ottomans*). Figure 209 shows the Prophet Mohammed (with turban) and the Angel Gabriel meeting Moses in Heaven (from Mustafa Zarir's *The Book of the Life of the Prophet*, ca. 1594).

24 Angela Fisher, *Africa Adorned* (New York: Harry N. Abrams, Inc., 1984), Fig. 199. The Muslim Tuareg, descendants of ancient Berbers, today roam the Tassili Mountains bordering Mali and Niger in the southern Sahara Desert. In addition to large, white turbans, Taureg men after puberty wear a *tagelmoust*, a twenty- to thirty-foot-long strip of cloth that covers the face, providing protection against desert heat and blowing sand. Susan J. Rasmussen ("Veiled Self, Transparent Meanings: Tuareg Headdress as Social Expression," *Ethnology* [April 1991], 101-17) maintains that the male turban and "face veil" indicate noble class identity and kinship roles, but that they may also be purely aesthetic expression when worn during courtship and festivals.

25 Cesare Vecellio, *Renaissance Costume Book* (*All 500 Woodcut Illustrations from the Famous Sixteenth-Century Compendium of World Costume*) (New York: Dover Publications, Inc., 1977), 110, 130.

26 The *niqāb* in Saudi Arabia consists of a rectangular piece of cloth with two holes for the eyes, attached to the back of the head by two strings. It may be heavily decorated with beads, embroidery or silver coins from a bride's dowry. Certain tribes use *niqābs* made of stiff leather stained with ground henna. Tribal affiliation is often determined by the *niqāb* style and decoration. For other examples of Saudi Arabian women's headgear, see John Topham, *Traditional Crafts of Saudi Arabia* (London: Stacey International, 1981), 104-11.

27 Jennifer M. Scarce, "The Development of Women's Veils in Persia and Afghanistan," *Costume* 9 (1975), 13. For another version, see Dawn Chatty, "The Burqa Face Cover: An Aspect of Dress in Southeastern Arabia," in *Languages of Dress in the Middle East*, eds. Nancy Lindisfarne-Tapper and Bruce Ingham (Richmond, Va.: Curzon Press, 1997), 127-48.

28 Folklife Programs and Renwick Gallery, National Museum of American Art, *Celebration: A World of Art and Ritual* (Washington, D.C.: Smithsonian Institution Press, 1982), 118.

29 David Cohen, ed., *The Circle of Life* (San Francisco: HarperCollins, 1991), 38.

30 *Celebration*, Figs. 137, 137a, 137b. See also Thérèsa Metzger and Mendel Metzger, *Jewish Life in the Middle Ages: Illuminated Hebrew Manuscripts of the Thirteenth to the Sixteenth Centuries* (New York: Alpine Fine Arts Collection, Ltd., 1982), 142, Fig. 197 for a late-fifteenth-century version of an Italian Jew wearing the *tallit* with *tsitsith* while carrying the Torah.

31 *Holy Bible*, RSV, 136-37. Curiously, while in the prehistoric era females associated with the Mother Goddess tradition apparently wore tassels (or fringes) near their lower sexual parts, in ancient Jewish tradition, dating back some 3,000 years, it is the men who wear tassels (or fringes) at the corners of their prayer shawls (see note 7). The words "tassels" and "fringes," found in many different biblical translations, seem to be used interchangeably. In the earlier RSV of 1946, the word "tassel" was used, while in this 1989 version "fringes" appears. By definition, a "tassel" is a pendent ornament ending in a tuft of loose threads. "Fringes," on the other hand, are usually the edging or trimming made from projecting ends of a fabric. Fringes can include loose threads twisted or plaited together at the top. Although modern *tallesium* usually have applied tassels, not fringes that are part of the fabric, translators have apparently used both words since no one really knows how *tallesium* were made during the ancient biblical eras. There is no confusion, however, about where the tassels (or fringes) were to be put, at the four corners of the *tallit*.

   Another translation variation is the word "blue" for the stripe on the *tallit* and tassel (fringes). Some translations refer to blue-violet (Everett Fox, *The Five Books of Moses*, [New York: Schocken Books, Inc., 1995], 736) and others use violet (*Jerusalem Bible* [New York: Doubleday & Co. Inc., 1966], 191). According to tradition, the dye used came from the mollusk *hhalazona*, and depending on the time of day when it is harvested, the dye could appear blue or violet.

32 The name *phylacteries*—derived from the Greek *phylacteria*, as used in the New Testament (Matthew XXIII:4, "Everything they do is done to attract attention, like wearing broader *phylacteries* and longer tassels")—means "things that guard" (amulets, talismans). However, Jewish *tefillin* are

not interpreted as amulets. The New Testament name may derive from an external resemblance between the *tefillin* and the Greek *phylacteria*.

33 "Laying on the *tefillin*" (used for morning prayers) is a ritual accompanied by appropriate benedictions and recitation of scriptural passages. First a box is fastened to the naked left arm above the elbow, with the strap wound around seven times below the elbow (in remembrance of the seven days of creation in Genesis). The other box is rested upon the forehead below the hair and between the eyes, with the strap knot being at the neck nape, and its ends pass over the shoulders hanging down on either side. Finally, the end of the arm *tefillin* strap is wound three times around the middle finger and around the hand. When removing *tefillin*, the box on the forehead is taken off first, then that of the arm. Both are placed into a bag for protecting sacred objects.

34 Rabbi Herbert C. Dobrinsky, *A Treasury of Sephardic Laws and Customs* (New York: Yeshiva University Press, 1986), 35.

35 *Holy Bible*, RSV, 167. Four biblical references emphasize that Jews should place a sign on the hand and between the eyes: Exodus 13:9 and 13:16; Deuteronomy 6:8 and 11:18.

36 Rubens, *History of Jewish Costume*, Fig. 179. "Wedding" —Painting by M. D. Oppenheim (in Israel Museum) with setting in Frankfurt, Germany, 1866-69. Notation indicates fashions on men date to a former time.

37 Rubens, *History of Jewish Costume*, 41, Fig. 45.

38 Roth, *Jewish Women*, 82 (bride in India); 91 (wedding couple in Ukraine).

39 Dobrinsky, *Treasury of Sephardic Laws*, 45 (Syrian Jews); 53 (Moroccan Jews). An early depiction where the *tallit* appears as a wedding *chupah* is printed in Thérèsa and Mendel

Metzger's *Jewish Life in the Middle Ages*, from an Italian manuscript dated 1438.

40 Rubens, *History of Jewish Costume*, 122, Fig. 165.

41 *Holy Bible*, RSV, 21 (Rebekah and Isaac); 26 (Jacob and Rachel).

42 Beverly Chico, "Yemenite Headdress Reflects Orthodox Jewish Values," *Artifacts* (winter 1986): 3.

43 Rubens, *History of Jewish Costume*, Figs. 71 and 72 show two magnificent Yemenite bridal *gargushes*.

44 Daniel B. Syme, *The Jewish Home: A Guide for Jewish Living* (Northvale, N.J., and London: Jason Aronson, Inc., 1989), 2. See also Lisa Aiken, *To Be a Jewish Woman* (Northvale, N.J., and London: Jason Aronson, Inc., 1992).

45 Roth, *Jewish Women,* 233, Leah Golomb preparing *challah* in Moshav Meor Modiím, an Israeli collective agricultural settlement.

46 Syme, *Jewish Home*, 106.

47 This tradition is associated with Rabbi Gamaliel's teachings dating to the first or second century C.E.

48 Feldman Mortuary personnel, interview by author, Denver, Colo., spring 1992. Within Jewish tradition, there may be other practices carried out by *chevra kaddisha* (members of traditional Jewish burial societies).

49 Saeeda Hamid (of Pakistan), interview by author in Denver, 10 September 1994.

50 Cohen, *Circle of Life*, 54-55.

51 Ibid., 56-57. See Wédad Zénié-Ziegler, *In Search of Shadows: Conversations with Egyptian Women* (London: Zed Books, 1988), 94-l02, for clinical definition and three forms of female circumcision.

52 Anne Cloudsley, *Women of Omdurman: Life, Love and the Cult of Virginity* (New York: St. Martin's Press, 1984), 105.

53 *Essentials of Muslim Prayer* (Washington, D.C.: The Islamic Center, n.d.), 15-16.

54 Andrea B. Rugh, *Reveal and Conceal: Dress in Contemporary Egypt* (Syracuse, N.Y.: Syracuse University Press, 1986), 149.

55 See Wiebke Walther, *Women in Islam: From Medieval to Modern Times* (Princeton and New York: Markus Wiener, 1993), 122, 190, 199, Fig. 154, for references to Sultana Raziyya who ruled Delhi from 1236 to 1240 C.E. and princesses in the seventeenth-century Mughal Court of India wearing turbans.

56 Rabbi Eve Ben-Ora, interview by author, Congregation Emmanuel, Denver, Colo., 2 September 1994.

57 Gershon Winkler, "They Called Her Rebbe," *Moment* (December 1993): 56-57, 98-100. For many references to rabbinic writings, *halakhic* (legal) texts and responsa addressing male and female roles in Judaism and the optional use of the *tallit* and *tefillin* by women, see Aviva Cayam, "Fringe Benefits: Women and *Tzitzit*," in *Jewish Legal Writings by Women*, eds. Micah D. Halpern and Chana Safrai (Jerusalem: Urim Publications, 1998), 119-42.

58 Artisans produce handmade women's *kippot* in Los Angeles, California, and in "Lifeline for the Old" (workshop for the elderly) in Jerusalem.

59 Diament, Carol, ed., *Moonbeams: A Hadassah Rosh Hodesh Guide* (Woodstock, Vt.: Jewish Lights Publishing, 2000), 15-35. Today some Jewish rabbis are beginning to take the position that women may wear *tefillin*. For an extensive legal discourse, see Aliza Berger, "Wrapped Attention: May Women Wear *Tefillin*?" in *Jewish Legal Writings by Women*, eds. Micah D. Halpern and Chana Safrai (Jerusalem: Urim Publications, 1998), 75-118.

60 Blu Greenberg, "Is Now the Time for Orthodox Women Rabbis?" *Moment* (December 1993): 50-53, 74, cover.

61 Huda Shaarawi, *Harem Years: Memoirs of an Egyptian Feminist*, trans. Margot Badran (New York: The Feminist Press, City University of New York, 1987). For early examples of unveiling in other countries such as Turkey (around 1910), Morocco (1940s), Iraq (1936), see Walther, *Women in Islam*, 226-27.

62 Soha Abdel Kader, *Egyptian Women in a Changing Society, 1899-1987* (Boulder, Colo., and London: Lynne Rienner, 1987), 73-89.

63 Rugh, *Reveal and Conceal*, 150-53.

64 Sherifa Zuhur, *Revealing Reveiling: Islamist Gender Ideology in Contemporary Egypt* (Albany: State University of New York, 1992), 59-61.

65 During October 1994 in Minneapolis, Minnesota, the police ticketed a completely covered Muslim woman wearing the *niqāb* (face veil) when she refused to uncover her face because she violated a 1963 state law against concealing one's identity in public. The law was originally passed to prevent thefts, bank robberies and shoplifting committed by people concealing their identity with masks or other disguises not intended for entertainment. The Muslim woman had a criminal record for shoplifting ("Muslims Angered Over Veil Ticketing," *The Denver Post*, 7 October 1994, p. 4A). Five years earlier, in Paris, France (where many former colonials from Algeria, Tunisia and Morocco reside), controversy flared up when two thirteen-year-old girls were expelled from a public school for wearing the Islamic veil because it was against school policy that prohibited wearing items of religious display in school. Newspaper headlines called it "The Scarf Affair."

66 Yvonne Yazbeck Haddad, "Islam, Women and Revolution in Twentieth-Century Arab Thought," *The Muslim World* LXXIV, nos. 3-4 (July/October 1984), 158. Haddad's conclusions were made after carrying out interviews with Muslim women in Egypt, Jordan, Oman, Kuwait and the United States from 1980 to 1984.

67 Jennifer Scarce, *Women's Costume of the Near and Middle East* (London: Unwin Hyman, 1987), 139, plate 94 (from a miniature painting in a manuscript of the Jami al-Tawarikh of Rashid al-Din).

68 Daniel Schofield, ed., *The Kingdom of Saudi Arabia* (London: Stacey International, 1986), 113. See also Scarce, "Development of Women's Veils," 5. In contrast, Wiebke Walther, *Women in Islam*, 71, points out that not all high-ranking women wore veils if some Persian miniatures are used for interpretation.

69 Jennifer Scarce, "Development of Women's Veils," 5. For a discussion of the veils worn by Berber women and Muslim urban dwellers, see Bouthaina Shaab, *Both Right and Left Handed: Arab Women Talk about Their Lives* (Bloomington and Indianapolis: Indiana University Press, 1988), 203.

70 Haddad, "Islam, Women and Revolution," 63.

71 Zuhur, *Revealing Reveiling*, 63.

72 Ibid., 64-65.

73 Ibid., 23.

74 Gelareh Asayesh, "Islamic Revolution Veils Face of Vibrant, Diversified Iran," *Denver Post*, 10 February 1991, p. 6A.

75 Iranian women after the 1979 revolution adopted the black *chador*. Commitment to the Islamist regime was displayed by one woman who attended a ceremony at Tehran stadium when troops were dispatched to the front lines during the war against Iraq. On her forehead over the *chador* were attached photos of the Iranian leaders Ayatollah Ruhollah Khomeini and President Sayyed Ali Khamenei.

76 Randi Jo Land, "Singing Sparks Clash at Wall," *The Jerusalem Post*, 7 July 1989, 6.

77 Joysa Maben Winter, "How I Became a *Kippa* Crusader," *Lilith* (summer 2000): 32-33.

78 Photo by Jacqueline Arzt (Associated Press), *Denver Post*, 4 May 1994, 9A.

BIBLIOGRAPHY

Aiken, Lisa. *To Be a Jewish Woman*. Northvale, N.J., and London: Jason Aronson, Inc., 1992.

Alireza, Marianne. "Women of Saudi Arabia." *National Geographic* (October 1987): 423-53.

Alloula, Malek. *The Colonial Harem*. Minneapolis, Minn: University of Minnesota Press, 1986.

Asayesh, Gelareh. "Islamic Revolution Veils Face of Vibrant, Diversified Iran." *Denver Post*, 10 February 1991, 6A.

Baizerman, Suzanne. "The Jewish *Kippa Sruga* and the Social Construction of Gender in Israel." In *Dress and Gender: Making and Meaning in Cultural Contexts*, edited by Ruth Barnes and Joanne B. Eicher. Providence and Oxford.: Berg, 1992.

Barber, E.J.W. "On the Antiquity of East European Bridal Clothing." In *Folk Dress in Europe and Anatolia: Beliefs about Protection and Fertility*, edited by Linda Welters. Oxford and New York: Berg, 1999.

Berger, Aliza. "Wrapped Attention: May Women Wear *Tefillin*?" In *Jewish Legal Writings by Women*, edited by Micah D. Halpern and Chana Safrai. Jerusalem: Urim Publications, 1998.

Björkman, W. "Turban." In *Encyclopaedia of Islam*. Vol. 4. Leyden: E. J. Brill, 1913.

Cayam, Aviva. "Fringe Benefits: Women

and *Tzitzit.*" In *Jewish Legal Writings by Women*, edited by Micah D. Halpern and Chana Safrai. Jerusalem: Urim Publications, 1998.

Charles, R. H., ed. *The Apocrypha and Pseudepigrapha of the Old Testament.* Oxford, England: Oxford at the Clarendon Press, 1913.

Chatty, Dawn. "The Burqa Face Cover: An Aspect of Dress in Southeastern Arabia." In *Languages of Dress in the Middle East,* edited by Nancy Lindisfarne-Tapper and Bruce Ingham. Richmond, Surrey Curzon Press, 1997.

Chico, Beverly. "Gender Headwear and Power in Judaic and Christian Traditions." *Dress* 17 (1990): 27-40.

———. "Yemenite Headdress Reflects Orthodox Jewish Values." *Artifacts* (winter 1986): 3.

Cloudsley, Anne. *Women of Omdurman: Life, Love and the Cult of Virginity.* New York: St. Martin's Press, 1984.

Cohen, David, ed. *The Circle of Life.* San Francisco: HarperCollins, 1991.

Davis, Eli, and Elise Davis. *Hats and Caps of the Jews.* Israel: Massada Ltd., 1983.

Diament, Carol, ed. *Moonbeams: A Hadassah Rosh Hodesh Guide.* Woodstock, Vt.: Jewish Lights Publishing, 2000.

Dobrinsky, Rabbi Herbert C. *A Treasury of Sephardic Laws and Customs.* New York: Yeshiva University Press, 1986.

El Guindi, Fadwa. *Veil: Modesty, Privacy and Resistance.* Oxford and New York: Berg, 1999.

Epstein, Rabbi Dr. I., ed. *The Babylonian Talmud, Berakoth.* London: Soncino Press, 1936.

Essentials of Muslim Prayer. Washington, D.C.: The Islamic Center, n.d.

Fisher, Angela. *Africa Adorned.* New York: Harry N. Abrams, Inc., 1984.

Folklife Programs and Renwick Gallery, National Museum of American Art. *Celebration: A World of Art and Ritual.* Washington, D.C.: Smithsonian Institution Press, l982.

Fox, Everett. *The Five Books of Moses.* New York: Schocken Books, Inc., 1995.

Frankel, Giza. "Notes on the Costume of the Jewish Woman in Eastern Europe." *Journal of Jewish Art* VII (1980): 50-57.

Greenberg, Blu. "Is Now the Time for Orthodox Women Rabbis?" *Moment* (December 1993): 50-53, 74.

Haddad, Yvonne Yazbeck. "Islam, Women and Revolution in Twentieth-Century Arab Thought." *The Muslim World* LXXIV, nos. 3-4 (July/October 1984):137-60.

Haddad, Yvonne Yazbeck, and John L. Esposito, eds. *Islam, Gender and Social Change.* New York and Oxford: Oxford University Press, 1998.

Holy Bible, Containing the Old and New Testaments. New Revised Standard Version. Iowa Falls, Iowa: World Bible Publishers, Inc., 1989.

Holy Koran. Revised and edited by the Presidency of Islamic Researches, IFTA, Kingdom of Saudi Arabia, A.H. 1413.

Joseph, Norma Baumel. "Hair Distractions: Women and Worship in the Responsa of Rabbi Moshe Feinstein." In *Jewish Legal Writings by Women,* edited by Micah D. Halpern and Chana Safrai. Jerusalem: Urim Publications, 1998.

Kader, Soha Abdel. *Egyptian Women in a Changing Society, 1899-1987.* Boulder, Colo., and London: Lynne Rienner, 1987.

Krauss, Samuel. "The Jewish Rite of Covering the Head." In *Beauty in Holiness: Studies in Jewish Customs and Ceremonial Art,* edited by Joseph Gutman. New York: KTAV Publishing House, 1970.

Land, Randi Jo. "Singing Sparks Clash at Wall." *The Jerusalem Post,* 7 July 1989, 6.

Meeks, Wayne A., ed. *The HarperCollins Study Bible.* New Revised Standard Version with the Apocryphal/ Deuterocanonical Books. New York: HarperCollins, 1993.

Metzger, Thérèsa, and Mendel Metzger. *Jewish Life in the Middle Ages: Illuminated Hebrew Manuscripts of the Thirteenth to the Sixteenth Centuries.* New York: Alpine Fine Arts Collection, Ltd., 1982.

Neusner, Jacob. *A History of the Mishnaic Law of Women, Part II: Ketubot.* Vol. 33. Leiden: E. J. Brill, 1980.

Petsopoulos, Yanni. *Tulips, Arabesques and Turbans: Decorative Arts from the Ottoman Empire.* New York: Abbeville Press, 1982.

Rasmussen, Susan J. "Veiled Self, Transparent Meanings: Tuareg Headdress as Social Expression." *Ethnology* (April 1991): 101-17.

Roth, Joan. *Jewish Women: A World of Tradition and Change.* New York: Jolen Press, 1995.

Rubens, Alfred. *A History of Jewish Costume.* New York: Crown Publishers, 1973.

Rugh, Andrea B. *Reveal and Conceal, Dress in Contemporary Egypt.* Syracuse, N.Y.: Syracuse University Press, 1986.

Scarce, Jennifer M. "The Development of Women's Veils in Persia and Afghanistan." *Costume* 9 (1975): 4-14.

———. *Women's Costume of the Near and Middle East.* London: Unwin Hyman, 1987.

Schofield, Daniel, ed. *The Kingdom of Saudi Arabia.* London: Stacey International, 1986.

Shaab, Bouthaina. *Both Right and Left Handed: Arab Women Talk about Their Lives.* Bloomington and Indianapolis: Indiana University Press, 1988.

Shaarawi, Huda. *Harem Years: Memoirs of an Egyptian Feminist.* Trans. Margot Badran. New York: The Feminist Press, City University of New York, 1987.

Steinhauer, Harry. "Holy Headgear." *The Antioch Review* 48, no.1 (winter 1990): 4-25.

Syme, Daniel B. *The Jewish Home: A Guide for Jewish Living*. Northvale, N.J., and London: Jason Aronson, Inc., 1989.

Topham, John. *Traditional Crafts of Saudi Arabia*. London: Stacey International, 1981.

Trasko, Mary. *Daring Do's: A History of Extraordinary Hair*. Paris and New York: Flammarion, 1994.

Vecellio, Cesare. *Renaissance Costume Book (All 500 Woodcut Illustrations from the Famous Sixteenth-Century Compendium of World Costume)*. New York: Dover Publications, Inc., 1977.

Walther, Wiebke. *Women in Islam: From Medieval to Modern Times*. Princeton and New York: Markus Wiener, 1993.

Winkler, Gershon. "They Called Her Rebbe." *Moment* (December 1993): 56-57, 98-100.

Winter, Joysa Maben. "How I Became a *Kippah* Crusader." *Lilith* (summer 2000): 32-33.

Zénié-Ziegler, Wédad. *In Search of Shadows: Conversations with Egyptian Women*. London: Zed Books, 1988.

Zuhur, Sherifa. *Revealing Reveiling: Islamist Gender Ideology in Contemporary Egypt*. Albany: State University of New York, 1992.

Gail Stein

Mr. John, "Emperor of Fashion"

Gail Stein is an archivist in the Doris Stein Research Center for Costume and Textiles at the Los Angeles County Museum of Art.

Mr. John (a.k.a. John P. John) referred to himself as the "Emperor of Fashion," an apt illustration of his life and career.[1] Upon John's death in 1993, the executors of his will donated his papers and other memorabilia to the Doris Stein Research Center for Costume and Textiles, Los Angeles County Museum of Art.[2] This material now comprises the Mr. John Archive (see Appendix).

Although a well-known creator of original and ingenious hats for the rich and famous for almost sixty years of the twentieth century, John has not yet been the subject of a comprehensive biography.[3] Therefore, this paper has two purposes: to acquaint colleagues with the scope of information available in the Mr. John Archive; and to present a review of Mr. John's life and work with information drawn predominantly from the primary sources in the Archive. Accordingly, this review will provide insight into John's talent as a milliner, his brilliant knack for self-promotion, and the uneven success of his business ventures, which nevertheless provided him with a self-proclaimed successful and satisfying career. Because Mr. John assembled the material in the Archive, it probably presents a summary of his life and work as he wished it to be seen: "I've enjoyed every minute of my career; no matter what's happened . . . I live in the illusion I created for myself."[4]

John was as imaginative with his biography as he was with his creations. Accounts differ as to his age and place of birth. One biography states that Hans Pico Harberger and his twin sister, Margarete, were born to Rose and Henry Harberger in Florence, Italy, March 14, 1906.[5] Another account states Munich or Cologne, Germany, as his birthplace in 1906.[6] His passport lists the year of birth as 1902 with his birthplace in Munich. Sometimes he spelled his parents' name as Harburger, and at other times Harberger. A few years after the birth of

John and his twin sister, the Harbergers had a third child, Elsa.[7]

According to John, his mother and maternal grandmother worked as milliners, designing for the court ladies of Vienna. His creativity became apparent at an early age. In the October 1956 issue of *Current Biography*, John stated that at the age of six he fell from a garden swing and landed in a sewing basket. To console him, Mrs. Harberger gave him fabrics with which he created a turban for his younger sister.[8] A *Good Housekeeping* article of 1957 gives another version of his early interest in hats. In the article John states that at the age of five he made a set of doll hats for the children of a poor family living nearby because he worried that they would not have presents at Christmas time. His sisters and their friends also benefited from his early creative skills when he made clothes for their dolls, too.[9] Although the veracity of the various anecdotes as to his first creations cannot be determined, it was quite apparent that Hans Pico Harberger's future would include a career as a designer.

At the end of World War I, the Harbergers immigrated to the United States, where they established a home in New Rochelle, New York. When they enrolled Hans in school, his classmates teased him about his name. He insisted that his parents Americanize it to John. In the early 1920s, Mrs. Harberger opened a millinery shop, *Madame Laurel,* on Madison Avenue, with her husband serving as its business manager. Mr. Harberger wanted their son to attend medical school and sent him to the University of Lucerne in Switzerland. However, John had his own ideas and transferred to the Sorbonne in Paris to study art. While there, he claims to have designed gowns and hats that he sold to Paris couturiers.[10]

After a year in Paris, his father sent him to Indianapolis, where he became a floorwalker in Mr. Harberger's friend's department store. To his father's chagrin, John could not stay out of the millinery workroom; he added to or removed decorations from the hats, personalizing them for each customer. His talent became apparent to the management, who appointed John as head of the millinery department. During his stay in Indianapolis, John also became interested in the theater and had occasional walk-on parts. This pursuit marked the beginning of his attraction to high society and the theatrical world.

Despite his success, John remained under his parents' influence. He left Indianapolis at the request of his father, who found a position for him as a fabric designer at the Pine Tree Silk Mills in Philadelphia. Again John demonstrated his talent and began to earn a large salary, $300 per week.[11] As in Indianapolis, the theatrical environment appealed to him, but apparently he had difficulty developing friendships with the actors and he felt lonely. "I wanted to mingle with the theatrical people, but didn't know how to meet them. . . . I was so lonely my family decided at last that I would be better off if I joined their business."[12]

John accompanied his mother to Paris to purchase materials and fabrics. This opportunity allowed him to spend time in the museums. Here John began his lifelong hobbies of painting and recreating miniature hats of the eighteenth, nineteenth and early twentieth centuries.[13] Before long, John replaced his mother on the annual business trip to Paris. Mrs. Harberger's and John's ideas often conflicted, and, since she soon would retire, John decided to follow his dream and start his own millinery establishment.[14]

At least two different accounts exist that describe the founding of his

Figure 1. Mr. John and his model, Lynn. Archives, Doris Stein Research Center, Los Angeles County Museum of Art.

business. In reference to the formation of his own company, one biography states that he opened his first salon, a two-and-a-half room apartment over Delman's Madison Avenue shoe store, by himself and afterwards formed a partnership with a young German named Frederic Hirst.[15] Another biography states that he established a partnership with Frederic Hirst and that, together, they opened this first store over Delman's.[16] Whichever version is correct, we know that John and Frederic established John-Frederics in the fall of 1928 and that the partnership endured until 1948.

It is difficult to find any documentation as to Frederic Hirst's design input, if any, to John-Frederics's creations. The small amount of data in the Mr. John Archive regarding this matter suggests that John focused on the design aspects of John-Frederics and left the business sector to Frederic Hirst. If this is true, John demonstrated a marked proficiency in knowing what society matrons desired. Word of mouth sent customers to the John-Frederics Salon. Their first customers, actress Mary Pickford and Mrs. Otis, of the elevator fortune, spread the word to their friends that they had discovered a new hat salon. At this time, the cost of a custom-made John-Frederics hat started at $35.[17]

John's intuition and talent guided him to success. His mother and her contemporaries fabricated hats from ready-made frames. John believed that a hat should be individually blocked to a personal size, "so that a hat would become practically part of a woman's head, as if she had grown it."[18] Rather than using hat molds, he designed hats by fitting fabric directly on a model's head (Figure 1). John emphasized and took pride in his method of creating hats:

> I never sketch. I design with materials directly on the head—and on only one head, Miss Lynn's. This woman is my one and only model, and although she is neither very young nor very beautiful, she gives life to every hat she wears. It's easy to design a hat for a beauty. I relish the challenge of designing a hat for an adult face.[19]

Before long, business increased and the John-Frederics boutique and workshop became *the* place to be seen. They expanded to other locations in Beverly Hills, Miami and Palm Beach, catering to society matrons and celebrities. John expressed the following about his clientele:

> My clients let me get closer to them the more successful I became. They wanted to know the artist personally. They made me a part of their lives. Before I made a hat for any of my women, I had to become familiar with them. I had to marry them, so to speak, to make hats that would please their husbands.[20]

Society matrons such as Lady Beatty, Princess Tasillo von Furstenberg, the Duchess of Windsor, and Mrs. Cornelius Vanderbilt Whitney regularly patronized the John-Frederics Salon.[21]

Two organizations established in 1930—The Associated Manufacturers of Los Angeles and Bernard Waldman's Modern Merchandising Bureau—promoted and popularized fashion designs via motion pictures. The public viewed new fashion trends in newsreels, such as Fox Movietones, in movie magazines, and more importantly, in the movies. In advance of a film's release, the movie studio supplied the organizations with sketches or photographs of styles that the actresses would wear in the upcoming production. Manufacturers contracted with the studio to produce

chosen styles to be available for retail sale at the same time the studio released the film. Often, a motion picture studio hired an established fashion designer as a film's costume designer. To this end, John joined with milliner Sally Victor to design hats for Walter Wanger's *Vogues of 1938*. The Modern Merchandising Bureau marketed copies of their creations.[22]

By 1938 the John-Frederics Salon caught the attention of some Hollywood studio executives, who hired the company to design hats to accessorize the

costumes that the actresses wore in various films. John especially enjoyed creating period hats, utilizing as models the miniature hats that he designed over the years. In 1939 David Selznick hired John to design the hats for *Gone with the Wind*. Mr. Selznick paid John-Frederics $20,000 for the hat that Rhett Butler brought Scarlett O'Hara from Paris (Figure 2).[23] One of the hats he designed for *Gone with the Wind* became a popular fashion trend: it had a "veil draped low and caught up with a piece of period

Figure 2. John-Frederics. Gone with the Wind *hat, 1939. Archives, Doris Stein Research Center, Los Angeles County Museum of Art.*

Figure 3. John-Frederics design for Goldwyn Girl Irene Vernon in The Secret Life of Walter Mitty, *1947. Archives, Doris Stein Research Center, Los Angeles County Museum of Art.*

jewelry." However, this fashion success proved to be a business misfortune for John. Another manufacturer "negotiated with the film company for the right not only to reproduce and sell hat styles from *Gone with the Wind* at the wholesale price of $12 per dozen, but also to use the John-Frederics name."[24] To further aggravate the loss, the motion picture industry was strongly unionized, which bound producers to extensive contractual rules. For unknown reasons, John had neglected to join the union and therefore never received on-screen credit.[25]

Many other actresses donned John-Frederics hats. Greta Garbo wore a John-Frederics turban in *The Painted Veil* in 1934; Goldwyn Girl Irene Vernon appeared in a John-Frederics turban in the film *The Secret Life of Walter Mitty.* (Figure 3); Marlene Dietrich donned a paradise-feather evening shell in *Shanghai Express*; Joan Crawford, Gloria Swanson, Gene Tierney, Paulette Goddard, Marilyn Monroe and countless others wore hats created by John-Frederics.[26]

John created the Charleston cloche, the wimple, the felt hat trimmed with pearls and jet, folding hats, the tailored hat trimmed with tulle, crocheted hats, hats with scarves attached, and the window veil. He also popularized the "convertible hat, a turban for country driving with a folding detachable brim to be added upon arrival."[27] The 1956 *Current Biography* attests, "other original ideas include the shoulder strap bag, stoles and ballet slippers for street wear."[28]

Enjoying the limelight, John worked and partied with his customers. He loved his vocation and delighted in viewing his creations in the movies, on the stage and in the fashion and society pages of newspapers and periodicals. His hats appealed to many and appeared on the cover of *Vogue* several times.[29]

As fashions changed, designers recognized that hat designs needed to complement the changing hairstyles. In 1941 John-Frederics, along with hat designers Lilly Daché and Sally Victor, formed Millinery Fashion Inspiration "to offer the public high-style hats at moderate prices, and . . . planned to cooperate with hairdressers in creating hat designs." [30]

During World War II, many designers incorporated patriotic themes in their creations, including John-Frederics. In 1943 John-Frederics, along with milliners Sally Victor and Lilly Daché, received the Coty Award in recognition of their patriotic contributions to the war effort.[31] At this time, John-Frederics designed the so-called "Johnny Jeep" hat for women.

While John expressed contentment with his creations during this time of prolific creativity, he disagreed with some of the business decisions of his partner, Frederic Hirst, and decided to dissolve their partnership. Several factors contributed to the breach of their business. Frederic convinced John that they should expand their business to include a perfume line, and the perfume *Chapeau* thus became a part of the John-Frederics line. But John wanted to limit their business to fashion and design. He stated that he made "no pretense at being a chemist, and that only trained chemists should dabble in perfumes."[32] In addition, John expressed concern over Frederic bringing in "high-salaried outside influences to handle the firm's perfume projects, without coordinating the ideas of the house with John."[33] Despite the fact that John-Frederics grossed approximately $1.6 million annually, selling 16,000 top-level hats, the firm suffered financially due to their perfume venture. They reinvested a large portion of their profits from the hat designs into *Chapeau*. More importantly, John believed that their entrance into the perfume field lowered the firm's prestige in the fashion domain.[34]

Still another factor contributing to the split was John's concern over the long-distance maintenance of custom millinery branches outside of New York. He disliked and resented "West Coast improvements on his designs" that questioned his creative integrity.[35] John and Frederic's dispute resulted in the dissolution of John-Frederics in 1948; with Frederic Hirst retaining all rights to the John-Frederics label, which continued

Figure 4. Mr. John, Inc. Salon and Studio, 53 East fifty-seventh Street, New York. Archives, Doris Stein Research Center, Los Angeles County Museum of Art.

to appear on accessories such as gloves, stockings, hairnets, scarves, stoles, *Golden Arrow* cologne for men and clothing for men and women.[36]

Although the exact date could not be found in the Archive, apparently John formed his own company, Mr. John, Inc., within the same year. Peter Brandon, a Yale-trained business executive and personal friend, became the Executive Vice-President. Former employees of John-Frederics split their loyalties between John and Frederic. Mr. John, Inc., had a staff of seventy-five and leased six floors at 53 East Fifty-seventh Street in New York. They called their salon "Mr. John's Royal Palace of Custom Fashion" (Figure 4). According to photographs and comments by clients, visitors and the press, John and Peter attempted to recreate the Palace of Versailles and more. They furnished the salon in the style of Louis XVI with many objects from John's personal collections. The interior featured mirrors, marble, fourteen-foot-high ceilings, huge crystal chandeliers, Corinthian columns, white and gilt paneled walls, a life-sized white porcelain cupid and paired doves, a stuffed leopard wearing a rhinestone collar, gilt statues of mythical creatures that were half-lion, live parrots, and blackamoors wearing jeweled costumes and holding plumes. Romantic pastel oil paintings by John adorned the walls. The millinery workroom, tailors' quarters for clothing production and rooms full of fabric bolts and trimmings occupied spaces inaccessible to the public.[37]

John's new venture proved successful. Early in his career, John had stated, "There's a difference between commerce and art. Reaching the unwashed masses is for someone concerned with the cash register. I never wanted that. I never created for the masses, rather for one wonderful woman."[38] This elitist sentiment expressed by John could not, and did not, endure. Beginning in the late 1950s, fashion trends changed and fewer women wore hats on a daily basis; many ceased wearing hats entirely. Accordingly, as society changed, so did John. He expressed the belief that "a top-notch milliner is duty-bound to build up the potential sales of retailers."[39] The reality, stated Peter Brandon, was that "you have to do that to survive."[40]

Thus, John broke down and decided not to separate wholesale and custom customers from the masses and opened his salon to the public. While continuing to create hats (Figure 5), he promoted a "total look" from top to toe. His creations now included ready-to-wear women's and men's clothes and accessories. The Mr. John, Inc., label expanded to include gloves, scarves, stockings, perfume, belts, furs, purses, children's hats and cosmetics. Men's accessories included hats, cravats, cologne, cuff links and shirts. Some of these items appeared under the labels Fredoras, Charmers, Sweet Young Things, Mr. Fred, Mr. John Juniorettes, Mr. John Deb Teens, Mr. John Boutique, Mr. John Custom Gifts for the Connoisseur, Mr. John Jr., Mr. John Boutique Hats and Mr. John Deb-Teens Hats. According to Peter, "We were like General Motors, with our Cadillac division, our Pontiac division, and so on down the line."[41]

John, with the able assistance of Peter, promoted Mr. John, Inc., arranging for his creations to appear before the public on a continuous basis, employing every opportunity to advertise their enterprise. They maintained organized records, which included photographs and data that they released to the press as often as possible. Beginning in 1952, they planned each collection around a central theme

Figure 5. Mr. John, Inc., ca. 1950. Archives, Doris Stein Research Center, Los Angeles County Museum of Art.

and gave every hat a name. Often they emphasized a specific color, fabric or pattern. Sometimes they incorporated social and political events into their themes. They named the Spring/Summer 1953 Collection, for example, the "Coronation of Spring: The Royal Garden Party" to commemorate Queen Elizabeth's coronation (Figure 6). For other themes, Mr. John used his vivid imagination. He named the Autumn/Winter 1955 Collection "Florentine," the Autumn/Winter 1958 Collection "Gainsborough," the Autumn/Winter 1961 Collection "La Belle Epoque," and the Spring/Summer 1956 Collection "Directoire." Each collection had its own

brochure, with sketches, photographs and an elaborate and complete description of John's creations for that season. The following is an excerpt from the brochure for the Fall/Winter 1952 Collection, titled "Heaven on Earth":

One Touch of Venus: At twilight, the first star in the heavens is Venus, and under her spell Mr. John has created a series of shadowy, romantic hats for twilight-time. Some are Stardust Caps and Magic Carpet Cloches of crumpled embroidered velvet; some are wispy Diana Turbans encrusted with heavy Lunar Fringe; some are Heavenly Haloes—a tiny toque enclosed . . . ."[42]

In addition, Mr. John, Inc., began releasing *Fashion News* by Mr. John, Emperor of Fashion.[43] This newsletter always espoused the talents of John, as well as how influential and important he was to the fashion industry. The ostentatious language in the newsletters and press releases illustrates John's flamboyant character. John and Peter had a cache of Mr. John, Inc., news releases from which to select their blurbs on new designs, such as the one that follows:

> Mr. John P. John society award-winning couturier-milliner, "Mr. John" realizes today's romantic traveler needs the assurance of feminine prettiness. He designed this packable and becoming Venetian Traveler to underwrite the wearer with fashionable travel insurance . . . [which] will delight your favorite masculine travel companion. This hat is

named . . . and is from Mr. John's new travel-inspired "Romance in Venice— 1953" Fall and Winter Collection.[44]

The biographical sketch of John released by Mr. John, Inc., refers to him as "John P. John, Internationally Famous Fashion Authority." His advertisements appeared in numerous American and foreign newspapers and journals. The press covered John's presence at many social functions, reporting on the socialites and celebrities he accompanied to events and those who frequented his salon. As Mr. John, Inc., grew, so too did his celebrity clientele. The Duchess of Kent, Princess Grace, Mrs. Nelson Rockefeller, Mrs. John N. Rosenkrans and Mrs. Gordon Getty frequented his salon, as well as many stage, motion picture and television actresses.[45]

In 1951 John and Mrs. Cornelius Vanderbilt Whitney attended a costume ball as Napoleon and Josephine. Thus was born the reference to John as the "Emperor of Fashion." He welcomed and adopted this moniker for himself and was frequently photographed in a Napoleonic pose both with and without the costume. Throughout the years, he also collected Napoleonic memorabilia. The Mr. John Archive holds photographs of John and Mrs. Whitney as Napoleon and Josephine, as well as correspondence between them in which they assumed the roles of the historical personalities.[46]

Another unique aspect to Mr. John, Inc., was its Victorian Hat Salon and Paris Gift Boutique located in the M. N. Ammann Hardware Store in Riverhead, Long Island. Peter Brandon's great-great-grandfather opened the store in 1816, and Peter restored it to "the old country store atmosphere as nearly as possible, much as it was back in 1816 when it was established by my family." Photographs of a section of the hardware store reveal a chic display of Mr. John, Inc., hats and accessories.[47]

John and Peter frequently traveled to Europe and to other exotic sites in search of new ideas, colors and fabrics. During their travels abroad, they made themselves and their models available for photo opportunities. The photo sessions began as they and their entourage boarded the ocean liner and ended when they returned to their salon. On top of all the aforementioned publicity tactics, they held a special showing for the press twice a year. In addition, Mr. John, Inc., orchestrated frequent fashion shows for the public and appeared on radio and television programs as well as at charitable events. Still another opportunity to advertise Mr. John, Inc., occurred when the City of

Figure 6. Mr. John, Inc. "Royal Garden Party" hat for the 1953 Coronation of Spring *collection. Archives, Doris Stein Research Center, Los Angeles County Museum of Art.*

Figure 7. Mr. John, Inc. "Ikette" hat, 1952. Archives, Doris Stein Research Center, Los Angeles County Museum of Art.

New York granted John permission to plant a Ginkgo tree in front of his salon. To welcome the tree, he held a "Tree Planting Ceremony," complete with floral vines and, in the salon's display window, added a life-size Flora, Goddess of Flowers, draped with leaves. Beautiful models and, of course, photographers, attended the celebration.[48]

Every occasion or special event led John to exhibit another, frequently whimsical, side to his creativity that generated commentary by the media. Aside from designing hats for the retail market, John tailored hats for special events and products, always exhibiting skilled workmanship. He designed the "General's Delight" hat in honor of General MacArthur, as well as the "Capital Airlines" hat, the "Ikette" hat, 1952 (Figure 7), the "Merry-Go-Round" hat of 1951 (Figure 8) and the "Banana Peel" and "Orange Peel" hats. He even went so far as to create hats for elephants and dogs. In 1950 John unveiled a hat for a baseball player that "protects his eyes from the sun, the back of his neck from the sun, his ears from the sun—and his pate from misguided missiles."[49] The *New Yorker* magazine characterized John in their cartoons as the official expert on hat styles.[50]

In 1953 John designed new summer and winter uniforms for New York state troopers. He stated, "the average trooper looks so dark, dreary and uncomfortable in his uniform that a person shies from him. . . . [He] shuddered at mention of the fact that the troopers now wear the same heavy uniform in the summer." The sketches for the new uniforms reveal a more practical costume that, according to Mr. John, permitted the state troopers more "freedom, comfort, dignity and far more eye-appeal."[51]

John's designs remained in demand and his business flourished into the early 1960s. The motion picture industry continued to employ him to design hats for many films. Unfortunately, his designs would be attributed to the designers Adrian, Travis Banton, Walter Plunkett, and William Travilla. John created the hats worn in the Metro-Goldwyn-Mayer movie *A New Kind of Love* with Paul Newman and Joanne Woodward (1963). However, Edith Head received the credit for all the costumes designed for this movie. His designs also appeared in the movies *Gentlemen Prefer Blondes* (1953) and *Death in Venice* (1971). In 1964 he served in an advisory role for the movie *My Fair Lady*.[52] Sketchbooks in the Mr. John Archive have hat designs with notations that designate them as creations for Adrian costumes. Furthermore, the hundreds of photographs of hats that are housed in the Archive with notations for

Figure 8. Mr. John, Inc. "Merry-Go-Round" hat, 1951. Archives, Doris Stein Research Center, Los Angeles County Museum of Art.

Brandon, needed some additional financing to expand its profitable licensee operations, because "all custom businesses are expensive to run and are not very profitable."[58] More than one factor contributed to the financial problems of Mr. John, Inc. The company was unable to obtain the loans that they had depended upon in the past to finance the production of a custom couture and accessory collection. Additionally, they had contracted with an Italian company to manufacture a new, very reasonably priced licensee dress collection that John had designed. Their planned profit evaporated when a worker's strike occurred in Italy and the factory burned. The Italian company requested that Mr. John, Inc., wait for two years while they relocated to another facility in Brazil. Unable to hold out, John and Peter looked elsewhere for financial aid.[59]

Correspondence, memos and court documents in the Archive contain the following information about the events that led to the collapse of Mr. John, Inc., as controlled by John and Peter. In 1975, during the time of their financial crisis, an acquaintance introduced John to Mr. Leonard Brown, Financial Resources Corporation, New Jersey. Brown convinced him that the Financial Resources Corporation had "unlimited funds to invest," and would gladly invest in Mr. John, Inc. Without obtaining legal advice, John naively signed a contract with Leonard Brown that allowed Brown to gain complete control of Mr. John, Inc.[60]

The agreement between Mr. John, Inc., and Brown's Financial Resources Corporation gave Brown fifty-five percent ownership of Mr. John, Inc., and forty-five percent to the parent company,

specific motion picture and stage productions offer additional evidence of John's copious contribution.[53]

By the mid-1960s, a Mr. John, Inc., suit and dress cost $395 and up, and hats cost upwards of $69.50.[54] Mr. John, Inc., grossed "close to $2,000,000 annually."[55] Notwithstanding the considerable amount of money that Mr. John, Inc., earned in the mid-1950s and 1960s, serious financial problems plagued the corporation. Fabricating and selling hats comprised a large percentage of the business costs. However, their expansion into other design areas affected the financial stability of Mr. John, Inc. Additionally, by this time hats had faded from fashion. In 1970, John closed his Fifty-Seventh Street salon, but continued "to design for special clients off and on for the next twenty years."[56] John declared, "that women no longer had character or chic, having sold-out to hairdressers who make orthopaedic hairdos and French-fried curls."[57]

The corporation, according to Peter

or to John personally. Financial Resources Corporation would develop a complete licensing program and arrange a capital loan of $50,000 to the parent company. In turn, one-third of the $50,000 would be advanced by the parent company to the New Corporation for advertising and start-up. All matters concerning fashion design, presentation and creativeness were to be presented to John for his approval.[61]

Quickly thereafter it became apparent that Brown had no intention of financially aiding Mr. John, Inc. Brown's charm and promises soon ceased to exist. He fired Peter Brandon, sold valued patterns of dresses and accessories and moved all of John's personal property from the salon to the Brown residence in New Jersey. In short, according to Peter Brandon, Brown destroyed Mr. John, Inc., as well as "demeaning" John.[62]

In 1977 Peter filed a complaint with the District Attorney for the County of New York against Leonard Brown claiming fraud by Brown. Brandon claimed that Brown failed to consult John on matters concerning fashion design, presentation and creativeness. John sued Brown, but due to threatening phone calls, "John was actually physically afraid to testify successfully against Brown" and dropped the case. Brown continued to hold the Mr. John label and collected as much as $60,000 annually from one licensee and well over a million dollars from the Mr. John label itself.[63]

In 1979 John opened a new salon in New York under the name Mr. John, King of Fashion, where he continued to design for several friends and loyal customers until his death, on June 25, 1993.[64]

[1] The expression "Emperor of Fashion" appears in press releases for Mr. John, Inc. Unfortunately, the majority of the press releases in the Archive are not dated. Mr. John Archive, Doris Stein Research Center for Costume and Textiles, Los Angeles County Museum of Art.

[2] Founded in 1987, the Doris Stein, Research Center is a comprehensive resource center for costume-and textile-related studies. Resources include a library of 10,000 volumes, including rare books and runs of over sixty-five journals and magazines; a 2,500 piece "hands-on" study collection; original prints, drawings, vintage fashion plates, sketches and manuscripts dating from the sixteenth through the nineteenth century; extensive files on regional dress, designers, costume and textile subjects and chronological history; and a collection of vintage photographs. The Center's mandate is to facilitate and contribute to scholarship, and to make a major collection accessible for study. Access is tempered by current, responsible, professional practice as outlined by the International Committee on Museums (I.C.O.M.) in order to protect and preserve the collection for future generations.

[3] The author has substituted the word "creator" for "designer" because John disdained the word designer: "I hate the word 'designer.' There are only six, maybe seven, in the world today who really create fashion. The others steal a sleeve from some creator with real talent, a neckline from another—this is creative ability? A real designer wouldn't know how to copy, it would take too long, he wouldn't have the patience." ("Fashion's Royalists in Dissent," *Sunday News*, ca. 1970. Photocopy of article in the Mr. John Archive.)

[4] Adrienn Scott, "The Milliner's Tale," *New York* (n.d.): 46. Mr. John Archive.

[5] "John, John P(ico)," *Current Biography: Who's News and Why* 17, no. 9 (October 1956): 47-48. Mr. John Archive.

[6] Richard Martin, ed., *Contemporary Fashion* (New York: St. James Press, 1995), 252-53.

[7] Nanette Kutner, "It Had to Be Hats: His Own Story by Mr. John," *Good Housekeeping* (June 1957): 72. Mr. John Archive.

[8] "John, John P(ico)," 47.

[9] Kutner, "It Had to Be Hats," 72.

[10] "John, John P(ico)," 47.

[11] Ibid.

[12] Kutner, "It Had to Be Hats," 73.

[13] Ibid. The original miniature hats are in the Mr. John Archive.

[14] Ibid.

[15] "John, John P(ico)," 48.

[16] Kutner, "It Had to Be Hats," 73.

[17] Amy Sullivan, "Million-Dollar Milliner," *Harper's Bazaar* (September 1993): 123-25. Mr. John Archive. Adjusted for inflation, a $35 hat would cost $336.10 in the year 2000 (http://www.westegg.com/inflation/).

[18] Kutner, "It Had to Be Hats," 73.

[19] Sullivan, "Million-Dollar Milliner," 125.

[20] Scott, "The Milliner's Tale," 43.

[21] Ibid., 42-46.

[22] Dilys E. Blum, "Ahead of Fashion: Hats of the 20th Century," *Philadelphia Museum of Art Bulletin* (summer/fall 1993): 26-27.

[23] Colin McDowell, *Hats: Status, Style and Glamour* (New York: Rizzoli International Publications, 1991), 159. The Department of Costume and Textiles, LACMA, holds the original working model of a John-Frederics hat for *Gone with the Wind*.

[24] Blum, "Ahead of Fashion," 27.

[25] Sullivan, "Million-Dollar Milliner," 124.

[26] Ibid. Photographs of actresses in these hats may be found in the Mr. John Archive.

[27] Ibid.

[28] "John, John P(ico)," 48.

[29] Blum, "Ahead of Fashion," 26. John-Frederics hats and Mr. John, Inc., hats appeared on the following *Vogue*

covers : June 15, 1943; October 15, 1944; January 15, 1946; August 1, 1946; and February 15, 1953.

30 Blum, "Ahead of Fashion," 32.

31 Ibid., 29. The Coty Award was the American fashion industry's equivalent of the Oscars. During his career John received the Coty American Fashion Critics Award, 1943; Neiman Marcus Award, 1950; Millinery Institute of America Award, 1956; Millinery Research Oscar for Best Fashion Show Hats of the Year, International Center of Arts and Costume, Palazzo Grassi, Venice, 1970; American Fashion Critics Award, 1970; and Honorary Citizen of Boys Town of Italy, 1970. He lectured on fashion at Columbia University, New York University, and at Hunter, Barnard, Vassar, Smith, Sarah Lawrence and Wheaton Colleges. ("John, John P(ico)," 48; miscellaneous undated articles in the Mr. John Archive.)

32 Charles Lehman, "Perfume Losses Caused John-Frederics Split," *Millinery Research: The Voice of the Millinery Industry* 11, no. 7 (7 July 1948): 1. Mr. John Archive.

33 Ibid.

34 Ibid.

35 Ibid.

36 Ibid.

37 Haskel Frankel, "A Baffled Male Reconnoiters Mr. John's Empire," *The National Observer* (1965). See also photographs and newsletters in the Mr. John Archive.

38 Sullivan, "Million-Dollar Milliner," 125.

39 Lehman, "Perfume Losses."

40 Bernadine Morris and Barbra Walz, *The Fashion Makers: An Inside Look at America's Leading Designers* (New York: Random House, 1978), 122.

41 Sullivan, "Million-Dollar Milliner," 125. See also photographs and newsletters and notes in the Mr. John Archive.

42 Brochure for the "Heaven On Earth" Collection 1952. Mr. John Archive.

43 The majority of the *Fashion News* issues in the Archive are undated. However, the first issues appear about 1952.

44 *Fashion News*, 1953. Mr. John Archive.

45 Miscellaneous notes, photographs and correspondence in Mr. John Archive.

46 Sullivan, "Million-Dollar Milliner," 124; correspondence in Mr. John Archive.

47 Photographs and notes. Mr. John Archive.

48 Ibid.

49 Murray Robinson, "Let's Give Baseball That 'Unburnt Look': Comes the Revolution, Our Diamond Heroes Will Be Style Horses," *New York World-Telegram The Sun* (8 April 1950), 2nd section. Mr. John Archive.

50 *New Yorker*, n.d. (photocopy). Mr. John Archive.

51 Weston Barclay, "Dressed to Kill," *World Telegram and Sun Saturday Magazine* (1953), 4. Sketch and article in Mr. John Archive.

52 Drake Stutesman, "Gives Good Face: Mr. John and the Power of Hats in Film," *Framework: The Journal of Cinema and Media* 41 (autumn 1999): 90-91. The issue of the lack of credit given to Mr. John for many of his hat designs for movies is referred to in some of the other biographical sources listed for this article. They too do not offer an explanation regarding this matter. Furthermore, inquiries to designer guilds about the absence of credit to Mr. John did not proffer answers.

53 Ibid.; see also photographs in the Mr. John Archive.

54 Adjusted for inflation, a $395 suit or dress would cost $2,119.21 in year 2000 dollars, while $69.50 would cost $372.87 in year 2000 (http://www.westegg.com/inflation/).

55 Frankel, "Mr. John's Empire."

56 Stutesman, "Gives Good Face," 102. There is no data in the Mr. John Archive, nor in any publication that states where Mr. John designed and manufactured hats and clothes after closing his salon.

57 McDowell, *Hats: Status, Style and Glamour*, 160.

58 Correspondence, memos and notes of Peter Brandon, n.d.

59 Ibid. There is no explanation in the Mr. John Archive as to why they could not obtain a loan.

60 Correspondence, memos, notes and court documents of Peter Brandon, John P. John and Mr. John, Inc., 1970s. Mr. John Archive.

61 Correspondence from Financial Resources Corporation to John P. John and Mr. John, Inc., 17 October 1975. Mr. John Archive.

62 Notes of Peter Brandon. Mr. John Archive. It is unclear as to which salon this note refers to because there is documentation that John closed his salon in 1970.

63 Correspondence from District Attorney of the County of New York to Peter Brandon, 5 May 1977; notes of Peter Brandon. Mr. John Archive.

64 Telephone conversation with Ms. Drake Stutesman, friend of Mr. John, on March 6, 2000; Martin, *Contemporary Fashion*, 252-53.

APPENDIX

Mr. John Archive

The Mr. John Archive encompasses the life and work of Mr. John (a.k.a. John P. John), hat designer. The Archive contains a biography, sketches, and miniature hat collection; photographs of John's hat, fur, costume and accessory designs, as well as photographs of John himself. Also included are brochures, correspondence, a client list, news releases, journal and news clips, greeting cards and other data that John amassed throughout his career. In addition to the photographs of his designs, John saved photographs of the society matrons and celebrities who frequented his salon. Photographs comprise the majority of the collection. Among the personal documents are records that define the last years of Mr. John and his enterprise: his passport, a General Power of Attorney, international certificates of vaccination, a health insurance card and legal documents and correspondence in reference to a lawsuit between Mr. John, Inc., and Leonard D. Brown Financial Resources.

The Mr. John Archive spans the years from 1906 to the 1980s, with the bulk of the collection dating to the 1950s and 1960s. The Doris Stein Research Center personnel arranged the archive into six series and edited the original consignment to seventy-two linear feet to eliminate duplicates. Archivist Gail Stein processed the collection with the assistance of Norma Green, Marion Kaplan, Pauline Kuntz, Siuin Morrissey, Susan Ogle, Sandra Rosenbaum and Betty Zucker.

The Department of Costume and Textiles, Los Angeles County Museum of Art, holds several of Mr. John's original hats.

BIBLIOGRAPHY

Arbus, Amy. *No Place Like Home*. Garden City, N.Y.: Doubleday and Company, 1986.

Blum, Dilys E. "Ahead of Fashion: Hats of the 20th Century." *Philadelphia Museum of Art Bulletin* (summer/fall 1993): 10-44.

Clark, Fiona. *Hats*. London: Anchor Press, 1982.

Ginsburg, Madeleine. *The Hat: Trends and Traditions*. Hauppauge, N.Y.: Barron's Educational Series, 1990.

Martin, Richard, ed. *Contemporary Fashion*. New York: St. James Press 1995.

McDowell, Colin. *Hats: Status, Style and Glamour*. New York: Rizzoli, 1991.

Morris, Bernadine, and Barbra Walz. *The Fashion Makers: An Inside Look at America's Leading Designers*. New York: Random House, 1978.

Reilly, Maureen, and Mary Beth Detrich. *Women's Hats of the Twentieth Century for Designers and Collectors*. Atglen, Penn.: Schiffer Publishing, 1997.

Shields, Jody. *Hats: A Stylish History and Collector's Guide*. New York: Clarkson Potter, 1991.

Smith, Desire. *Hats with Values*. Atglen, Penn.: Schiffer Publishing, 1996.

Stegemeyer, Anne. *Who's Who in Fashion*. 3rd ed. New York: Fairchild Publications, 1996.

Stutesman, Drake. "Gives Good Face: Mr. John and the Power of Hats in Film." *Framework: The Journal of Cinema and Media* 41 (autumn 1999): 89-104.

MR. JOHN ARCHIVE

Barclay, Weston. "Dressed to Kill." *World Telegram and Sun Saturday Magazine* (1953).

Frankel, Haskel. "A Baffled Male Reconnoiters Mr. John's Empire." *The National Observor* (1965).

"John, John P(ico)." *Current Biography: Who's News and Why* 17, no. 9 (October 1956): 47-48.

Kutner, Nanette. "It Had to Be Hats: His Own Story by Mr. John." *Good Housekeeping* (June 1957): 70-77, 162-66.

Lehman, Charles. "Perfume Losses Caused John-Frederics Split." *Millinery Research: The Voice of the Millinery Industry* 11, no. 7 (7 July 1948): 1.

Robinson, Murray. "Let's Give Baseball That 'Unburnt Look': Comes the Revolution, Our Diamond Heroes Will Be Style Horses." *New York World-Telegram The Sun* (8 April 1950).

Scott, Adrienn. "The Milliner's Tale." *New York* (n.d.): 42-46.

Sullivan, Amy. "Million-Dollar Milliner." *Harper's Bazaar* (September 1993): 123-25.

Christina Bates

Women's Hats and the Millinery Trade, 1840-1940
An Annotated Bibliography

Christina Bates is curator and historian at the Canadian Museum of Civilization, Hull, Quebec. She recently organized a panel presentation on dressmaking and millinery for the CSA national symposium, 2001.

Introduction

This annotated bibliography was developed during the course of a research project on the history of the millinery trade in Ontario, Canada. The impetus for this research is a collection of five-hundred hats at the Canadian Museum of Civilization, mostly dating from the 1920s, all from one millinery shop in Sarnia, Ontario. Along with analysis of the collection itself, I traced the millinery trade through documentary sources. The research period starts in 1840, when millinery became a trade separate from dressmaking and when publications on millinery techniques began to proliferate, and ends in 1940, when the trade showed signs of decline. Primary sources such as census returns, city directories and newspapers established the basic parameters of the trade. To enhance the statistical information, I consulted material published during this period relating directly to the millinery trade. These titles, along with works written on the history of women's hats and the millinery trade, make up this bibliography.

The first section of the bibliography lists occupational guides produced for youth groups or schools, where millinery was included as a possible career choice. Although biased toward positive endorsement of the trade, these instructional books provide useful information describing the aptitudes required for the work, average wages and promotional facilities. This section of the bibliography also includes labor studies of the trade that outline the economic factors in the millinery retail and wholesale trades, including the problem of seasonal, rather than year-round, employment. The studies also address directly, or indirectly, the ramifications of the gender bias in the millinery trade. The most useful volumes in the first section are by Edna Bryner, Marjory MacMurchy and Lorinda Perry.

The second section lists the technical hatmaking manuals I consulted to understand the milliner's métier and techniques. The heyday for custom millinery was between the years 1890 and 1925, and most of the manuals date to this period. Up to the 1890s directions are sketchy and mostly limited to fabric hats with foundations of cane, straw or cardboard. After the 1890s, when millinery entered the trade-school curriculum and well-known milliners established their own schools, technical instruction became more standardized and thorough. The manuals for the period from 1890 to 1920 have lengthy directions for wire-frame construction (Figure 1), a traditional technique that was slowly dying out. By the 1920s many milliners used ready-made foundations, and the popularity of felt for women's hats created the need for new techniques in blocking. The most comprehensive manuals include those by Anna Ben-Yusuf, Violet Brand and Beatrice Mussared, and Rosalind Weiss.

This bibliography concentrates on handmade millinery, rather than industrial or machine production. However, some workshops employed scores of "copyists" to make hats by hand in quantity. The section on wholesale millinery and merchandizing concentrates on the large-scale production and sale of hats including works on straw hat production, usually a large-scale enterprise. The book by Charlotte Rankin Aiken has proved very useful for identification of millinery materials and for tips on choosing styles for customers.

Works on the history of hats and the millinery trade define the final section of the bibliography. Included are a few contemporary hatmaking manuals that describe historical techniques. I have chosen French titles, which are

Figure 1. Visual instructions for making wire hat frames. Florence Anslow, Practical Millinery *(London: Sir Isaac Pitman, 1922): 57. All instruction manuals included chapters on wire frame construction until the 1930s, when this traditional technique was phased out.*

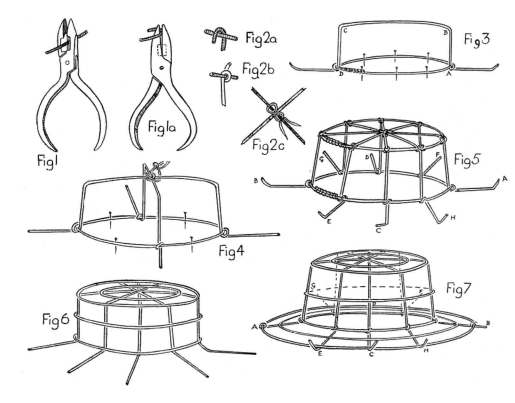

particularly worthwhile for their illustrations and information on the millinery trade. Of the books on design chronology, the best are by Fiona Clark and Madeleine Ginsburg. In the last few years historians and curators have shown serious interest in the millinery trade in terms of regional, labor and women's history, including Christina Bates, Christie Dailey, Wendy Gamber, Christine Godin, Claire Gonzales, Janet Loverin and Glendyne Wergland. A section on biographies of milliners follows the general listings of secondary sources. While most biographies deal more with celebrities than the trade, the careers of Yvette Brillon and Aage Thaarup are worth reading.

Trade periodicals are fruitful sources for the history of the millinery trade, although they are slanted toward manufacturers, wholesalers and large retailers, usually male. For a list of English and American trade catalogues, consult Fiona Clark and Kevin L. Seligman, respectively. For Canada, the English-language sources are the Toronto *Canadian Milliner* and the Toronto and Montreal *Dry Goods Review*, which contained a millinery report in virtually every issue.

Millinery and its sister trade, dressmaking, allowed women to transform female skills into lucrative occupations. The interest in the history of millinery and dressmaking has increased in the last few years, and it is hoped that this bibliography will serve as an aid for future researchers.

Occupational Guides and Studies, 1840-1940

Babcock, L. M. "Employments for Women—No. 6: Millinery." *The Delineator* (Oct. 1894): 50-52.
◆ Short article in a women's journal on the suitability of the trade for women, the skills required, divisions of work and types of establishments.

Bryner, Edna. *Dressmaking and Millinery.* Cleveland, Ohio: Survey Committee of the Cleveland Foundation, 1916.
◆ Results of a survey of the trades in Cleveland, Ohio, with reference to surveys in other parts of the United States. Chapters on training, conditions of work, comparison between retail and wholesale. Detailed and informative.

Carter, Lillian. *Plastic Millinery and Miniature Dressmaking.* London: Cassell, 1911.
◆ Course designed to encourage aptitude among schoolgirls for dressmaking and millinery. Directions for modelling miniature hats first from plasticene, clay or crepe paper, then from fabric.

[Devlin, James]. *The Guide to the Trade: The Dress-maker and the Milliner.* London: Charles Knight, 1843.
◆ Advice on aptitude, apprenticeship, tasks and physical requirements.

Dodge, Harriet Hazen. *Survey of Occupations Open to the Girl of Fourteen to Sixteen Years.* Boston: Girls Trade Education League, 1912.
◆ General discussion of young female

employment, mostly in industrial trades. With a chart that lists wages, training, qualifications, advancement, disadvantages, seasons and hours for millinery (pp. 24-25).

MacMurchy, Marjory. *The Canadian Girl at Work*: *A Book of Vocational Guidance*. Toronto: A. T. Wilgress, 1919.
◆ Chapter on millinery training, wages and working conditions. Also contains advice on starting a business, including how to be independent by budgeting earnings.

Massachusetts Minimum Wage Commission. *Report on the Wages of Women in the Millinery Industry*. Bulletin 20. Boston: Wright and Potter Printing, 1919.
◆ Emphasis on industrial employment in straw hat, artificial flower and feather factories, as well as on wholesale millinery. Includes information on millinery retailing. Numerous tables.

Nienburg, Bertha Marie von der. *Conditions in the Millinery Industry in the United States*. Washington, D.C.: Government Printing Office, 1939.
◆ Department of Labor study of the millinery industry in cities across the United States. The study attributes the industry's losses between the years 1936 and 1939 to poor resources and lack of knowledge of sound business methods or market conditions. Details on numbers, salaries and sex of millinery factory workers.

Ontario Department of Labour. *Vocational Opportunities in the Industries of Ontario: A Survey*. Bulletin 1, *General Introduction*. Bulletin 3, *Dressmaking and Millinery*. Toronto: Ryerson Press, 1920.
◆ School occupational manual containing information on numbers of millinery workers, consumer demand, scope of the field, apprenticeship, seasonal work, hours, wages and opportunity for proprietorship.

Perry, Lorinda. *Millinery as a Trade for Women*. Studies in the Economic Relations of Women, vol. 5. New York: Longmans, Green and Company, 1916.
◆ Very thorough study for the Women's Educational and Industrial Union of Boston on all aspects of the trade—wholesale and retail—in Boston and Philadelphia.

Philo [pseud.]. *Twelve Letters to a Young Milliner*. New York: Hill Brothers, 1883.
◆ Lengthy advice on the location and setting up of a store, ordering and displaying stock, pricing goods, hiring assistants, bookkeeping and good business practice. Written in a paternalistic manner for aspiring or practicing female milliners by the editors of Hill's *Milliner Gazette*, the promotional journal of Hill Brothers millinery wholesalers.

[Robinson, Mary Viola]. *Primer of Problems in the Millinery Industry*. Washington, D.C.: Government Printing Office, 1941.
◆ Analysis of problems in large-scale millinery manufacturing, conducted because "the industry was sick . . . and the death rate among millinery firms was high." One of the last attempts to deal with problems in seasonality, competition and marketing. Excellent presentation of the relationships among job categories, salaries and gender.

Tobey, Evelyn Smith. "The Educated Woman in Millinery." In *Vocations for the Trained Woman: Opportunities Other Than Teaching*, edited by Agnes F. Perkins. Boston: Women's Educational and Industrial Union, 1920.
◆ Requirements and training for teachers of millinery and for the retail milliner who works out of her home or shop. Advice on the necessity for aesthetic sensibilities and understanding of Parisian style.

U.S. Federal Trade Commission. *Report to the President of the United States on Distribution Methods in the Millinery Industry*. 21 November 1939.
◆ Outlines the change over the last fifteen years in manufacturing, distribution, retailing and its effect on workers and consumers. The industry "in a chaotic condition," due to the rise of syndicates.

Van Kleeck, Mary. *A Seasonal Industry: A Study of the Millinery Trade in New York*. New York: Russell Sage Foundation, 1917.
◆ Informative study by a foundation for improvement of social and living conditions. Examines the economic position of women, training, wages, work conditions and the problem of seasonal employment in millinery shops, large and small. Fascinating photographs of milliners at work.

Weaver, E. W. *Profitable Vocations for Girls*. New York: A. S. Barnes, 1915.
◆ Chapter on dressmaking and millinery includes advice on aptitude, apprenticeship, seasonal trade and wages.

Woman's Institute of Domestic Arts and Sciences. *The Millinery Shop*. Scranton, Penn.: Woman's Institute, 1923.
◆ Informative booklet on how to set up a business, aptitude, location, fixtures and supplies, managing the business, selling goods and managing employees.

Technical Instruction Manuals, 1840-1940

Anslow, Florence. *Practical Millinery.* London: Sir Isaac Pitman, 1922.
- ◆ Historical introduction, with detailed instructions on construction, pattern making, draping, straw working, trimming, children's millinery and renovations. Excellent, clear illustrations (Figure 1).

Babcock, L. M. "Employments for Women—No. 6: Millinery." *The Delineator* (Oct. 1894): 50-52.
- ◆ Short description of preparing and trimming a straw hat in a women's fashion journal.

Ben-Ysuf, Anna. *Edwardian Hats: The Art of Millinery.* 1909. Reprint, Mendocino, Calif.: R. L. Shep, 1982.
- ◆ Facsimile reprint of *The Art of Millinery, a Complete Series of Practical Lessons for the Artiste and Amateur* with additional period illustrations of fashions. Very thorough, with seventeen lessons on millinery processes and sections on trimming, mourning millinery, children's millinery, stock-keeping, starting a millinery business and the designer in the workroom (Figure 2). Glossary

of millinery and dry goods terms. By a leading milliner whose career spanned Paris, London and New York.

Bottomley, Julia, ed. *A Complete Course in Millinery: Twenty-Four Practical Lessons Detailing the Processes for Mastering the Art of Millinery.* New York: The Illustrated Milliner Company, 1919.
- ◆ Revised version of Bottomley, *Practical Millinery Lessons* (1914); further revised by Burke as *Perfect Course in Millinery* (1925).

Bottomley, Julia, ed. *The Milliners' Guide: A Complete Handy Reference Book for the Workroom.* New York: The Illustrated Milliner Company, [1917].
- ◆ Guide to renovating, tinting, stain removal, cleaning and sewing hints (not hatmaking) by two experienced milliners.

Bottomley, Julia. *Practical Millinery Lessons: A Complete Course of Lessons in the Art of Millinery.* New York: The Illustrated Milliner Company, 1914.
- ◆ Thorough how-to in twenty-four lessons, with list of tools and equipment; diagrams and photographs of patterns and process. Revised version of *Practical Millinery Lessons* (1905).

Brand, Violet, and Beatrice Mussared. *Millinery.* London: Sir Isaac Pitman and Sons, 1935.
- ◆ Thorough guide on new and old techniques by English technical college teachers. Includes information on tools and materials, pattern and shape making, covering,

Figure 2. Pressing a straw hat brim. Anna Ben-Ysuf, Edwardian Hats: The Art of Millinery, reprint of The Art of Millinery, a Complete Series of Practical Lessons for the Artiste and Amateur, 1909 (Mendocino, Calif.: R. L. Shep, 1982): 222.

lining, felt, straws, stitched hats, children's millinery and ribbon trimmings. Supplement shows twenty-two different kinds of straw, detailed photographs of processes and finished hats with photos and instructions.

Brown, Carlotta M. *Millinery Processes.* Boston: Ginn and Company, 1930.
- ◆ Thorough description of hatmaking with diagrams and photographs by instructor of millinery at the University of Minnesota.

Burke, Emma Maxwell. *A Perfect Course in Millinery.* New York: The Illustrated Milliner Company, 1925.
- ◆ Later edition of Bottomley, *Practical Millinery Lessons.* Has twenty-eight lessons in millinery, descriptions of tools and equipment and diagrams and photographs of patterns and processes.

Campbell, Agnes. *Lessons in Millinery.* Extension Bulletin 46. Winnipeg, Canada: Manitoba Farmer's Library, 1920.
- ◆ One of a series of bulletins on agricultural and sanitary matters from the Manitoba Department of Agriculture, intended as part of a class on making millinery in the farm home. Brief description of processes with numerous drawings.

[Devlin, James]. *The Guide to the Trade: The Dress-maker and the Milliner.* London: Charles Knight, 1843.
- ◆ Directions on wiring and covering chip bonnets; making and covering bonnet foundations; drawn, transparent and mourning bonnets; caps, dress hats and turbans.

Hill, Clara. *Millinery: Theoretical and Practical.* London: Methuen and Co., 1900.
- ◆ Contains information on trimming, straw and wire shapes; patterns, draping and lining; drawn silk

hats and bonnets; renovating and cleaning; stitches; materials; glossary. Also includes rare information for this period on color, form and pattern drafting. By instructress of the Leeds (England) school board. Went through many editions.

Howell, Mrs. M. J. *The Handbook of Millinery, Comprised in a Series of Lessons for the Formation of Bonnets, Capotes, Turbans, Caps, Bows.* London: Simpkin, Marshall, 1847.
◆ A series of lessons on drawn and transparent bonnets; lining straw and other bonnets, caps, turbans and toques; and selection of colors and materials. This handbook is more technical and detailed than most of the early guides.

Innes, Isabella. *Scientific Dressmaking and Millinery.* Toronto: I. Innes, 1913.
◆ Rare Canadian manual, with diagrams and instructions for making about fifty hats. Has geometrical drafting and sewing instructions. Also with hand drawings by the principal of the costumer's art school, Toronto.

Kaye, Georgina Kerr. *Millinery for Everywoman: A Complete Course in the Millinery Art.* 1926. Reprint, Berkeley, Calif.: Lacis Publications, 1992.
◆ Basic series of lessons in foundations, draping and finishing.

Kintzel, Margaret, and Mary M. Lunt. *Complete Guide to Millinery of Kintzel Millinery School.* Philadelphia: Dando Printing, 1915.
◆ Brief instructions for millinery construction, draping, trimming and care of materials. No illustrations.

The Ladies' Hand-Book of Millinery and Dressmaking, with Plain Instructions for Making the Most Useful Articles of Dress and Attire. New York: J. S. Redfield, 1844.
◆ Sketchy discussion of materials and the making of bonnets, including drawn, silk, children's and mourning styles.

The Ladies' Self Instructor in Millinery and Mantua Making, Embroidery and Appliqué, Canvas-work, Knitting, Netting and Crochet-work. 1850. Reprint, Fort Bragee, Calif.: R. L. Shep Publications, 1988.
◆ Brief discussion of color, fashion and materials. Sketchy directions for making bonnets. Engravings show two finished bonnets.

Loewen, Jane. *Millinery.* New York: Macmillan, 1925.
◆ Thorough instructions, with drawings, of all processes for foundation and fabric hats; turbans; trimmings; cleaning and remodelling; and color and line harmony.

Lyon, Hester B. *Modern Millinery: A Workroom Text Book.* New York: Millinery Trade Publishing, 1922.
◆ Basic textbook with excellent illustrations comparing hat frame and finished hat.

Ortner, Jessica. *Practical Millinery.* London: Whittaker, 1897.
◆ Historical introduction, with directions for construction, trimming, straw working and infants' millinery.

Patty, Virgina C. *Hats and How to Make Them.* Chicago: Rand McNally, 1925.
◆ Thorough instructions for construction, trimming and renovation by home economics professor, University of Washington.

Practical Millinery Lessons. New York: Grosvenor K. Glenn, 1905.
◆ Nineteen lessons in millinery. Instructions for tools and equipment, starting in business, store and workroom supplies and décor, stock and recipes for cleaning and renovation. Diagrams, drawings and photographs. See later versions by Bottomley and Burke.

Pullen, Marion M. *Beadle's Dime Guide to Dress-Making and Millinery.* New York: Beadle, [1860].
◆ Chapter on bonnets discusses design and color, materials and covering with fabric. Directions sketchy, as usual for this period.

Rosée, Madame. *The Handbook of Millinery: A Practical Manual of Instruction for Ladies.* London: L. Upcott Gill, 1895.
◆ General instructions with drawings, by the principal of the School of Millinery, London.

Van Cleef Bros. *Millinery Without Sewing.* Chicago: Van Cleef Bros., 1919.
◆ Advertising booklet for Snow White Millinery Cement. Directions on how to cover frames with fabric, ribbon and feathers, and on how to make millinery ornaments using the product.

Weiss, Rosalind. *How to Make Hats.* New York: McGraw-Hill, 1931.
◆ Trade-school series of lessons on all aspects of custom millinery, with clear line drawings. Shows transition from wire-frame construction, "now on the decline," to blocking techniques (Figure 3).

Woman's Institute of Domestic Arts and Sciences. *Millinery* (1920), *Millinery for Misses and Children* (1924), *Millinery Materials* (1927), *Millinery for Mature Women* (1923). Scranton, Penn.: Woman's Institute of Domestic Arts and Sciences.
◆ Series of very informative booklets set out as instruction papers with examination questions. Produced by a home-study institution teaching dressmaking, millinery and cookery.

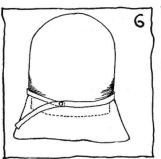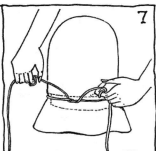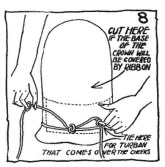

Figure 3. Visual instructions for blocking the crown of a hat on a wooden mould. Rosalind Weiss, How to Make Hats *(New York: McGraw-Hill, 1931), 8. By the 1930s, technical manuals began to include instructions for direct moulding.*

The Workwoman's Guide. 1840. Reprint, Sudbury, Suffolk, Eng.: Bloomfield Books, 1973.
- ◆ General English guide on sewing and needlework. Contains directions for making pieced caps, bonnets and caleches.

Wholesale Millinery and Merchandising, 1840-1940

Aiken, Charlotte Rankin. *The Millinery Department.* Department Store Merchandise Manuals. New York: The Ronald Press, 1918.
- ◆ Thorough discussion of the wide variety of millinery materials, including straw, felt, velvet and other fabrics, as well as trimmings. Also has advice on how to set up a millinery department and workroom, color and form in hat design and hints to salespeople (Figure 4).

Inwards, Harry. *Straw Hats, Their History and Manufacture.* London: Sir Isaac Pitman and Sons, 1922.
- ◆ A still-relevant, early history of the straw hat industry principally in England, with detailed descriptions of methods and technology. Valuable information on women's hats.

Murphy, William S., ed. *Modern Drapery and the Allied Trades, Wholesale and Retail.*

Vols. 1 and 2. London: Gresham Publishing Company, 1914.
- ◆ Chapters on the millinery department, workroom, wholesale, retail, materials, business practice and training. With illustrations of millinery materials and showrooms.

Nelson, Michael Louis. *Millinery Merchandising.* Minneapolis, Minn.: Colwell Press, 1928.
- ◆ Advocates "modern methods" in setting out millinery shops and departments. Contains information on advertising, management, correct color and form harmony.

Philo [pseud.]. *Twelve Letters to a Young*

Milliner. New York: Hill Brothers, 1883.
- ◆ Lengthy advice on the location and setting up of a store, ordering and displaying stock, pricing goods, hiring assistants, bookkeeping and good business practice. Written in a paternalistic manner for aspiring or practicing female milliners by the editors of Hill's *Milliner Gazette*, the promotional journal of Hill Brothers millinery wholesalers.

Van Cleef Bros. *Millinery Without Sewing.* Chicago: Van Cleef Bros., 1919.
- ◆ Advertising booklet produced by the manufacturers of Snow White Millinery Cement with directions on how to use their product.

Weil, Claire, ed. *Glossary of French Millinery Terms.* New York: Style Magazines, Inc., and Contemporary Modes, 1939.
- ◆ Includes detailed glossaries of terms related to color, fabric, silk, straw and lace.

Woman's Institute of Domestic arts and Sciences. *The Millinery Shop.* Scranton, Penn.: Woman's Institute, 1923.
- ◆ Informative booklet on how to set

Figure 4. How to choose a becoming hat for the full-faced or snub nosed. Charlotte Rankin Aiken, The Millinery Department *(New York: The Ronald Press, 1918): 146. Books on millinery merchandising often included hints on millinery style, color and form.*

up in business, aptitude, location, fixtures and supplies, managing the business, selling goods and managing employees.

The Workwoman's Guide. 1840. Reprint, Sudbury, Suffolk, Eng.: Bloomfield Books, 1973.
◆ General guide on sewing and needlework with directions on straw platting and straw bonnet-making.

Secondary Sources on the History of Women's Hats and the Millinery Trade

Albrizio, Ann, and Osnat Lustig. *Classical Millinery Techniques: A Complete Guide to Making and Designing Today's Hats.* Asheville, N.C.: Lark Books, 1998.
◆ A good guide for modern-day instructions on many traditional millinery techniques.

Alto, Vonnie R. "The Business of Female Fripperies and the Fashionable Lady: Women's Millinery in America, 1620-1920, and the Oregon Experience: A Proprietorship Study of Hats and Hatmaking." Master's thesis. University of Portland, 1992.
◆ History of the millinery trade, fashion and etiquette. With chapters on milliners in Oregon and an extensive bibliography.

Amplett, Hilda. *Hats: A History of Fashion in Headwear.* Chalfont St. Giles: Sadler, 1974.
◆ Encyclopedic, from 100 A.D. Illustrated.

Baldwin, Betsey. "The Millinery Tradition in Decline, 1900-1930: The Displacement of Hat-Making as a Professional Art at Eaton's." Report on file, History Division, Canadian Museum of Civilization, 1999.
◆ Based on an analysis of the Eaton's catalogue.

Ball, Carlos H. "A Palmleaf Hat Manufactory." *Chronicle of the Early American Industries Association* 40, no. 2 (June 1987): 20-21.
◆ This factory made women's hats out of various organic materials.

Bates, Christina. "Wearing Two Hats: An Interdisciplinary Approach to the Millinery Trade in Ontario, 1850-1930." *Material History Review* 51 (spring 2000): 16-25.
◆ Combines methodologies of historical research and material culture analysis to explore trade. Based on a collection of five hundred 1920s/1930s hats from a Sarnia millinery shop.

Bates, Christina. "Creative Abilities and Business Sense: The Millinery Trade in Ontario." In *A Century Stronger: A History of Women in the Twentieth Century,* edited by Sharon Anne Cook, Kate O'Rourke and Lorna McLean. Montreal, McGill-Queens Press, 2001.
◆ Focused on training, demographics, pay and the rise and decline of the trade.

Bawden, Juliet. *The Hat Book: Creating Hats for Every Occasion.* Asheville, N.C.: Lark Books, 1992.
◆ Detailed and well-illustrated instructions on making folk hats and international styles.

Blum, Dilys E. *Ahead of Fashion: Hats of the Twentieth Century.* Philadelphia: Philadelphia Museum of Art, 1993.
◆ Exhibition catalogue on high-fashion hats by American and European designers, organized thematically. Discussion of the millinery business.

Bolomier, Élaine. *Cents ans de chapeaux, 1870-1970.* Chazelles-sur-Lyon, France: Musée du chapeau, [1993].
◆ Chronological history of women's

hats, with one chapter on men's, based on the museum's collections. Written by museum curator and ethnologist. Beautifully illustrated.

Bolomier, Élaine. *Le Chapeau: Grand art et savoir-faire.* Paris: Musée du chapeau and Somogy éditions d'art, 1996.
◆ Beautifully illustrated history of hatmaking, somewhat anecdotal; organized thematically. Chapters on the history of felt, felt hats, Chazelles-sur-Lyon industries, straw hatmaking, millinery techniques, hat-block makers, trimming industries and men'shatters. Written by museum curator and ethnologist.

Campione, Adele. *Women's Hats; Il cappello da donna.* San Francisco: Chronicle Books, 1989.
◆ Picture book of hats, from 1880 to 1969.

Clark, Fiona. *Hats.* The Costume Accessories Series. London: B. T. Batsford, 1982.
◆ Chronological study of women's and men's hats and caps in England, from 1600 to the 1960s, illustrated by museum collections. Two chapters on the millinery trade. Glossary.

Courtais, Georgine de. *Women's Headdress and Hairstyles in England from A.D. 600 to the Present Day.* London: B. T. Batsford, 1973.
◆ For the late-nineteenth and twentieth centuries (about one-third of the book). Discussion and clear drawings of hairstyles, caps, bonnets and hats.

Dailey, Christie. "A Woman's Concern: Millinery in Central Iowa, 1870-1880." *Journal of the West* 21, no. 2 (April 1982): 26-32.
◆ Analysis of the millinery trade based on census records and newspapers, including comparison with other female occupations, age, marital status, demography and social status.

Darnell, Paula Jean. *Victorian Millinery: Ladies' Hats, 1850-1900*. Reno, Nev.: Fabric Fancies, 1995.
◆ Discussion of women's fashion, bonnet and hat styles, trimmings and hair dressing for each decade, with illustrations and quotes from *Harper's Bazar*, the *Delineator* and other women's fashion journals.

Davis, Jean. *Straw Plait*. Aylesbury, Bucks, England: Shire Publications, 1981.
◆ Brief history of the straw hat industry in the south Midlands, England.

Delpierre, Madeleine. *Chapeaux, 1750-1960*. Paris: Musée de la mode et du costume, 1980.
◆ Exhibition catalogue.

Dreher, Denis. *From the Neck Up: An Illustrated Guide to Hatmaking*. Minneapolis, Minn.: Madhatter Press, 1981.
◆ Comprehensive instructions and patterns for historical, theatrical and modern headwear. Illustrated glossary and extensive bibliography.

Dugald Costume Museum. *From Hats to Hems*. Dugald, Manitoba, Canada: Dugald Costume Museum, 1986.
◆ Small booklet based on an exhibition, with drawings of hats in the museum's collection, from 1800 to 1986.

Gamber, Wendy. *The Female Economy: The Millinery and Dressmaking Trades, 1860-1930*. Urbana, Ill.: University of Illinois Press, 1997.
◆ Seminal work by a cultural historian. Traces the gendered nature of millinery work and the trend toward mass production, with emphasis on the eastern United States. Sources include a wide range of documentary material. Extensive notes and bibliography. Based on Ph.D. dissertation of the same name (Brandeis University, 1990).

Gamber, Wendy. "Gendered Concerns: Thoughts on the History of Business and the History of Women." *Business and Economic History* 23 (fall 1994): 129-40.
◆ Based on Ph.D. dissertation (see above).

Gamber, Wendy. "A Precarious Independence: Milliners and Dressmakers in Boston, 1860-1890." *Journal of Women's History* 4 (spring 1992): 60-88.
◆ Based on Ph.D. dissertation (see above).

Genin, John N. *An Illustrated History of the Hat*. New York: Genin, 1850.
◆ History of hats and hatmaking, mostly men's, but some women's, from ancient times to the nineteenth century. Well-researched for its time.

Ginsburg, Madeleine. *The Hat: Trends and Traditions*. Hauppauge, N.Y.: Barron's Educational Series, 1990.
◆ Chronological popular history of women's and men's hats, from medieval times to the twentieth century. Good glossary.

[Godin, Christine]. *Les chapeaux feminins d'hier et d'aujourd'hui; Women's Hats, Yesterday and Today*. Montréal: La société d'archeologie et de numismatique de Montreal, 1989.
◆ Exhibition catalogue from the Musée Chateau Ramezay, with essays on hatmaking in Canada, both industrial and homemade, from the eighteenth to the twentieth centuries and changing millinery fashions. Also includes interviews with Quebec milliners. Good bibliography.

Godin, Christine. "Les femmes au chapeau." *Cap-aux-diamants* 4, no. 2 (summer 1988): 25-28.
◆ Article by an ethnologist on the sociology of hats, past and present, with quotes from Quebec milliners.

Godin, Christine. "Créer des chapeau." *Cap-aux-diamants* 4, no. 2 (summer 1988), 51-54.
◆ Article by an ethnologist on the milliner's métier, based on accounts by Quebec milliners.

Gonzales, Claire L. *Dressmaking and Millinery in Lansing, Michigan, 1847-1910*. Master's thesis. Michigan State University, 1983.
◆ Analysis of extant dresses and hats according to E. McClung Fleming's artifact study model. Demographic profile of dressmakers and milliners and their production and marketing methods.

Gordon, Joleen. *Handwoven Hats: A History of Straw, Wood and Rush Hats in the Nova Scotia Museum*. Halifax: The Nova Scotia Museum, 1981.
◆ History of the straw hat industries in Europe and North America, with little-known information on the straw plait and hat cottage and wholesale industry in Nova Scotia. Instructions on making women's straw, rush and chip hats and on renovating straw hats.

Harrison, Michael. *The History of the Hat*. London: Herbert Jenkins, 1960.
◆ Chronology, from ancient Etruscan to 1950. Illustrated with scant drawings.

Hats. A Pepin Press Design Book. New York: Costume and Fashion Press, 1998.
◆ Over 300 pages of drawings and prints of hats from the Middle Ages to the 1920s, taken from costume books, fashion plates and catalogues. Unfortunately, the sources for the illustrations are not identified.

Hopkins, Susie. *The Century of Hats: Headturning Style of the Twentieth Century*. London: Aurum, 1999.
◆ Chronological popular history of mostly women's hats, with profiles of famous milliners and celebrities.

Kilgour, Ruth Edwards. *A Pageant of Hats, Ancient and Modern*. New York: R. M. McBride, 1958.
◆ Ethnographic.

Langley, Susan, and John Dowling. *Vintage Hats and Bonnets, 1770-1970*. Paducah, Ken.: Collector Books, 1998.
◆ Lavishly illustrated price guide, with costume history notes.

Lintner, Mildred Doris. "The Height of Fashion: The Construction of Ladies' Fashion Headwear, 1830-1914." Ph.D. dissertation. University of Michigan, 1979.
◆ Dissertation for the department of theater. A fashion history of hats, with useful categorization of hat types and construction methods.

Loverin, Janet I., and Robert A. Nylen. "Creating a Fashionable Society: Comstock Needleworkers from 1860 to 1880." In *Comstock Women: The Making of a Mining Community*, edited by Ronald M. James and C. Elizabeth Raymond. Reno, Nev.: University of Nevada Press, 1998.
◆ Analysis of census records, city directories and newspapers show that milliners and dressmakers in the precarious and transient environments of western mining communities created a fashionable society. Rare details about individual milliners and excellent notes.

Maux, Nicole Le. *Histoire du chapeau féminin*. Paris: Editions Massin, 2000.
◆ Popular history from the late eighteenth century to the present, based on the author's collection of 500 hats.

McClellan, Mary Elizabeth. *Felt, Silk and Straw Handmade Hats: Tools and Processes*. Doylestown, Penn.: Bucks County Historical Society, 1977.
◆ Eighteenth- and nineteenth-century felt, silk plush and straw women's and men's hats and bonnets. Illustrated by tools in the Bucks County Historical Society collection.

McDowell, Colin. *Hats: Status, Style and Glamour*. New York: Rizzoli, 1992.
◆ Popular sociology of hats from around the world.

Mendes, Valerie D. "Hats as Art: A Glance at the V&A's 20th-Century Collection." *The V&A Album* (spring 1989): 55-62.
◆ Discussion and illustration of a selection of hats from the Victoria and Albert Museum, London, by the museum curator. Mostly hats from the 1940s to the 1980s made by high fashion milliners.

Mills, Ruth. "Miss Newton Hat Collection Report: An Analysis of Fabrication Techniques." Report on file, History Division, Canadian Museum of Civilization, 1999.
◆ Results of a study of a collection of 500 hats of the 1920s and 1930s with respect to techniques, materials and style.

Muller, Florence, and Lydia Kamitsis. *Les chapeaux: une histoire de tête*. Paris: Syros Alternatives, 1993.
◆ Thematic discussion of hats and hatmaking by two art historians, illustrated by several museum collections. Anecdotal history.

The Paris Hat, 1885-1910. San Francisco: Fine Arts Museums and the Los Angeles County Museum of Art, [1983].
◆ Brochure catalogue with descriptions of hats in the exhibit, some illustrated. A map shows locations of Parisian milliners.

Probert, Christina. *Hats in Vogue Since 1910*. New York: Abbeville Press, 1981.
◆ Mostly pictures from *Vogue* magazine, organized chronologically, from 1910 to 1980, with some text on changing styles and influences.

Reilly, Maureen, and Mary Beth Detrich. *Women's Hats of the Twentieth Century for Designers and Collectors*. Atglen, Penn.: Schiffer Publishing, 1997.
◆ Basically a price guide lavishly illustrated, with some information on costume history and designers.

Rendell, T. J. "Millinery Techniques in the 1920s." *Costume* 10 (1976): 86-94.
◆ Reminiscence of author's apprenticeship with Liberty and Co., London, including working conditions, pay, division of labor and the types of hats made. Patterns and instructions for a cloche and child's sunbonnet.

Ridley, J. "Stylistic Changes in American Women's Hats with Identification Criteria for the Years 1900 to 1950." Master's thesis. Oklahoma State University, 1981.
◆ Quantitative study based on the Sears Roebuck catalogue to determine distinguishing features of hats. Procedural model developed to classify and catalogue historic collections.

Rivera, Betty. "Art: Les Chapeaux, Millinery Allure Mirrored in Figurative Painting." *Architectural Digest* 4, no. 3 (March 1983): 100-105.
◆ Hats in painting, from 1885 to 1920.

Roger-Miles, L. *Les créateurs de la mode*. Paris: [n.p.], 1910.
◆ Beautiful sepia-toned photographs of millinery shops and workrooms in Paris.

Seligman, Kevin L. *Cutting for All: The Sartorial Arts, Related Crafts, and the Commercial Paper Pattern: A Bibliographic Reference Guide for Designers,*

Technicians and Historians. Carbondale, Ill.: Southern Illinois University Press, [1996].

◆ Chapter on millinery has excellent listing of publications found in American libraries and other institutions, with details of publishing data.

Severa, Bill. *Here's Your Hat.* New York: David McKay Co., 1963.

◆ Popular book with some anecdotal historical information and chapters on hat makers and fashion.

Shields, Jody. *Hats: A Stylish History and Collector's Guide.* New York: Clarkson Potter, 1991.

◆ More than a collector's guide. Includes text on changing hat styles in the context of general fashion history, with illustrations from fashion magazines and trade journals and photographs of hats. Glossary of hat types.

Smith, Desire. *Hats with Values.* Atglen, Penn.: Schiffer Publishing, 1996.

◆ Lavishly illustrated price guide, mainly twentieth century.

Sullivan, Brian. *Romance of the Straw Bonnet.* Westborough, Mass.: Whipple House, 1986.

◆ Brief history of the straw hat industry in New England.

Victoria Magazine, ed. *The Romance of Hats.* New York: Hearst Books, 1994.

◆ Historical styles for today. Profiles of four hatmakers in the U.S. and instructions on the care of hats.

Wergland, Glendyne R. "Designing Women: Massachusetts Milliners in the Nineteenth Century." In *Textiles in Early New England: Design, Production, and Consumption.* Dublin Seminar for New England Folklife Conference Proceedings. Boston: Boston University Press, 1999.

◆ Based on the R. G. Dun credit reports, public records, city directories and newspapers. Shows that millinery could be a lucrative and lasting trade for women. Discusses how milliners failed due to bad image, credit, marketing and business practices.

Wilcox, R. Turner. *The Mode in Hats and Headdress, Including Hair Styles, Cosmetics and Jewelry.* New York: Charles Scribner's Sons, 1959.

◆ Encyclopedic history, from ancient Egypt to 1959. Multitude of drawings of hat styles by the author.

Yesterday's Headlines: The Hat Collection of the Stoke-on-Trent City Museum and Art Gallery. Stoke on Trent, England: City Museum and Art Gallery, 1987.

◆ Photographs and catalogue data on 234 hats in the museum's collection, from 1770 to 1986.

Milliners' Biographies

Daché, Lily. *Talking Through My Hats.* New York: Coward-McCann, 1946.

◆ Popularized autobiography of a famous New York milliner.

Garling, Carol. "Old Hat." *Craftnews* (July/Aug. 1995): 14.

◆ Brief biography of 1950s-1990s Toronto milliner Ina Shale.

Giroux, Jacqueline. *Yvette Brillon, femme de coeur et femme de têtes.* Longueuil, Quebec: La société historique de Marigot de Longueuil, 1989.

◆ Engaging biography written by the niece of the well-known Montréal modiste, born 1907. Brillon apprenticed at twelve years old in a hat store, became head milliner in fashionable department stores, and, in 1933, established her own shop.

Rendell, T. J. "Millinery Techniques in the 1920s." *Costume* 10 (1976): 86-94.

◆ Reminiscences of work in the millinery department of Liberty's, London.

Thaarup, Aage. *Heads and Tales.* Lincoln: John Gifford, 1946.

◆ Autobiography of London milliner who made hats for the Queen Mother and celebrities. Many details about the workroom and his design sources.

Woods, Caroline H. [Belle Otis]. *The Diary of a Milliner.* New York: Hurd and Houghton, 1867.

◆ Fictionalized autobiography dealing with personal philosophy, rising above the moral frailties of her customers, and the difficulties for women in business.

Acknowledgements

Thanks to Beverly Chico, Ruth Mills and the competent and genial staff at the Canadian Museum of Civilization library for their expertise, contributions and assistance.

Joanne B. Eicher

The Anthropology of Dress

Since beginning to study the use, significance, and meaning of dress, I have been intrigued with the wide variety of disciplines such as art history, history, anthropology, sociology, folklore, philosophy, economics, and women's studies that contribute to the topic of dress. I am also amazed by the insularity of many scholars who do not venture beyond the boundaries of their disciplines when accessing bibliographic sources for their own research. Thus, I have chosen to highlight anthropology because I suspect that the scope of writing in that discipline may come as a surprise to many scholars writing about dress (and perhaps even to many anthropologists who would not expect the topic to exist).[1] Anthropology contributes scholarship that relates to understanding the place of dress in culture, and I define the anthropology of dress simply as the study of dress by anthropologists.[2]

In this article, I concentrate on published writings in English from anthropologists and exclude other writings even though they may have an "anthropological approach."[3] I highlight four aspects of anthropology (holism, culture, fieldwork, and women's involvement) that have contributed to the study of dress. I follow this with a chronological survey of published works on dress by anthropologists, both articles and books, from the roots of the field at the end of the nineteenth century through 1999.

Contributions from Anthropology for Studying Dress

Anthropologists study human behavior, or as Tim Ingold says in the *Companion Encyclopedia of Anthropology*:

> Anthropologists study people . . . [but] it is not so obvious how—if at all, anthropology may be distinguished from the many other

branches of the human sciences, all of which could claim to be studying people in one way or another. Medicine is concerned with the workings of the human body, psychology with those of the mind, history studies people's activities in the past, sociology their institutional arrangements in the present, and so on. The list could be extended almost indefinitely. What then, is the distinctively *anthropological* way of studying people?[4]

Holism

Ingold answers his question by stating that this distinction is partially a result of the importance of anthropology's subfields, for they give anthropology the gift of holism. The four subfields interconnect the biological, social, historical and cultural dimensions of human life that might otherwise be divided among several disciplines.[5] This commitment to holism is the first contribution of anthropology to the study of dress; holism forces us to look at dressing the body within a larger sociocultural context of such factors as kinship, the political economy, lack or presence of hierarchy, and ideological belief systems.

Culture

The second contribution of anthropology is the concept of culture with its obvious implication of cultural diversity. Culture, as an idea or theory, has been thoroughly scrutinized over the years. One example is the mid-twentieth century book by Alfred Kroeber and Clyde Kluckhohn, titled *Culture: A Critical Review of Concepts and Definitions,* in which they analyzed and categorized 164 definitions.[6] A more recent one is *Culture: The Anthropologists' Account* by Adam Kuper.[7] Culture as an idea is about how human beings teach and learn "proper conduct" within a specific setting. Through language and role models, humans learn how to behave from other human beings, and

Joanne B. Eicher is Regents' Professor in the Department of Design, Housing, and Apparel at the University of Minnesota.

this transmission of knowledge carries across generations. Thus, culture and history are closely intertwined, for we are taught how to behave; we are not programmed genetically. We learn to wear fur or feathers (or to despise or avoid wearing them); we are not born with them. Furthermore, we can decide to change our minds or be persuaded to change our minds about wearing or not wearing them. By accepting the idea that culture is about teaching and learning "proper conduct" within a specific setting, we can learn about cultural diversity. We see that other people do not live by our rules. "Our ways" of learning how to treat family, friends and neighbors or about what to wear and not to wear and how to sit and stand can be completely different from others. They can feel as strongly about the rightness of their choices as we feel about the rightness of ours. Thus, the concepts of culture and cultural diversity are important contributions from anthropology in analyzing the meaning of dress.

Fieldwork

A third contribution from anthropology is fieldwork. This contribution is attributed to Bronislaw Malinowski who is known for his extended research in the Trobriand Islands from 1914 to 1918 (Figure 1).[8] As most anthropologists agree, this process of living among a group and learning the indigenous language is necessary for real understanding of human behavior in another culture. Fieldwork allows us to observe people firsthand and become engaged with them in order to understand and interpret their behavior rather than relying on the observations and comments of others. The practice of fieldwork is shared by researchers in other disciplines; the direct observation of dress and associated behavior, along

Figure 1. Detail, Trobriand women from Bronislaw Malinowski's Argonauts of the Western Pacific (1922).

with learning the indigenous words and phrases that define actual items of dress and related practices, allows a more thorough understanding of what I call the "complex act of dress."[9]

Women's Involvement

A fourth contribution of anthropology is women's involvement. When reading early histories of many disciplines, one might assume that only men, especially white men, made contributions to any given field. A surge of interest in many disciplines about women's involvement in the sciences and humanities exposes women's early contributions to anthropology.[10] Most interestingly, Franz Boas wrote in 1920 to a colleague: "I have had a curious experience: All my best graduate students are women."[11] In fact, during Boas's tenure at Columbia University, over twenty women received doctoral degrees, the majority of them doing fieldwork in the Southwest.[12] However, as in other disciplines, only in the last twenty-five years have women

anthropologists been recognized for their work.[13] In Women Writing Culture, Ruth Behar chides Clifford and Marcus for the overwhelming absence of women contributors in Writing Culture: The Poetics and Politics of Ethnography and declares that the contributions of Elsie Clews Parsons (1875-1941) qualify her to be designated the "mother" of American anthropology.[14] Heightened interest in the contributions of women and gender issues have become important in the anthropology of dress. Biological differences are socially interpreted categories that provoke strong cultural interpretations related to dress; clearly, in the following chronological review, more women than men have chosen to study dress.

Chronological Survey

I present a comprehensive, but not exhaustive, bibliographic survey of anthropologists who write on dress, in English, from the discipline's inception through 1999, a period of approximately

125 years. This survey emerges from my own extensive library and from searching additional works cited in bibliographies. However, certain areas still need systematic plumbing, such as the early ethnographies from the American Southwest and careful searching of specific area studies such as Latin America and Asia.[15] Since my intent is to expose the continuous thread of anthropological research and writing on dress, I concentrate on providing brief descriptions of the written works and not a thematic classification.

The first publications on the topic of dress appeared during the late nineteenth century, a time in

Figure 2. Ernest Crawley's title page from Dress, Drinks, and Drums: Further Studies of Savages and Sex *(1931).*

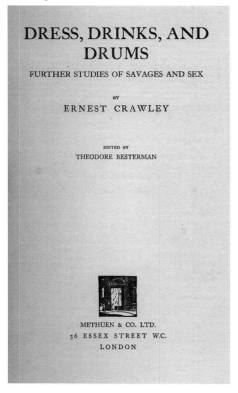

anthropology often designated as the "curio cabinet" stage. At that time, both facts about and artifacts from other peoples of the world were gathered by travelers and then studied by anthropologists who rarely conducted field research. Two well-known names, Sir Edward Burnett Tylor and Sir James Frazer, along with Ernest Crawley, epitomize this phase.[16] Crawley considered dress and its importance to humans in detail by writing a lengthy essay titled "Dress" in 1912 for the *Encyclopedia of Religion* (later reprinted in a volume titled *Dress, Drinks, and Drums: Further Studies of Savages and Sex*).[17] (See Figure 2.) Supported by cross-cultural examples, his discussion developed various theories about the origins of dress and astutely concluded: "Speculation alone is possible when dealing with the genesis of dress."[18]

Noteworthy sections of his essay included dress symbolism, the social psychology of dress, nakedness and dress, dress and social grade (or dress through the life course), sexual dress, and sacred dress. However, much of Crawley's writing smacked of the social evolutionism popular in that era as found in his usage of words such as "savages." Also typical of his time, he was insensitive to concerns about gender. Shortcomings aside, Crawley keenly observed the use of dress in social and cultural terms:

> The great bifurcation of dress is sexual.[19]

> [D]ress is the most distinctive expression in a material form of the various grades of social life. The biological period thus becomes a social period of existence.[20]

The cross-cultural and cross-temporal implications of his generalizations anticipated our continued research and analysis. Indeed, gendered dress is ubiquitous and becomes salient in socializing and enculturating children into adulthood.

Crawley saw no area of the study of dress and the body as off-limits. He scrutinized dress of the dead and mourning dress with vivid examples of various customs, topics generally avoided or ignored in later work. As modern medicine contributes to longer life spans, death is not always sad and sudden, for dress can play a part in death and dying and provide clues to understanding human values and key family relationships.[21] Another area little pursued since his essay is that of nudity and dress. Crawley declared: "When clothing is firmly established as a permanent social habit, temporary nudity is the most violent negation possible of the clothed state."[22] His observation is still intriguing and worthy of research, for there are many instances where temporary nudity or stripping oneself of clothing is considered violently antisocial. However, in our contemporary Euro-American world, public near-nudity or what I have called the "display of skin,"[23] particularly for younger women, seems to be newsworthy and attention getting.[24] Crawley noted the importance of global exchange at the time he wrote, which diminishes any ethnocentric idea we may have that globalization is a recent phenomenon:

> A remarkable tendency is observable at the present day, which is due to increased facilities of travel and inter-communication, towards a cosmopolitan type of dress, European in form.[25]

The curio cabinet period of anthropology stretched into what is acknowledged as the fieldwork era begun by Malinowski. However, fieldwork by women anthropologists in the Southwest flourished at the turn of the century. As one example, Alice Fletcher worked with Francis La Flesche, an Omaha Indian man, to publish a voluminous work on the Omaha in 1911 that included analyzing the significance

Figure 3. Alice Fletcher and Francis La Flesche analyzed the meaning communicated in the various types of wrappings within Omaha dress practices in "The Omaha Tribe" (1911).

of different ways of wearing and wrapping garments (Figure 3).[26] In another example, Matilda Coxe Stevenson reported her findings on Pueblo Indian dress.[27]

Alfred Kroeber took a different approach to the anthropology of dress by exploring the concept of order in that early period. He measured women's evening gowns from 1844 through 1919 and concluded that "regularity in social change" exists, and later conducted similar research with Jane Richardson in 1940.[28] His devotion to the idea of anthropology as a science and his use of quantitative research also importantly contributed to the study of dress.

Alfred Radcliffe-Brown's early research on the body decoration practices of the Andaman Islanders was an example of the fieldwork approach and structural-functional analysis. He interpreted these practices as a desire for protection and display, marking "the relation of the individual to the society and to that force or power in the society to which he owes his well-being and happiness."[29]

Although fieldwork was firmly established in anthropology by the 1930s, the three anthropologists who wrote entries for the *Encyclopedia of the Social Sciences*, Ruth Benedict on "Dress," Ruth Bunzel on "Ornament," and Edward Sapir on "Fashion," included some armchair theorizing divorced from fieldwork about such topics as origins and functions.[30] Some apt observations emerged, such as Sapir's statement that "Fashion is custom in the guise of departure from custom."[31]

Many ethnographies through the 1960s included a chapter or section describing dress, no doubt influenced by the then-bible of fieldwork, *Notes and Queries on Anthropology*, that instructed researchers about what data to collect on the topic.[32] *Mongol Costumes* in 1950 is possibly the first European ethnography on dress published in English.[33] Henny Harald Hansen, a Danish anthropologist, combined her talents as a painter, tailor's cutter in Paris, and anthropologist to analyze 400 items that had been collected on expeditions in the 1930s to Mongolia by Henning Haslund-Christensen, a Danish explorer. She meticulously measured, described and assessed each item according to an earlier scheme developed by Gudmund Hatt on Arctic skin dress to provide exemplary documentation and a theoretical perspective for understanding the production and use of garments in another cultural setting.[34] In addition, her analysis and the excellent color photographs of the 1983 edition of various ensembles inspire ideas for top-notch museum displays.

In the 1950s and 1960s, four examples emerged that analyzed the meaning of dress, rather than merely describing it. Paul Bohannon's article, "Beauty and Scarification amongst the Tiv," came from his research in Nigeria and documented changing fashions in scarring, but also pointed out that the tactile sensations resulting from scarring carry significance in intimate interactions.[35] Simon Messing analyzed the detailed meaning associated with different ways of wrapping garments in Ethiopia in "The Non-Verbal Language of the Ethiopian Toga" and Robert Murphy, the use of the veil by Tuareg men, not women, in "Social Distance and the Veil."[36] Terrence Turner scrutinized the significance of body painting practices within the social structure of Brazil's Tchikrin people.[37]

In contrast to the above examples in which dress appeared to be a sideline

interest, Sidney M. Mead, a Maori, chose the topic as his focus in *Traditional Maori Clothing*.[38] He worked from a structural-functional perspective and gave a detailed analysis of the various forms of Maori clothing and changes over time, perhaps the first indigenous ethnography of dress in English written by a trained anthropologist.[39] His book foreshadowed many publications that followed in the next three decades with a variety of thematic theoretical perspectives arising in the discipline almost simultaneously (such as semiotics, symbolism, reflexivity, gender studies, Marxism, and interpretivism).[40]

In the early 1970s, two monographs, again apparently sidelines of original field research, appeared. One is *Self-Decoration in Mount Hagen* by Andrew and Marilyn Strathern, and the other *Nuba Personal Art* by James Faris.[41] The Strathern book, with exquisite detail, dwells on the "primary emphasis which Hageners place on adorning their own bodies."[42] They provided examples of body painting, feathered headdress, wigs and tally marker necklaces worn in festivals, which they related to two central values of Hagen society—the first, clan solidarity and prestige; the second, individual wealth and well-being. The Stratherns summarized as follows:

> Dances themselves provide an opportunity for demonstrating both clan solidarity and individual excellence . . . [for] the prestige of the clan coincides with that of its members. It is themselves that they decorate, for it is through men's personal achievements that renown is brought to them and their clan alike.[43]

Faris's research on the Nuba offered different findings. Body painting, oiling, and hair design are carried out by the Southeastern Nuba of Sudan, a classless society, primarily for aesthetic reasons to show off the body, rather than for

symbolic, functional or ritual ones. Faris concluded:

> The principal exercise is the celebration and exposure of the strong and healthy body. And it is probably in the concern with health that we find the material origin of the art tradition. A paramount emphasis of this study is that aesthetics stem from material origins and are not independently existing ideas.[44]

Hilda Kuper, in a thoughtful article titled "Costume and Identity," documented clothing as a symbol of social differentiation in Swaziland with examples of the conflicts that emerged when Western ideas of fashion were introduced into the seemingly traditional scene.[45] In 1978, two books by Ted Polhemus, one on the body and another (with Lynn Proctor) entitled *Fashion and Anti-Fashion: An Anthropology of Clothing and Adornment,* forecast his continuing dedication to the study of the dressed body.[46]

In 1979, *The Decorated Body* by Robert Brain and *Fabrics of Culture: An Anthropology of Dress,* co-edited by Justine Cordwell and Ronald Schwarz, were published.[47] The first stressed the multitude of body modifications around the world, anticipating the outpouring of books in the 1990s on body piercing and tattooing by a wide variety of popular writers. In the second, Cordwell and Schwarz introduced their book by declaring that anthropologists "are relatively silent about the meaning and function of dress and adornment . . . [but] In contrast, the natives *(sic)* who are the subject of our queries are generally cognizant of how they and others are dressed."[48] Their volume also anticipated the flurry of publications on the anthropology of dress that continues into the twenty-first century. Thirteen of the twenty-three authors came from disciplines other than anthropology, acknowledging that theoretical, comparative, and ethnographic approaches arose from a wide academic world and encompassed a wide range of cultures.

The 1980s began with Patricia Anawalt's work on late pre-Hispanic and MesoAmerican dress as analyzed from the Aztec codices in Mexico.[49] In 1983, Liza Dalby included a chapter on kimono in her book on *Geisha*.[50] And in 1989, three books added momentum to publications. Annette Weiner and Jane Schneider co-edited *Cloth and Human Experience*, another interdisciplinary volume with four of the eleven contributors being non-anthropologists.[51] Although this volume focused on cloth, the works of several contributors centered on the role of clothing, such as the chapter by Gillian Feeley-Harnik on how Malagasy dress separated the living from the dead, and Bernard Cohn's chapter on the role of attire in nineteenth century colonial India.[52] The other two books undergirded Museum of Mankind exhibits in London. One was by Michael O'Hanlon, *Reading the Skin: Adornment, Display and Society among the Wahgi*, based on his fieldwork in Papua New Guinea, which resulted in an exhibit titled "Paradise."[53] Shelagh Weir's outstanding book *Palestinian Costume* also accompanied an exhibit of the same name.[54] She emphasized that her initial assumptions of "one village, one style" and a contrast of traditional and modern dress were not upheld. She narrowed her research site to one village known for its fashion leadership in the Jaffa region, Beit Dajan. She discovered that change occurred in so-called traditional dress. Many books by anthropologists appeared in the 1990s—ethnographic monographs that stemmed from field research centering on dress as well as edited volumes that supplied cross-cultural and single-culture examples. Substantial publications on dress from museum exhibits continued, as shown in Margot

Schevill's *Maya Textiles of Guatemala* in which she analyzed the 252 textiles collected by Gustavus Eisen in 1902 for the Phoebe Hearst Museum of Anthropology.[55] She supplemented his collection notes with data from her own Guatemalan fieldwork. Carol Hendrickson supplied a perspective of contemporary Guatemalan dress in *Weaving Identities: Construction of Dress and Self in a Highland Guatemala Town*.[56] Her rationale for studying Guatemalan dress typified the intent of several of the authors of the 1990s regarding a focus on dress as part of material culture:

> The material world must be understood as a cultural system, that objects reflect a wealth of cultural categories, and that meaningful patterns relate all "objects" with a cultural universe.[57]

Also in 1993, Liza Dalby in her book *Kimono* delved into the history and use of kimono and style changes and stated that the Japanese perceived the kimono as a primary form of clothing only after contact with the Western world, from 1868 onward.[58] Sandra Niessen, in *Batak Cloth and Clothing: A Dynamic Indonesian Tradition*, analyzed the dynamics of how Malay-Muslim, Christian missionary, and European colonial dress influenced and changed the dress of nineteenth-century Bataks in the highlands of north central Sumatra.[59] Through these examples, the authors recognized that "ethnic" dress begins when group members compare and contrast their dress to that of others.

In *From the Land of the Thunder Dragon: Textile Arts of Bhutan*, Diana Myers and Susan Bean also documented through an exhibit that the textiles used in Bhutan "are an evolving art and have been for centuries, changing as their role in Bhutanese life has evolved."[60] Similarly, Ted Polhemus's catalog that accompanied the Victoria and Albert Museum exhibit titled *Streetstyle: From*

Sidewalk to Catwalk provoked interest in the contemporary "styletribes" of the United Kingdom and the United States.[61] Thoughtful articles on dress in the 1990s included those by Karen Hansen on second-hand clothing in Zambia and by Joseph Nevadomsky on dress and identity in Benin.[62] Several editors narrowed their volumes to one area or continent of the world. For example, in *Clothing and Difference: Embodied Identities in Colonial and Post-Colonial Africa*, the authors emphasized the interplay of indigenous forms of African dress and Western influences.[63] *Languages of Dress in the Middle East* included nine diverse ethnographic papers on this regional area.[64] *Outward Appearances: Dressing State and Society in Indonesia* assessed many facets of Indonesian dress history and contemporary life.[65] Judith Perani and Norma Wolff concentrated primarily on Nigerian examples in *Cloth, Dress, and Art Patronage in Africa*.[66] *Beauty Queens on the Global Stage: Gender, Contests and Power* focused on the Western phenomenon of the beauty pageant now popular all over the world, with obvious implications about body and dress.[67] In addition, anthropologists contributed chapters to *Dress and Gender* by Barnes and Eicher, *Dress and Ethnicity* by Eicher, and *Beads and Bead Makers: Gender, Material Culture and Meaning* by Sciama and Eicher.[68]

Single-authored books also appeared, such as Polhemus's *Style Surfing: What to Wear in the Third Millennium* and Emma Tarlo's work on Gujarat in *Clothing Matters: Dress and Identity in India*.[69] *Cloth That Does Not Die* by Elisha Renne developed the argument that the making and wearing of cloth by the Bunu Yoruba paralleled changing conditions in modern Nigeria, for the use of handwoven cloth continued even though production dwindled markedly.[70] In 1997, Dorinne Kondo deconstructed gender, race and "Orientalism" in *About Face: Performing Race in Fashion and Theater*.[71] Michaele Haynes scrutinized an elite ritual of dress in *Dressing Up Debutantes: Pageantry and Glitz in Texas* (Figure 4).[72] Fadwa El Guindi, in *Veil: Modesty, Privacy and Resistance*, provided another breakthrough in untangling some of the multifaceted aspects of covering the head, the face and/or body (Figure 5).[73] In these volumes, the writers developed new interpretations about meaning and the place of dress in negotiating identity, moving from analysis of a bounded culture to focusing on global interconnections.[74]

Gendered craft production within a global market was another major and rich theme that arose in the 1990s. Two Latin American examples included *Kuna Crafts, Gender, and the Global Economy* by Karin Tice, and *Crafts in the World Market: The Impact of Global Exchange on Middle American Artisans*, an edited volume by June Nash.[75] While these two works focused on the production and exchange of textiles such as Kuna *mola* appliques or Guatemalan backstrap-loom-woven textiles, they also analyzed the use of these textiles as dress. For example, Robert Carlsen illustrated that textile production becomes an important aspect of culture in contemporary highland Guatemala; a multiplicity of ethnic identities are constructed through the use of these textiles as dress.[76]

The role of museums and work by anthropologists in museum settings needs acknowledgement. Mounting exhibits of artifacts collected from or based on field research enriches viewers' visual experience and knowledge. An exhibit provides opportunities to experience the impact of both single items and total ensembles of dress by seeing the color, silhouette and materials used from culture to culture. The accompanying museum publications,

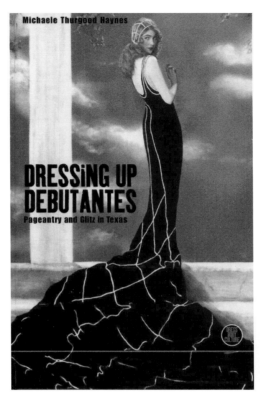

Figure 4. Michaele Haynes's book cover for Dressing Up Debutantes: Pageantry and Glitz in Texas *(1998)*.

usually published as books rather than as catalog lists, permit the idea of the exhibit to live beyond the exhibit itself. These exhibits extend knowledge into public communities-at-large, beyond the academic "ivory towers."

Conclusion

In the above survey of writings in English by anthropologists on dress, the four contributions (holism, culture, fieldwork, and women's involvement) I attribute to anthropology are virtually self-evident. Throughout the writings, the concept of holism is paramount: dress is analyzed, as part of a larger configuration of human behavior of a specific people in a

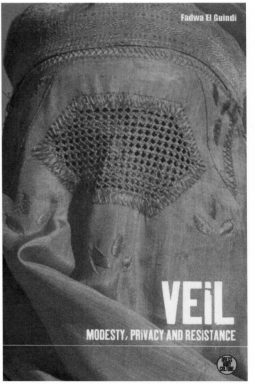

Figure 5. Fadwa El Guindi's book cover for Veil: Modesty, Privacy and Resistance *(1999)*.

specified time and place. The culture of specific people in relation to their habits of dress is also analyzed, with cultural diversity in dress from group to group becoming readily apparent. Fieldwork as a method of collecting data encouraged rich descriptions and analyses of the many variations and permutations of meanings attached to dress. The exceptions to fieldwork-based analyses are limited to such examples as those in the curio-cabinet stage and the essays written by Benedict, Bunzel, and Sapir. The role of women in anthropology, their attention to gender issues and interest in the topic of dress has resulted in more research and publications on the topic by women than by men. For example, the majority of books noted above from 1989 to 1999 were written, co-authored or co-edited by women. Women's sensitivity and attention to the topic of dress fairly obviously stems from the subcultural milieu of women and their frequent involvement in, concern and care for their own and others' dress.

The history of the anthropology of dress mirrors the history of anthropology itself, proceeding from cross-cultural examples from the curio-cabinet era to in-depth interpretive studies of one culture. A thread of agreement runs through these books and articles in that dress is presented as an effective communication system about personal and sociocultural identities.

[1] This paper was first written for presentation as a Distinguished Scholar Lecture at the 1999 International Textile and Apparel Association meeting. In my introduction, I commented on my perception of a significant difference between the goals of textiles and clothing scholars and the goals of anthropologists in studying dress. The interdisciplinary field of textiles and clothing originated in the U.S. in colleges as "Home Economics," based on a concern with solving problems of everyday life and improving the human condition. Scholars from this background center on textiles and clothing as subject matter, just as dress historians and museum curators do. In contrast, anthropologists focus generally on human beings as sociocultural animals and study dress from that perspective. I want to thank my research assistants, Susan J. Torntore and Theresa M. Winge, for their help, and Helen Callaway, Lidia Sciama, Linda Welters, and the four anonymous reviewers who made thoughtful and useful suggestions.

[2] I arbitrarily define "anthropologists" as individuals either with degrees in anthropology or who identify themselves as such.

[3] The topic will be greatly enhanced by a survey of anthropological writings in other languages.

[4] Tim Ingold, Companion Encyclopedia of Anthropology (London: Routledge, 1994), xiii.

[5] Ibid., xv.

[6] Alfred L. Kroeber and Clyde Kluckhohn, Culture: A Critical Review of Concepts and Definitions (New York: Vintage Books, 1952).

[7] Adam Kuper, Culture: The Anthropologists' Account (Cambridge, Mass.: Harvard University Press, 1999).

[8] Bronislaw Malinowski, Argonauts of the Western Pacific (London: G. Routledge & Sons, Ltd., 1922).

[9] Joanne B. Eicher, "Dress, Identity, Culture, and Choice: The Complex Act of Dress," in Proceedings of the International Textile and Apparel Association (Monument, Colo.: International Textile and Apparel Association, 1995), 8-11.

[10] Ute Gacs, Women Anthropologists: A Biographical Dictionary (New York: Greenwood Press, 1988); Barbara A. Babcock and Nancy J. Parezo, Daughters of the Desert: Women Anthropologists and the Native American Southwest (Albuquerque: University of New Mexico, 1988); Nancy J. Parezo, ed., Hidden Scholars: Women Anthropologists and the Native American Southwest (Albuquerque: University of New Mexico Press, 1993); Ruth Behar and Deborah A. Gordon, eds., Women Writing Culture (Berkeley and Los Angeles: University of California Press, 1995); Sherry B. Ortner, Making Gender: The Politics and Erotics of Culture (Boston: Beacon Press, 1996).

[11] Babcock and Parezo, Daughters of the Desert, 2.

[12] Ibid.

[13] Books such as Michelle Rosaldo and Louise Lamphere's Woman, Culture and Society (Stanford: Stanford University Press, 1974) were strategically written and titled to offset Harry L. Shapiro's Man, Culture and Society (New York: Oxford University Press, 1956). Shirley Ardener's edited volumes Defining Females: The Nature of Women in Society (New York: John Wiley and Sons, 1975), Perceiving Women (New York: John Wiley and Sons, 1975), and Women and Space: Ground Rules and Social Maps (1981; reprint, Oxford and New York: Berg, 1997), with Jackie Waldren, are other examples.

[14] Behar and Gordon, Women Writing Culture; James Clifford and George E. Marcus, eds., Writing Culture: The Poetics and Politics of Ethnography (Berkeley and Los Angeles: University of California Press, 1986), 17.

[15] My knowledge of African sources may be the most complete at this writing.

[16] Sir Edward Burnett Tylor, Primitive Culture: Researches into the Development of Mythology, Philosophy, Religion, Art, and Custom (1873; reprint, New York: Harper, 1958); Sir James G. Frazer, The Golden Bough: A Study in Magic and Religion (1890; reprint, New York: Macmillan, 1998).

17 Ernest Crawley, "Dress," in *Encyclopedia of Religion and Ethics,* ed. James Hastings (New York: Charles Scribner's Sons, 1912), 40-72; Ernest Crawley, *Dress, Drinks, and Drums: Further Studies of Savages and Sex* (London: Methuen and Co., Ltd., 1931).

18 Crawley, *Dress, Drinks, and Drums,* 2.

19 Ibid., 54.

20 Ibid., 117.

21 For example, a hospice nurse told me that her terminal patients were willing and eager to discuss what they wanted to wear in the coffin.

22 Crawley, *Dress, Drinks, and Drums,* 111-12.

23 Joanne B. Eicher, "Dress, Gender, and the Public Display of Skin," in *Dress and the Embodied Self,* eds. Elizabeth Wilson and Joanne Entwhistle (Oxford and New York: Berg, forthcoming in 2001).

24 Examples include movie star and model Elizabeth Hurley at the Academy Awards (1994) in Versace's safety-pin dress; rap artist Lil' Kim at the MTV Video Music Awards (1999) in a jumper, of her own design, that exposed one breast; and movie star and pop artist Jennifer Lopez at the Grammy Awards (2000) in Versace's transparent and open below the navel dress.

25 Crawley, *Dress, Drinks, and Drums,* 172.

26 Alice Fletcher and Francis La Flesche, "The Omaha Tribe," in *Twenty-Seventh Annual Report of the Bureau of American Ethnology to the Secretary of the Smithsonian Institution, 1905-1906* (Washington, D.C.: Government Printing Office, 1911): 17-672.

27 Matilda Coxe Stevenson, *Dress and Adornment of the Pueblo Indians,* Ms. No. 2093, Bureau of American Ethnology Archives. (Washington D.C.: National Anthropological Archives, 1911).

28 Alfred L. Kroeber, "On the Principle of Order in Civilization as Exemplified by Changes of Fashion," *The American Anthropologist* 21 (1919): 235-63; Alfred Kroeber and Jane Richardson, "Three Centuries of Women's Dress Fashion: A Quantitative Analysis," *Anthropological Records* 5, no. 2 (1940): 111-53.

29 Alfred R. Radcliffe-Brown, *The Andaman Islander: A Study in Anthropology* (Cambridge, Mass.: The Harvard University Press, 1922), 319.

30 Ruth Benedict, "Dress," in *Encyclopedia of the Social Sciences,* 235-37; Ruth Bunzel, "Ornament," in *Encyclopedia of the Social Sciences,* 496-97; Edward Sapir, "Fashion," in *Encyclopedia of the Social Sciences,* 139-44 (New York: Macmillan, 1931).

31 Sapir, "Fashion," 140.

32 Committee of the Royal Anthropological Institute of Great Britain and Ireland, *Notes and Queries on Anthropology* (1874; 6th ed., reprint, London: Routledge and Kegan Ltd., 1960). One example of following the *Notes and Queries* format is Allan R. Holmberg, *Nomads of the Long Bow: The Siriono of Eastern Bolivia* (Washington, D. C.: U. S. Government Print Office, 1950).

33 Henny Harald Hansen, *Mongol Costumes* (1950; reprint, London: Thames and Hudson, 1983).

34 Gudmund Hatt, *Arktiske Skinddragter i Eurasien og Amerika* (Copenhagen: J. H. Schultz, 1914); an English edition, *Arctic Skin Clothing in Eurasia and America,* was published in 1969.

35 Paul Bohannan, "Beauty and Scarification amongst the Tiv," *Man* 56 (September 1956): 117-21.

36 Simon D. Messing, "The Non-Verbal Language of the Ethiopian Toga," *Anthropos* 55, nos. 3-4 (1960): 558-60; Robert Murphy, "Social Distance and the Veil," *American Anthropologist* 66, no. 6 (1964): 1257-74.

37 Terrence Turner, "Tchikrin: A Central Brazilian Tribe and Its Symbolic Language of Bodily Adornment," *Natural History* 78, no. 8 (1969): 50-59; 70.

38 Sidney Moko Mead, *Traditional Maori Clothing* (Wellington: A. H. and A. W. Reed, 1969).

39 Although Petr Bogatyrev, a Slovak, wrote *Functions of Folk Costume in Moravian Slovakia* in 1937, the original was published in Slovak and only became available in English in 1971, when it was translated by Richard Crum.

40 See Alan Barnard, *History and Theory in Anthropology* (London: Routledge, 2000) for an appreciation of the development of the many orientations and analytical approaches.

41 Andrew Strathern and Marilyn Strathern, *Self-Decoration on Mount Hagen* (London: Gerald Duckworth and Co., Ltd., 1972); James Faris, *Nuba Personal Art* (London: Gerald Duckworth and Co., Ltd., 1971).

42 Strathern and Strathern, *Self-Decoration on Mount Hagen,* 1.

43 Ibid., 173.

44 Faris, *Nuba Personal Art,* 114.

45 Hilda Kuper, "Costume and Identity," *Comparative Studies in Society and History* 15, no. 3 (1973): 348-67.

46 Ted Polhemus, ed., *The Body Reader: Social Aspects of the Human Body* (New York: Pantheon, 1978); Ted Polhemus and Lynn Proctor, *Fashion and Anti-Fashion: An Anthropology of Clothing and Adornment* (London: Thames and Hudson, 1978).

47 Robert Brain, *The Decorated Body* (London: Hutchinson, 1979); Justine M. Cordwell and Ronald A. Schwarz, eds., *The Fabrics of Culture: The Anthropology of Clothing and Adornment* (The Hague: Mouton Publishers, 1979).

48 Cordwell and Schwarz, *Fabrics of Culture,* 1.

49 Patricia Rieff Anawalt, *Indian Clothing Before Cortes: MesoAmerican Costumes from the Codices* (Norman: University of Oklahoma Press, 1981).

50 Liza C. Dalby, *Geisha* (Berkeley and Los Angeles: University of California Press, 1983).

51 Annette B. Weiner and Jane Schneider, eds., *Cloth and Human Experience* (Washington, D.C.: Smithsonian Institution Press, 1989).

52 Gillian Feeley-Harnik, "Cloth and the Creation of Ancestors in Madagascar," in Weiner and Schneider, *Cloth and Human Experience,* 73-116; and B. S. Cohn, "Cloth, Clothes and Colonialism: India in the Nineteenth Century," in Weiner and Schneider, *Cloth and Human Experience,* 301-355.

53 Michael O'Hanlon, *Reading the Skin: Adornment, Display, and Society among the Wahgi* (London: British Museum Publications, 1989); *Paradise: Portraying the New Guinea Highlands* (London: British Museum Press, 1993).

54 Shelagh Weir, *Palestinian Costume* (London: British Museum Publications, 1989).

55 Margot Schevill, *Maya Textiles of Guatemala* (Austin: University of Texas Press, 1992).

56 Carol Hendrickson, *Weaving Identities: Construction of Dress and Self in a Highland Guatemala Town* (Austin: University of Texas Press, 1993).

57 Ibid., 40.

58 Liza C. Dalby, *Kimono: Fashioning Culture* (New Haven: Yale University Press, 1993).

59 Sandra A. Niessen, *Batak Cloth and Clothing: A Dynamic Indonesian Tradition* (Kuala Lumpur: Oxford University Press, 1993).

60 Diana Myers and Susan Bean, eds., *From the Land of the Thunder Dragon: Textile Arts of Bhutan* (London: Serindia Publications, 1994), 20.

61 Ted Polhemus, *Streetstyle: From Sidewalk to Catwalk* (New York: Thames and Hudson, 1994).

62 Karen Hansen, "Dealing with Clothing: *Salaula* and the Construction of Identity in Zambia's Third Republic," *Public Culture* 6, no. 3 (1994): 503-23; Karen Hansen, "Transnational Biographies and Local Meanings: Used Clothing Practices in Lusaka," *Journal of Southern African Studies* 21, no. 1 (1995): 131-45; Karen Hansen, "Other People's Clothes? The International Second-hand Clothing Trade and Dress Practices in Zambia," *Fashion Theory* 4, no. 3 (2000): 245-76; Joseph Nevadomsky, "The Clothing of Political Identity: Costume and Scarification in the Benin Kingdom," *African Arts* (winter 1995): 62-73, 100.

63 Hildi Hendrickson, ed., *Clothing and Difference: Embodied Identities in Colonial and Post-Colonial Africa* (Durham, N.C.: Duke University Press, 1996).

64 Nancy Lindisfarne-Tapper and Bruce Ingham, eds., *Languages of Dress in the Middle East* (Surrey, England: Curzon, 1997).

65 Henk Schulte Nordholt, *Outward Appearances: Dressing State and Society in Indonesia* (Leiden: KITLV Press, 1997).

66 Judith Perani and Norma H. Wolff, *Cloth, Dress and Art Patronage in Africa* (Oxford and New York: Berg, 1999).

67 Colleen B. Cohen, Richard Wilk and Beverly Stoeltje, eds., *Beauty Queens on the Global Stage: Gender, Contests and Power* (New York: Routledge, 1996).

68 Ruth Barnes and Joanne B. Eicher, eds., *Dress and Gender: Making and Meaning in Cultural Contexts* (Oxford and New York: Berg, 1992); Joanne B. Eicher, ed., *Dress and Ethnicity: Change across Space and Time* (Oxford and New York: Berg, 1995; reprint, 1999); Lidia D. Sciama and Joanne B. Eicher, eds., *Beads and Bead Makers: Gender, Material Culture and Meaning* (Oxford and New York: Berg, 1998).

69 Ted Polhemus, *Style Surfing: What to Wear in the Third Millennium* (New York: Thames and Hudson, 1996); Emma Tarlo, *Clothing Matters: Dress and Identity in India* (Chicago: Chicago University Press, 1996).

70 Elisha Renne, *Cloth That Does Not Die: The Meaning of Cloth in Bunu Social Life* (Seattle: University of Washington Press, 1995).

71 Dorinne K. Kondo, *About Face: Performing Race in Fashion and Theater* (New York: Routledge, 1997).

72 Michaele Thurgood Haynes, *Dressing Up Debutantes: Pageantry and Glitz in Texas* (Oxford and New York: Berg, 1998).

73 Fadwa El Guindi, *Veil: Modesty, Privacy and Resistance* (Oxford and New York: Berg, 1999).

74 A detailed discussion, not possible within the space constraints of an article, will be forthcoming in a book underway with the working title *The Anthropology of Dress* (Oxford and New York: Berg).

75 Karen E. Tice, *Kuna Crafts, Gender, and the Global Economy* (Austin: University of Texas Press, 1995); June Nash, ed., *Crafts in the World Market: The Impact of Global Exchange on Middle American Artisans* (Albany: State University of New York, 1993).

76 Robert S. Carlsen, "Discontinuous Warps: Textile Production and Ethnicity in Contemporary Highland Guatemala," in Nash, *Crafts in the World Market,* 199-222.

BIBLIOGRAPHY

Anawalt, Patricia Rieff. *Indian Clothing Before Cortes: MesoAmerican Costumes from the Codices.* Norman: University of Oklahoma Press, 1981.

Ardener, Shirley, ed. *Defining Females: The Nature of Women in Society.* New York: John Wiley and Sons, 1975.

———, ed. *Perceiving Women.* New York: John Wiley and Sons, 1975.

Ardener, Shirley, and Jackie Waldren, eds. *Women and Space: Ground Rules and Social Maps.* 1981. Reprint, Oxford and New York: Berg, 1997.

Babcock, Barbara A., and Nancy J. Parezo. *Daughters of the Desert: Women Anthropologists and the Native American*

Southwest. Albuquerque: University of New Mexico Press, 1988.

Barnard, Alan. *History and Theory in Anthropology.* London: Routledge, 2000.

Barnes, Ruth, and Joanne B. Eicher, eds. *Dress and Gender: Making and Meaning in Cultural Contexts.* Oxford and New York: Berg, 1992.

Behar, Ruth, and Deborah A. Gordon, eds. *Women Writing Culture.* Berkeley and Los Angeles: University of California Press, 1995.

Benedict, Ruth. "Dress." In *Encyclopedia of the Social Sciences.* New York: Macmillan, 1931.

Bogatyrev, Petr. *Functions of Folk Costume in Moravian Slovakia.* 1937. Translated by Richard Crum. Reprint, The Hague and Paris: 1971.

Bohannan, Paul. "Beauty and Scarification amongst the Tiv." *Man* 56 (September 1956): 117-21.

Brain, Robert. *The Decorated Body.* London: Hutchinson, 1979.

Bunzel, Ruth. "Ornament." In *Encyclopedia of the Social Sciences.* New York: Macmillan, 1931.

Carlsen, Robert S. "Discontinuous Warps: Textile Production and Ethnicity in Contemporary Highland Guatemala." In *Crafts in the World Market: The Impact of Global Exchange on Middle American Artisans,* edited by June Nash. Albany: State University of New York, 1993.

Clifford, James, and George E. Marcus, eds. *Writing Culture: The Poetics and Politics of Ethnography.* Berkeley and Los Angeles: University of California Press, 1986.

Cohen, Colleen B., Richard Wilk, and Beverly Stoeltje, eds. *Beauty Queens on the Global Stage: Gender, Contests and Power.* New York: Routledge, 1996.

Cohn, B. S. "Cloth, Clothes and Colonialism: India in the Nineteenth Century." In *Cloth and Human Experience,* edited by Annette B. Weiner and Jane Schneider.

Washington, D.C.: Smithsonian Institution Press, 1989.

Committee of the Royal Anthropological Institute of Great Britain and Ireland. *Notes and Queries on Anthropology.* 1874. 6th ed. Reprint, London: Routledge and Kegan, Ltd. (1960).

Cordwell, Justine M., and Ronald A. Schwarz, eds. *The Fabrics of Culture: The Anthropology of Clothing and Adornment.* The Hague: Mouton Publishers, 1979.

Crawley, Ernest. "Dress." In *Encyclopedia of Religion and Ethics,* edited by James Hastings. New York: Charles Scribner's Sons, 1912.

———. *Dress, Drinks, and Drums: Further Studies of Savages and Sex.* London: Methuen and Co., Ltd., 1931.

Dalby, Liza C. *Geisha.* Berkeley and Los Angeles: University of California Press, 1983.

———. *Kimono: Fashioning Culture.* New Haven: Yale University Press, 1993.

Eicher, Joanne B., ed. *Dress and Ethnicity: Change across Space and Time.* 1995. Reprint, Oxford and New York: Berg, 1999.

———. "Dress, Identity, Culture, and Choice: The Complex Act of Dress." In *Proceedings of the International Textile and Apparel Association.* Monument, Colo.: International Textile and Apparel Association (1995): 8-11.

———. "Dress, the Sexed Body, and the Public Display of Skin." In *Dress and the Embodied Self,* edited by Elizabeth Wilson and Joanne Entwhistle. Oxford and New York: Berg, forthcoming.

———. *The Anthropology of Dress* (working title). Oxford and New York: Berg, forthcoming.

El Guindi, Fadwa. *Veil: Modesty, Privacy and Resistance.* Oxford and New York: Berg, 1999.

Faris, James. *Nuba Personal Art.* London: Gerald Duckworth and Co., Ltd, 1972.

Feeley-Harnik, Gillian. "Cloth and the Creation of Ancestors in Madagascar." In *Cloth and Human Experience,* edited

by Annette B. Weiner and Jane Schneider. Washington, D.C.: Smithsonian Institution Press, 1989.

Fletcher, Alice, and Francis La Flesche. "The Omaha Tribe." In *Twenty-seventh Annual Report of the Bureau of American Ethnology to the Secretary of the Smithsonian Institution, 1905-1906,* Washington, D.C.: Government Printing Office, 1911.

Frazer, Sir James G. *The Golden Bough: A Study in Magic and Religion.* 1890. Reprint, New York: Macmillan, 1998.

Gacs, Ute. *Women Anthropologists: A Biographical Dictionary.* New York: Greenwood Press, 1988.

Hansen, Henny Harald. *Mongol Costumes.* 1950. Reprint, London: Thames and Hudson, 1983.

Hansen, Karen. "Dealing with Clothing: *Salaula* and the Construction of Identity in Zambia's Third Republic." *Public Culture* 6, no. 3 (1994): 503-23.

———. "Transnational Biographies and Local Meanings: Used Clothing Practices in Lusaka." *Journal of Southern African Studies* 21, no. 1 (1995): 131-45.

Hatt, Gudmund. *Arktiske Skinddragter i Eurasien og Amerika.* Copenhagen: J. H. Schultz, 1914.

Haynes, Michaele Thurgood. *Dressing Up Debutantes: Pageantry and Glitz in Texas.* Oxford and New York: Berg, 1998.

Hendrickson, Carol. *Weaving Identities: Construction of Dress and Self in a Highland Guatemala Town.* Austin: University of Texas Press, 1993.

Hendrickson, Hildi, ed. *Clothing and Difference: Embodied Identities in Colonial and Post-Colonial Africa.* Durham, N.C.: Duke University Press, 1996.

Holmberg, Allan R. *Nomads of the Long Bow: The Siriono of Eastern Bolivia.* Washington, D.C.: U.S. Government Print Office, 1950.

Ingold, Tim. *Companion Encyclopedia of Anthropology.* London: Routledge, 1994.

Kondo, Dorinne K. *About Face: Performing Race in Fashion and Theater*. New York: Routledge, 1997.

Kroeber, Alfred L. "On the Principle of Order in Civilization as Exemplified by Changes of Fashion." *The American Anthropologist* 21 (1919): 235-63.

Kroeber, Alfred L., and Clyde Kluckhohn. *Culture: A Critical Review of Concepts and Definitions*. New York: Vintage Books, 1952.

Kroeber, Alfred L., and Jane Richardson. "Three Centuries of Women's Dress Fashion: A Quantitative Analysis." *Anthropological Records* 5, no. 2 (1940): 111-53.

Kuper, Adam. *Culture: The Anthropologists' Account*. Cambridge, Mass.: Harvard University Press, 1999.

Kuper, Hilda. "Costume and Identity." *Comparative Studies in Society and History* 15, no. 3 (1973): 348-67.

Lindisfarne-Tapper, Nancy, and Bruce Ingham, eds. *Languages of Dress in the Middle East*. Surrey, England: Curzon, 1997.

Malinowski, Bronislaw. *Argonauts of the Western Pacific*. London: G. Routledge & Sons, Ltd., 1922.

Mead, Sidney M. *Traditional Maori Clothing*. Wellington: A. H. and A. W. Reed, 1969.

Messing, Simon D. "The Non-Verbal Language of the Ethiopian Toga." *Anthropos* 55, nos. 3-4 (1960): 558-60.

Murphy, Robert. "Social Distance and the Veil." *American Anthropologist* 66, no. 6 (1964): 1257-74.

Myers, Diana, and Susan Bean, eds. *From the Land of the Thunder Dragon: Textile Arts of Bhutan*. London: Serindia Publications, 1994.

Nash, June, ed. *Crafts in the World Market: The Impact of Global Exchange on Middle American Artisans*. Albany: State University of New York, 1993.

Nevadomsky, Joseph. "The Clothing of Political Identity: Costume and Scarification in the Benin Kingdom."

African Arts (winter 1995): 62-73, 100.

Niessen, Sandra A. *Batak Cloth and Clothing: A Dynamic Indonesian Tradition*. Kuala Lumpur: Oxford University Press, 1993.

Nordholt, Henk Schulte. *Outward Appearances: Dressing State and Society in Indonesia*. Leiden: KITLV Press, 1997.

O'Hanlon, Michael. *Paradise: Portraying the New Guinea Highlands*. London: British Museum Press, 1993.

———. *Reading the Skin: Adornment, Display, and Society among the Wahgi*. London: British Museum Publications, 1989.

Ortner, Sherry B. *Making Gender: The Politics and Erotics of Culture*. Boston: Beacon Press, 1996.

Parezo, Nancy J., ed. *Hidden Scholars: Women Anthropologists and the Native American Southwest*. Albuquerque: University of New Mexico Press, 1993.

Perani, Judith, and Norma H. Wolff. *Cloth, Dress and Art Patronage in Africa*. Oxford and New York: Berg, 1999.

Polhemus, Ted, ed. *The Body Reader: Social Aspects of the Human Body*. New York: Pantheon, 1978.

———. *Streetstyle: From Sidewalk to Catwalk*. New York: Thames and Hudson, 1994.

———. *Style Surfing: What to Wear in the Third Millennium*. New York: Thames and Hudson, 1996.

Polhemus, Ted, and Lynn Proctor. *Fashion and Anti-Fashion: An Anthropology of Clothing and Adornment*. London: Thames and Hudson, 1978.

Radcliffe-Brown, Alfred R. *The Andaman Islander: A Study in Anthropology*. Cambridge, Mass.: The Harvard University Press, 1922.

Renne, Elisha. *Cloth That Does Not Die: The Meaning of Cloth in Bunu Social Life*. Seattle: University of Washington Press, 1995.

Rosaldo, Michelle, and Louise Lamphere.

Women, Culture and Society. Stanford: Stanford University Press, 1974.

Sapir, Edward. "Fashion." In *Encyclopedia of the Social Sciences*. New York: Macmillan, 1931.

Schevill, Margot. *Maya Textiles of Guatemala*. Austin: University of Texas Press, 1992.

Sciama, Lidia D., and Joanne B. Eicher, eds. *Beads and Bead Makers: Gender, Material Culture and Meaning*. Oxford and New York: Berg, 1998.

Shapiro, Harry L. *Man, Culture and Society*. New York: Oxford University Press, 1956.

Stevenson, Matilda Coxe. *Dress and Adornment of the Pueblo Indians*. Ms. No. 2093, Bureau of American Ethnology Archives. Washington, D.C.: National Anthropological Archives, 1911.

Strathern, Andrew, and Marilyn Strathern. *Self-Decoration on Mount Hagen*. London: Gerald Duckworth and Co. Ltd., 1971.

Tarlo, Emma. *Clothing Matters: Dress and Identity in India*. Chicago: Chicago University Press, 1996.

Tice, Karen E. *Kuna Crafts, Gender, and the Global Economy*. Austin: University of Texas Press, 1995.

Turner, Terrence. "Tchikrin: A Central Brazilian Tribe and Its Symbolic Language of Bodily Adornment." *Natural History* 78, no. 8 (1969): 50-59, 70.

Tylor, Sir Edward Burnett. *Primitive Culture: Researches into the Development of Mythology, Philosophy, Religion, Art, and Custom*. 1873. Reprint, New York: Harper, 1958.

Weiner, Annette B., and Jane Schneider, eds. *Cloth and Human Experience*. Washington, D.C.: Smithsonian Institution Press, 1989.

Weir, Shelagh. *Palestinian Costume*. London: British Museum Publications, 1989.

Laurie Shade

Short Report

Figure 1. Ansel and Adeline Easton. *Courtesy, Columbus-America Discovery Group, Inc.*

Shipwreck: Ansel and Adeline Easton's Honeymoon Voyage of 1857

As the sun slipped below the horizon, vibrant shades of red, orange, and purple were reflected in ominous clouds and the turbulent sea. Ansel Ives Easton stood on the wheelhouse of the SS *Central America* with the captain and officers wearing an overcoat atop his life jacket and suit of clothes.[1] He watched the ship *Marine*, carrying all the women and children, including his bride of three weeks, move farther and farther away in the rough sea.[2] The captain asked Easton for his cigar to light the last rocket. As he turned to hand the cigar to the captain, the ship gave a great lurch. Easton found himself being swept into the water, as a vacuum created by the ship's weight pulled him and others down with her.[3] Those aboard the *Marine* watched in horror as the SS *Central America* disappeared beneath the waves.

There were 578 passengers and crew aboard the SS *Central America* when she left Havana for New York on September 8, 1857.[4] On September 12, she sank in water a mile and a half deep off the Carolina coast, taking with her 425 lives and over $1.2 million in commercial goods.[5] In the fall of 1990, the SS *Central America* sidewheeler recaptured the attention of Americans when researchers from Columbus-America Discovery Group, Inc., recovered a trunk from the debris field of

the shipwreck site using a remotely operated vehicle. During the removal of the items from the trunk, one shirt stood out, for written in ink on the right front side was the name "A. Ives Easton." The majority of the contents of the trunk were identified as Mr. Easton's while some items were identified as belonging to Mrs. Easton. (Clothing belonging to Mrs. Easton consisted of chemises, drawers, stockings, dressing gowns and a gown.) Contextual analysis of such finds demonstrates the utility of historical archaeology for enhancing our understanding of the history of dress.[6]

This paper focuses on Mr. Easton's clothing. Historically, much more attention has been paid to a bride's trousseau than to a groom's wardrobe.[7] Many sources of the period describe the trousseau items a bride would take with her on her honeymoon, but none mention what a groom packed for his journey. A gentleman to be married living in San Francisco during the 1850s had access to a variety of items to choose from right in the city itself.[8] Thus, we can expect his honeymoon wardrobe to be typical of any cosmopolitan American bridegroom.[9]

Ansel Ives Easton moved to San Francisco in 1849 or 1850 and established a company that provided laundry services, refilled mattresses, and furnished dry goods for the Pacific Mail Steamship Company.[10] Prior to moving to San Francisco he was a proprietor of

Laurie Shade earned a Ph.D. from The Ohio State University in 1994.

the Cronton Hotel in New York City. He met Adeline Mills in San Francisco (Figure 1).

Miss Mills was the sister of D. O. Mills, who would become the president and co-founder of the Bank of California.[11] Mr. Ansel Easton and Miss Adeline Mills were married in San Francisco on August 20, 1857. They left for their honeymoon voyage that same morning aboard the steamship *Sonora*, taking with them trunks of clothing and hampers of food and wine.[12] From San Francisco their itinerary took them to Panama, where they traversed the isthmus by rail and then boarded the SS *Central America* bound for New York via Havana, Cuba. Both were saved from the disaster separately and reunited six long days after the shipwreck, surviving with little more than the clothing they wore. Little did the Eastons know that over 134 years later one of their trunks, the stateroom trunk, would be recovered and the contents documented and studied. Mr. Easton may have brought the stateroom trunk on deck to transfer it to a rescue vessel, but as the ship sank, so did the trunk. This explanation accounts for its presence in the wreck's debris field.

Textile archaeologists recovered six layers of clothing and other artifacts, 109 pieces of which were dress items, from the Easton trunk.[13] Much of the clothing was rolled rather than folded. Additional artifacts consisted of jewelry, including gold cuff links and a watch fob, wrapped presents, and toilet items such as a comb, hairbrush, toothbrush and mustache brush.[14] A portion of a fruit loaf or cake that had been wrapped between an undershirt and a robe was found within the top layer of clothing.[15]

A combination of techniques was employed to analyze the garments. All dress items were examined, documented, sketched and photographed following the considerations outlined in Gardin's

archaeological constructs model.[16] The study included the development of an attribute examination record. A checklist designed with reference to primary and secondary visual and written documents of the period was used to record attributes that could serve as indicators of style, function and fashionability of men's outergarments during the mid-nineteenth century. Together with scholarly written and visual information, the attributes were studied to aid in the identification of the function and style of the dress items. Other types of men's outergarments from the same period were also examined.[17]

While only one of the Easton's trunks was retrieved from the shipwreck site, the items within the trunk represent at least two men's outfits that could have been modified with changes in shirt, waistcoat and neckwear. In addition to the suit of clothes Easton had on when he was rescued, these ensembles were in all likelihood the ones he wore on his wedding cruise. These outfits, however, represent only a portion of the clothing packed to be worn on his honeymoon. Additionally, he had given Mrs. Easton an overcoat with important papers in the pockets before her rescue. The Eastons' other trunks were stored in the hold of the ship, and were inaccessible during the trip.

In looking at Mr. Easton's outer garments, it appears that he was a robust man of short stature, perhaps 5'4" or 5'5". The inseam of both pairs of trousers measures 26 3/4" and 27" and 27 1/2" and 27 1/2", respectively. In addition, on a pair of suspenders analyzed in conjunction with one pair of trousers, the metal fastenings had been placed into the shortest eyelets. The waistband on each pair of trousers measures 37", and the majority of his shirts are voluminous in body.

The first example of a fashionable ensemble (Figure 2) consisted of a

Figure 2. Fashionable outfit Mr. Easton may have worn on his honeymoon cruise. *Double-breasted frock coat, white linen shirt, plaid tie, brown twill trousers with suspenders and gloves. Illustration by Julie Reeder.*

Figure 3. Fashionable informal outfit Mr. Easton may have worn on his honeymoon cruise. *Brown Paletot-sac coat worn with white linen shirt, double-breasted white waistcoat with brown floral motif, blue napped trousers, gold ascot with purple fishhook design, and a pair of gloves. Illustration by Julie Reeder.*

brown wool double-breasted frock coat (#29148), white linen shirt (#29066), pair of formal brown wool trousers (#29049) with canvas suspenders (#29322), single-breasted brown silk waistcoat with gold design (#29178), plaid cotton tie (#29296), pair of drawers (#29062), undershirt (#29054), and pair of white cotton socks with Easton's initials stamped or printed in red at the top edge (#29212). Accessory items included a pair of white kid gloves (#29282),[18] handkerchief (#29129), and three gold studs (#29202). No shoes or hats were found in the trunk.

The second outfit (Figure 3) consisted of a brown Paletot-sac coat for casual or seaside wear (#29168), white linen shirt (#29067), pair of formal blue wool trousers (#29164, recovered from the trunk inside out), double-breasted white cotton waistcoat with brown floral motif (#29181), gold silk ascot (or scarf) with purple fishhook design (#29096), pair of long underwear (#29174), and pair of white socks (#29213). Accessory items included a pair of white kid gloves (#29211) and a handkerchief (#29130). The outfit would have been completed, of course, with shoes and a hat.

As the dress items were analyzed, specific attributes began to emerge (Tables 1 and 2).[19] Both pairs of trousers and one waistcoat have remnants of manufacturer's marks: the trousers bear nearly illegible stamps which read "York" and "New York," while the waistcoat has a faded tailor's label. One shirt (#29066) has "A. Ives Easton 4" written in ink, perhaps to identify the owner when it was sent to be cleaned. All but one of the items from the two outfits have hand-sewn top stitching.

The majority of the clothing—coats, waistcoats, trousers and neckwear—is made of fabric with complex weave structures that incorporate float yarns or additional warp or weft yarns. In some cases, such as the brown wool trousers, red and gold yarns created the desired patterning. The fabric was then brushed to create a napped surface making the fabric patterning even more subtle. Both shirts and one tie,

Table 1: Attributes of Man's Outfit in Figure 2.

I.D.# Style	Label Manufactured	Top Stitching	Fabric Structure	Pattern	Design	Fiber Type
29148 DB Frock Coat	No	Hand	Unbalanced simple float weave	Float	None	Wool
29066 Shirt	No	Hand	Balanced simple plain weave	None	None	Linen
29049 Trousers	Yes	Hand	Unbalanced compound plain weave	Float yarns warp faced	None Color change Variation in # of yarns	Wool
29178 Waistcoat	Yes	Hand	Unbalanced compound plain weave	Float	Woven Variation in # of yarns	Silk
29296 Tie	No	None	Balanced simple plain weave	None	Applied linear printed	Cotton

Figure 4. Tie with tan and black printed plaid design on plain-weave white fabric ground. Illustration by Julie Reeder.

however, are made of a balanced plain weave fabric.

Some of the plain weave fabrics were printed with a design. The tie (#29296) illustrated in Figure 4, for example, is printed with a plaid design of tan and black. Another neckwear item, an ascot or scarf, has a printed purple fishhook design on a gold balanced plain-weave fabric.

Most of the fabrics in the garments had typical fiber contents for menswear of this period (Tables 1 and 2). While the frock coat and trousers are wool, the Paletot-sac coat's outer fabric is a blend of silk and wool fibers. Both coats have silk linings. In each pair of trousers the waist linings are made of silk and the lower-leg linings of flax (linen). Both shirts are made of fine linen. The suspenders are made of canvas, implying use as day wear.[20]

The two coats vary in stylistic details but measure similar lengths and shoulder widths. Both waistcoats have shawl collars, two welt pockets, six buttons down the center front and a half belt at the center back (Figure 5). The silk waistcoat (#29178) has leather foreparts. When recovered, it had a pen quill tip in one welt pocket and a plaid tie (#29296) in the other.[21] Both pairs of trousers have two cash pockets at the waist, one on either side of the body, a watch pocket at the right front side, and a half belt at the center back (Figure 6). The fashionable belt buckles, stamped "1857," were new at the time of the trip.

The shirts have collars with square ends and pleats on either side of the placket. The number and width of the pleats varies. One shirt (#29066) has three pleats or tucks on each side of the placket, and five to seven inches down from the neckband to the placket there are pin marks where perhaps a stick pin had secured Easton's ascot or scarf. This shirt, with buttonholes on both sides of the placket for studs, would be considered the more formal of the two analyzed. The other shirt (#29067) has buttonholes on one side of the placket and buttons on the other, as well as seventeen pleats or tucks

Figure 5. Single-breasted waistcoat. Illustration by Julie Reeder.

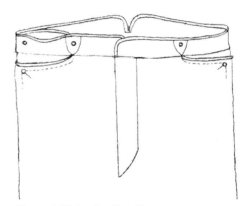

Figure 6. Waist details of brown trousers. Illustration by Julie Reeder.

Table 2: Attributes of Man's Outfit in Figure 3.

I.D.# Style	Label Manufactured	Top Stitching	Fabric Structure	Pattern	Design	Fiber Type
29168 Paletot-sac Coat	No	Hand	Balanced compound plain weave with complementary warp yarns	Float color change variation in weft yarn size	Woven stripe linear embroidery and pile	Wool/Silk
29067 Shirt	Yes	Hand	Balanced simple plain weave	None	None	Linen
29164 Trousers	Yes	Hand	Unbalanced compound float weave	Float warp faced yarns	None	Wool
29181 Waistcoat	No	Hand	Balanced compound, plain weave with complementary warp and weft yarns	Float color change variation in weft yarn size	Woven	Cotton
29096 Ascot	No	Hand	Balanced simple plain weave	Variation in warp/weft yarns	Woven/applied bar linear/curvilinear printed	Silk

in varying widths on either side of the placket. Both shirts have hand-rolled edges and are of generous proportion.

The neckwear items represent different styles, one being a tie and the other an ascot or scarf. The tie, recovered inside one of the welt pockets of the waistcoat (#29178), measures 43 1/2" in length and 5 1/2" in width, though it appears to have been folded in half, making it about 2 1/2" wide when worn. The ascot, which resembles a large square scarf, seems to have been folded diagonally when it was stored in the trunk.

Each of the two outfits recovered from the Easton trunk would have been worn for day wear, though the sac-coat ensemble is the less formal of the two. Mr. Easton may have changed his shirt, neckwear, and waistcoat, also considered day wear, and worn them with the frock coat as evening wear on the ship, since he had brought only one of his trunks to his stateroom, while the other trunks were in the hold of the ship. Both outfits would be considered fashionable dress for the period of 1857. Only the waistcoats manifest certain characteristics that reflect a style fashionable early in the 1850s. A photograph depicting two shipping merchants and their business associates from California of circa 1850 shows dress similar in style to Mr. Easton's two outfits (Figure 7). All five men wear coats, waistcoats, shirts, neckwear and trousers somewhat similar to Easton's. The status and position of Jacob Leese (seated left) and Thomas Larkin (seated center), prominent landowners and shipping merchants in the San Francisco area during the late 1840s and early 1850s, approximated that of landowner and businessman Ansel Ives Easton.

Mr. Easton's garments represent the type of clothing a wealthy man would pack and wear on his wedding voyage. Though the revolution of ready-made clothing had already begun in the 1850s with the advent of the

Figure 7. Five men from Monterey, California, *ca. 1850. Courtesy, Bancroft Library, University of California, Berkeley.*

sewing machine, the majority of Easton's two outfits were hand sewn, a feature that would take more time to produce. These items would, therefore, be more expensive. Only one of his shirts, out of fourteen recovered from the trunk, and all three detachable collars were ready-made. Interestingly, the collar of one hand-sewn shirt had been cut off, and straight pins had been placed to make the neck circumference smaller. Perhaps Easton was trying out one of his new ready-made detachable collars.

Mr. Easton's clothing is not unusual considering the context in which it was worn. It is similar to what other men of his position wore for business day wear: coats and trousers made of wool and lined in silk, waistcoats and neckwear items made of either cotton or silk fabrics, and hand-sewn shirts made of fine linen cloth.[22] The majority of Easton's dress may have been fashionable for the period, but perhaps not representative of the latest fashions available, with the exception of his two pairs of trousers. Some of the latest fashions available to men in 1857 included matched suits, consisting of coat, waistcoat, and trousers

called "ditto suits."[23] The sack coat also became fashionable at this time. Being a well-to-do man on his honeymoon voyage, Easton may have preferred to dress conservatively, in accordance with tastes dictated by his class and economic level that were slightly behind the innovative fashions of the day.

Conclusion

The find of a trunk of clothing from the year 1857 is a time capsule of dress items and personal effects. The analysis of such a collection allows us to glean a better understanding of the culture and social group to which Mr. Easton belonged. Easton, a man of relatively high status, was a prominent businessman living in San Francisco, California. His clothing reflects his social status and supports evidence that the group to which he belonged chose to wear clothing that was hand-made even when standardized ready-made clothing was new and available. At this time in San Francisco, a wide variety of clothing was available to men of all social positions. During the mid-nineteenth century, merchants from all over the world shipped large quantities of goods to San Francisco, often selling them on their ships that they converted into stationary stores. The examination of Mr. Easton's outergarments makes it clear that, despite the depiction in 1850s primary documents of men of position changing their clothing several times a day, these men also chose to wear the same coat and trousers for day wear and evening wear, changing only their shirt, neckwear and waistcoat to suit the occasion. This may not have been the case all the time, but perhaps it was for much of the time. The collection of outergarments recovered from Mr. Easton's trunk may reflect how gentlemen really dressed during this time in history, as well as documenting what a groom would pack for his honeymoon, a topic of speculation. Another fact of note is that all of Easton's clothing was new except his waistcoats, which have mended areas and represent a style fashionable in the earlier part of the decade. Perhaps the waistcoats are the one class of clothing from Mr. Easton's trunk that reflect who he was, items that he felt comfortable wearing.

Acknowledgements

This work is dedicated in memorium to Dr. Lucy R. Sibley, my advisor and friend, who inspired me with her passion and love of historic costume. My sincere appreciation also goes to researchers from Columbus-America Discovery Group, Inc., for making the contents of the Easton trunk available to me for study. Specifically, I would like to thank Thomas G. Thompson, President; Robert Evans, Science Director; Debra Willaman, Assistant to Robert Evans; Milton Butterworth, Director of Photography; and Judith Conrad, Historian. Thanks also to Julie Reeder for her illustrations. A special thanks to my husband, Scott; son, Louis; daughter, Sophie; and my mother, Carole Jeanne Crawford, for their encouragement, patience and support of this project.

1 Grace Jarrett Easton. Notes on the Eastons given to Anne Adams Helms, 1977. Private collection.

2 Mrs. Easton offered the Captain of the *Marine* money if he would send a boat back for her husband. Adeline Mills Easton to Jenny Page, 4 October 1857, 6. Adeline Mills Easton and Nellie Olmstead Lincoln, *The Story of Our Wedding Journey* (San Francisco: n.p., 1911), 27.

3 Easton, Notes.

4 The SS *Central America* left Aspinwall, Panama, on September 3, 1857, and headed for Havana. On September 8, 1857, she left Havana on the final leg of her journey bound for New York. Easton and Lincoln, *The Story of Our Wedding Journey*, 14.

5 Newspapers at the time printed very different figures for the amount of California gold and other goods, as well as the number of lives lost during the disaster. After much research, investigators estimated that the loss of commercial treasure reached approximately $1.2 million and 425 people lost their lives. Judy Conrad, *Story of an American Tragedy: Survivors' Accounts of the Sinking of the Steamship Central America*. (Columbus, Ohio: Columbus-America Discovery Group, 1988), xiv.

6 Much of the background information related to this story comes from two sources: Easton and Lincoln, *The Story of Our Wedding Journey*; and Conrad, *Story of an American Tragedy*.

7 A bride's trousseau, part of her dowry, was thought to be more important than her wedding dress. Usually it was composed of clothing and household linens intended to last several years. Penelope Byrde, *Nineteenth-Century Fashion* (London: B. T. Batsford, 1992), 151.

8 For the years 1856-57, the *San Francisco Alta* lists numerous dry goods stores advertising a wide variety of goods and services available to men of varying occupations.

9 Claudia B. Kidwell and Margaret C. Christman, *Suiting Everyone: The Democratization of Clothing in America* (Washington,D.C.: Smithsonian Institution Press, 1974), 63.

10 Originally from New York, Mr. Easton made his fortune in San Francisco prior to marrying Mrs. Easton. Easton, Notes.

11 Because of his business with the bank, D. O. Mills shipped gold frequently from San Francisco to New York. A $34,000 shipment of gold was lost when the SS *Central America* sank. In the early 1860s D. O. Mills and William Ralston established the Bank of California. Warren A. Beck and David A. Williams, *California: A History of the Golden State* (Garden City, New York: Doubleday, 1972); Conrad, *Story of an American Tragedy*. Strangely enough, a shirt with the name "W. Ralston" stamped or printed in ink on the right front side was recovered from the Easton trunk, wrapped in newspaper and tied with string. The newspaper was an issue of the *New York News*.

12 Based on letters and memories from Mrs. Easton, friends and family had given the couple hampers of biscuits, cakes and wine. There were also presents and beautiful clothes packed in trunks in the hold. Easton and Lincoln, *The Story of Our Wedding Journey*, 10.

13 Materials recovered from the trunk are listed in the order that they were found in the trunk. Laurie Crawford, "The Mid-Nineteenth Century Analysis of Men's Outer-Garments Recovered from a Deep Ocean Site" (Ph.D. diss., Ohio State University, 1994).

14 Perhaps the gifts were wedding presents or perhaps the Eastons had brought them to give to family members in New York.

15 The Easton family history does not

document what type of wedding cake the Eastons had or whether they placed a portion of cake in one of the trunks when they left on their honeymoon voyage. During the mid-nineteenth century, fruit cake was a popular choice for wedding cake. Arlene Hamilton Stewart, *A Bride's Book of Wedding Traditions* (New York: Hearst Books, 1995), 236.

[16] J. C. Gardin, *Archaeological Constructs: An Aspect of Theoretical Archaeology* (Cambridge, England: Cambridge University Press, 1980).

[17] Primary sources examined for this study include *Godey's Lady's Book,* 1857; *Peterson's Magazine,* 1857; *Hutchings' Illustrated California Magazine,* 1856-59; *Ehrichs Fashion Quarterly,* 1870s; *New York Daily News,* 1856-57; *Harpers Weekly,* 1857; *San Francisco Alta,* 1857; and *Leslie's Illustrated Weekly Newspaper,* 1857. Similar men's outer dress items (coats, waistcoats, trousers, neckwear, shirts, and collars) were observed at five different museums in the State of Ohio: Cincinnati Museum of Art, Kent State Museum, The Ohio Historical Society, The Western Reserve Historical Society, and the Kelton House (Columbus).

[18] Made of white kid leather, Mr.Easton's gloves have three points on the back. Good gloves are still finished with three lines of pointing on the back, a vestige of the embroidery that first appeared in 1780. Gloves worn during this period were meant to be fitted; in some cases the fingernail could be seen through the glove. Paul Keers, *A Gentleman's Wardrobe: Classic Clothes and the Modern Man* (New York: Harmony Books, 1988), 94.

[19] Specific attributes present in the garments can aid in identification of characteristics indicative of the status of the owner. In this case, because Mr. Easton's status was already known, the undertaking was a good test of the process. Crawford, "The Mid-Nineteenth Century Analysis of Men's Outer-Garments Recovered from a Deep Ocean Site".

[20] Canvas suspenders have been associated with day wear, while finely embroidered suspenders would have been worn for evening wear. Keers, *A Gentleman's Wardrobe,* 76.

[21] Waistcoats with leather facings or ties at the back were characteristic of a style that was popular in 1845. Waistcoats with borders edged with piping were fashionable beginning in 1839 but not after 1855. Foreparts are constructed by joining side seams to back-pieces which were united by a midline seam extending from neck to waist. Anne Buck, *Victorian Costume and Costume Accessories* (Bedford, England: Ruth Bean, 1984), 194-95. Cecil Willett Cunnington and Phillis Cunnington, *Handbook of English Costume in the Nineteenth Century* (London: Faber and Faber, 1966), 42-43.

[22] Penelope Byrde, *The Male Image: Men's Fashion in Britian, 1300-1970* (London: B.t. Batsford, 1979); Mr. Easton's double-breasted frock coat is similar in style and fiber content to a collection of frock coats analyzed from Virginia City, Montana, 1865. Deborah D. C. Meyer and Laurel E. Wilson, "Bringing Civilization to the Frontier: The Role of Men's Coats in 1865 Virginia City, Montana, Territory," *Clothing and Textiles Research Journal* 16, no 1 (1998): 26.

[23] Blanche Payne, Geitel Winakor and Jane Farrell-Beck, *History of Costume* (New York: Harper Collins, 1992), 497, 504.

BIBLIOGRAPHY

Beck, Warren A., and David A. Williams. *California: A History of the Golden State.* Garden City, New York: Doubleday, 1972.

Buck, Anne. *Victorian Costume and Costume Accessories.* Bedford, England: Ruth Bean, 1984.

Byrde, Penelope. *Nineteenth Century Fashion.* London: B.T. Batsford, 1992.

_____. *The Male Image: Men's Fashion in Britain, 1300-1970.* London: B.T. Batsford, 1979.

Conrad, Judy. *Story of an American Tragedy: Survivors' Accounts of the Sinking of the Steamship Central America.* Columbus, Ohio: Columbus-America Discovery Group, 1988.

Crawford, Laurie. "The Mid-Nineteenth Century Analysis of Men's Outer-Garments Recovered from a Deep Ocean Site." Ph.D. diss., Ohio State University, 1994.

Cunnington, Cecil Willett, and Phillis Cunnington. *Handbook of English Costume in the Nineteenth Century.* London: Faber and Faber, 1966.

Easton, Adeline Mills, and Nellie Olmstead Lincoln. *The Story of Our Wedding Journey.* San Francisco n.p., 1911.

Gardin, J. C. *Archaeological Constructs: An Aspect of Theoretical Archaeology.* Cambridge, England: Cambridge University Press, 1980.

Keers, Paul. *A Gentleman's Wardrobe: Classic Clothes and the Modern Man.* New York: Harmony Books, 1988.

Kidwell, Claudia B., and Margaret C. Christman. *Suiting Everyone: The Democratization of Clothing in America.* Washington, D.C.: Smithsonian Institution Press, 1974.

Meyer, Deborah J. C., and Laurel E. Wilson. "Bringing Civilization to the Frontier: The Role of Men's Coats in 1865 Virginia City, Montana Territory." *Clothing and Textiles Research Journal* 16, 1(1998): 19-26.

Payne, Blanche, Geitel Winakor and Jane Farrell-Beck. *The History of Costume from the Ancient Egyptians through the Twentieth Century.* New York: HarperCollins, 1992.

Stewart, Arlene Hamilton. *A Bride's Book of Wedding Traditions.* New York: Hearst Books, 1995.

Stella Blum Grant Report

Dominique Cocuzza is a recent M.A. graduate from the Fashion Institute of Technology. She recently relocated to Washington, D.C., where she is a Mellon Fellow in ethnographic textile conservation at the Smithsonian National Museum of the American Indian.

The Costume Society of America awards the Stella Blum Research Grant in memory of Stella Blum, curator, educator, writer, scholar and founding member of the Society. The purpose of the grant is to support original student research on North American dress.

The Dress of Free Women of Color in New Orleans, 1780-1840

The topic of my research is the dress of free women of color in New Orleans, Louisiana from 1780 to 1840. This report opens with a historical introduction to Spanish colonial New Orleans and proceeds to discuss the occupations of free women of color and their role as fashion makers in society. Racial miscegenation and the root of prevailing patriarchal ideas concerning women of color will be explored as well as legislation created during the Spanish colonial period (1763-1803) that attempted to limit their dress. Above all, this investigation focuses on how free women of color chose to appear in the public eye.

Unfortunately, no garments belonging to free women of color and only a few images of these women survive. Among free women of color, the appearance and dress of quadroon women were most frequently mentioned in primary sources.[1] The most detailed descriptions of their dress are found in contemporary travel journals, many of which were written from the perspective of European males.[2] To provide a more complete picture, this research explores primary sources written by and concerning women and people of color, slave testimonies, letters written by free women of color, novels and poems written by free people of color, Creole proverbs and slave songs.

During Louisiana's Spanish colonial period, a cohesive population of free people of color emerged. These people of African descent made significant advances in terms of legal rights, demographic expansion, labor and social standing. Many free people of color were Creoles of racially mixed heritage. The term *Creole* has had several meanings, depending on time period and locality.[3]

Creole as used here designates people born in New Orleans who were one or more of the following: American Indian, French, Spanish and/or African. New Orleans represented "an anomaly among the colonies because it refused to function according to any solidified social stratification based on race, class or legal status."[4] Masters and slaves of every color existed, and slaves were owned by all segments of the population, including whites, American Indians and free people of color. New Orleans was a unique city in which many cultures came into contact and blended.[5]

Throughout most of the eighteenth century, the slave population consistently outnumbered whites, and a unique and highly cohesive slave culture developed.[6] The labor of slaves generated the wealth of the Southern economy, and Southern families often received their greatest revenues by hiring out their slaves.[7] The urban slaves of New Orleans generally had greater geographic and social mobility than rural plantation slaves of Louisiana. Urban slaves had increased opportunities to gain valuable skills that would later enable them to buy their freedom. Slave women often worked as domestics in New Orleans, and many were engaged in tasks related to clothing and dress. In fact, female slaves were often marketed for their sewing and laundering skills.[8]

Spain officially gained control over Louisiana in 1763, during the reign of Charles III. During this period Louisiana began to flourish. The economy expanded sharply, and New Orleans became a bustling port city in which many goods from around the world changed hands. A cosmopolitan city developed in which many cultures interacted and assimilated. The rights of slaves were significantly extended under Spanish rule.[9] Slaves were able to buy their own freedom through a Spanish mandate called *coartacion*, enabling many urban slaves to find avenues to freedom for themselves or loved ones through profits generated by skilled labor.[10] The Spanish manumitted more slaves than other colonial powers, and one of the largest free black populations of the South emerged in New Orleans.

Due to a long history of miscegenation, many free people of color in New Orleans were racially mixed. These people often occupied the fringes of society; they were related to both the white and slave communities, yet were accepted by neither.[11] The following passage from a contemporary source illustrates the awkward position of two free women of color aboard a Mississippi riverboat:

> They were dressed much more expensively than either of the white ladies onboard – silks, lace, and feathers, white ornaments of jewelry of various kinds, being worn by them. . . . So equivocal . . . was the position of these colored ladies, that they could not be placed at either of the tables . . . so they had to retire to their pantry, where they took their meals standing; and the contrast of their finery of dress and ornament with the place in which they took their isolated and separate meal, was painfully striking.[12]

One writer on black fashion pointed out that fashion was an expression of liberation for people of color:

> Living and working in a racially segregated environment where domination of black folks via dramas of humiliation and disregard were the norm, dressing up, expressing one's style, was a declaration of one's independence.[13]

Race was not simply a matter of biology in New Orleans.[14] It was based on a complex formula that combined many factors, including physical features, clothing style, language, religion, family reputation and occupation. In general, free people of color distanced themselves from slavery as much as possible and identified with the values of the hegemonic white population.[15] Affluent people of color frequently intermingled with upper-class whites, blurring the social lines of distinction.[16] Many free people of color were able to attain economic independence as skilled laborers, farmers of small plots, slave owners, traders and business persons.[17]

Free women of color invested in jewelry, personal goods, real estate and slaves.[18] They worked to accumulate property and owned farms or even plantations. They also purchased slave women who had income-producing skills and often worked beside them.[19] Like whites, some free women of color avoided the appearance of working by having their slaves work for an income.[20]

Free women of color generally monopolized gender-specific occupations and extended their domestic world to that of the public.[21] Many were recognized as highly skilled weavers, seamstresses, laundresses and cooks.[22] The unique voice of these women is found in a book entitled *Chained to the Rock of Adversity*, the only published collection of letters written by free women of color, who in this case earned their living as seamstresses.[23]

Free women of color were important fashion producers who planned the gowns of elegant white women.[24] We find examples of free women of color who were known for their good taste and skills as hairdressers in the novels of George Washington Cable.[25] A traveler to New Orleans described contemporary fashions and referred to the quadroon hairdresser as "a refinement in which the richest ladies in Boston would not think of indulging."[26] The extraordinary tale of a free woman of color who traveled throughout the colonies and Europe dressing the hair of affluent white women is found in Eliza Potter's memoirs entitled *A Hairdresser's Experience in the High Life*. Free women of color were able to gain opportunities for social and geographic mobility through these kinds of occupations. Although free women generally earned less than free men, they were able to accumulate more wealth.[27]

Though quadroon women formed a small segment of the population of free women of color, this particular group of women captured the attention of many.[28] They were often referred to as "yellow ladies" because of their light complexion; their praises were sung in the popular song "The Yellow Rose of Texas." Quadroons became a favorite topic of abolition fiction authors, and a genre of novels emerged in which the quadroon was depicted as a tragic figure with an inevitable sad fate. These women were immortalized in myth and scandal because of their relationships with white men. Young quadroon girls were trained to develop their natural charm in preparation for their role in the illegal institution of *plaçage*, a "left-handed" marriage in which free women of color were "placed" with white men.[29]

Quadroon women and white men would rendezvous at the infamous Quadroon Balls, which were at their height during the first half of the nineteenth century. Both white women and men of color were excluded from these secretive and elitist social functions. However, one finds advertisements for these affairs tucked away in

Figure 1. Grand Ball Paré. *Advertisement for a ball inviting free women of color.* Le Moniteur, August 22, 1807.

inconspicuous sections of contemporary newspapers (Figure 1).[30] A mother's guilt associated with "placing" her daughter with a white man is expressed in the poem entitled *Epigram*, written by a free man of color named Armand Lanusse.[31] Although some of these illegal unions lasted a lifetime, others ended in heartbreak and abandonment.

Plaçage was also a form of "whitening" associated with social mobility.[32] This Creole song exemplifies the satire aimed at free women of color who attempted to "pass for white":

> Tou-Cou-Tou
> They know you,
> You are a black-a-moor!
> There is no soap,
> White enough,
> To bleach your skin.
> Even at the theater,
> When you take a loge,
> As white as you look,
> They will make you go to the balcony. . . .[33]

During the sixteenth and seventeenth centuries, interracial unions were generally tolerated, but the Spanish aristocracy responded defensively in the eighteenth century when increasingly affluent free women of color began to intermarry within their class.[34] These unions, which produced mixed-race children, threatened the social order because they challenged efforts to keep bloodlines "pure", marriages legitimate and women subordinate.[35] Women of color were to blame in the eyes of the community. The myth that they were naturally seductive followed these women from slavery into freedom and continued to significantly influence their experiences.[36] To better understand the source of these projected images, it is useful to examine the root of miscegenation in the non-consensual unions between master and slave. In the rare testimonial entitled *Incidents in the Life of a Slave Girl*, Harriet Jacobs described beauty as a curse for the female

Figure 2. Although this image is from a later period, the women vividly illustrate the continuity of resplendent dress worn by free women of color. Watercolor of free women of color. *Edouard Marquis, ca. 1870. Louisiana State Museum, New Orleans (1982.1.10.6).*

slave: "If God has bestowed beauty upon her, it will prove her greatest curse. That which commands admiration in the white woman only hastens the degradation of female slaves."[37] White men effectively escaped responsibility for their actions and justified the exploitation of these women by deeming them to be naturally erotic and seductive.[38]

In 1786 acting Governor Miro passed a set of forty-three legal articles in his inaugural proclamation.[39] Articles four through six were targeted at unmarried free women of color. Articles four and five concerned concubinage, while article six concerned the dress of mulattos and quadroons in particular. Miro warned that the extravagant luxury of their dress, which was already excessive, would compel him to investigate the mores of those who persisted in such display.[40] Quadroon women were renowned for their love of vivid colors and extravagant dress (Figure 2). One traveler described

Figure 3. Madras tignon worn by slaves. Louisiana State Museum, New Orleans (1981.33.73).

the dress of these women as being very different from the dress of white women.[41] A wonderful example of their lively style is found in an article entitled "A Quadroon's Taste" published in the *Daily Picayune*:

> . . . a handsome Quadroon, was attired, as well as we could make out, in the following dress . . . one white satin gown, neatly made and decorated with flounces, cut and fringed, and broad hems in the skirt, one crimson belt or zone, one pink neck handkerchief, one pair blue hose, one pair white satin shoes, with large shining buckles and a profusion of bows, ribbon and braid, one large bunch of artificial flowers in her [hair], one black veil, one yellow pocket handkerchief, one green umbrella with brown border with lilac fringe.[42]

Article six mentioned the distinction that existed in the hairdressing of people of color and stated that mulatto and quadroon women were forbidden to wear feathers or curls in their raised coiffures. The hair of these women was to be covered with a head kerchief when it was combed high, as was formerly the custom (Figure 3).[43] Spanish colonial sumptuary laws typically prohibited women of color from wearing silks, gold,

silver, pearls and mantillas.[44] Some Spanish colonial legislation went even farther, prohibiting women of color from wearing slippers ornamented with silver bells, from owning canopied beds, and from sitting on rugs or cushions while attending church.[45]

The headdress that Miro was referring to was the *tignon*, a fabric head wrap commonly worn by slaves and servants in the Southern colonies (Figure 4). The restriction was instituted for several reasons. It was an attempt to render these women less beautiful by limiting their use of ornament. One scholar pointed out that "hair exemplifies the sexual self far more for women than it does for men."[46] Covering the head thus neutralized the outward expression of sexuality. Whites

Figure 4. Servant of the Douglas Family, ca. 1850. Attributed to Julian Hudson, free woman of color. Louisiana State Museum, New Orleans (11943.54).

also perceived grooming and personal adornment as a privilege to be held only by the ruling majority.

> Hair grooming equates with leisure time; that is the more leisure one has, the more time one has to care for the hair. For most of the enslaved, their only free time to attend to personal chores was during some part of the weekend. . . . well groomed hair constituted an important outward form of status. . . .[47]

The *tignon* was also a signifier of racial status that could clearly identify the woman of color, preventing a light-complexioned woman from "passing for white." In addition, the mandate attempted to return the free woman of color, visibly and symbolically, to a subordinate and inferior status associated with slavery.[48]

> Free women of color who had become too light skinned or too clean or who dressed too elegantly, or who, in reality, competed too freely with white women and thus threatened the social order, were to express their ties to slavery through a simple head kerchief.[49]

New Orleans oral history says that the *tignon* was brought to Louisiana from Martinique and St. Domingue (Figure 5).

Figure 5. Free people of color of St. Dominque. Labrousse, 1790. Louisiana State Museum, New Orleans (1956.375).

Creole women of Martinique and Guadaloupe also wore elaborate head wraps called *tetes*.[50] Like *tetes*, *tignons* were commonly made of brightly colored cotton madras. This excerpt from a contemporary source describes a lavishly attired woman of color with her head wrapped in madras cloth, in addition to detailing the finery of her pet poodle:

> Directly in front of me sat a handsome yellow "lady," her head surmounted by an orange and scarlet plaid handkerchief, bound about it Turkish-turban fashion; a style that prevails here among Creole servants. . . . upon her neck was a richly worked black lace scarf; her dress was plain colored silk made in the most costliest manner. Her olive hands, which had very tapering fingers and remarkably oval nails, were covered with rings, chiefly plain gold ones. In one hand, she held a handsome parasol and in the other fondled a snow white French poodle upon her lap, said poodle having the tips of its ears tied with knots of pink ribbon, and a collar of pink silk quilled, and made like a ruff, while the end of its tail was adorned with a bow of blue ribbon, in the tastiest style; and as if his poodleship were not sufficiently decorated to be taken to the city to visit his town cousins, it had a nice bow of red satin tied about each of its four ankles.[51]

The act of wrapping the head has evoked multiple layers of meaning throughout time. The type of fabric used and the manner in which it was tied indicated status within the black community. Head wraps in Martinique spoke in a highly specific visual language that could convey a woman's occupation, among other things.[52] *Tignons* may have been used to either cover undone hair or to preserve an elaborate hairdo. The head wrap also kept hair clean and absorbed perspiration during the workday. The *tignon* was worn to protect the head from the scorching southern sun and may have functioned as a metaphorical form of protection as well.[53] In many West African cultures, the head is perceived as the seat of one's spirit. With that in mind, one begins to understand the importance of covering the head. Bold colors like yellow, red, green and white used in voodoo signified different spiritual concepts as well. New Orleans voodoo was a female-dominated religion. The city's most famous voodoo queen, Marie Laveaux, was a quadroon (Figure 6). Associations between quadroon women and voodoo were echoed in contemporary novels as well; the *tignon*-wearing quadroon named Palmyra Philosophy in Cable's *Grandissimes* was a voodoo priestess. A New Orleans oral historian, Barbara Trevigne, described a particular manner in which women tied

Figure 6. Believed to be a likeness of Marie Laveaux, the famous voodoo queen of New Orleans. This painting is a copy of the original, which is no longer in existence. It was painted by the reputed copyist F. Schneider.
Portrait of Marie Laveaux. F. Schneider. *Louisiana State Museum, New Orleans (11537).*

Figure 7. This image portrays the elaborate jewel-adorned coiffures worn by a woman who is believed to be a free person of color.
Marianne Celeste Dragon. *Attributed to the school of Salazar, ca. 1796. Louisiana State Museum, New Orleans (5750).*

their *tignons* with seven knots as a symbolic form of protection associated with voodoo.[54]

Other important items that protected the skin from the sun included gloves, veils, parasols and mantillas. These items aided women of color in maintaining a lighter complexion. They could also help to obscure racial identity. An example of how women used dress to conceal is found in this passage from a newspaper article about an elopement between a white man and a slave:

> The woman was most gorgeously attired, being dressed in a rich black silk robe, hung with innumerable floating flounces. A magnificent set of furs graced her shoulders and neck; while over her interesting physiognomy hung a thick green veil. Thus equipped, no one ever suspected her of being of Ethiopian extraction. . . .[55]

The jewelry of free women of color is often mentioned in primary sources (Figure 7). The use of coral, carnelian and gold were popular among these women.

Figure 8. Portrait of a free woman of color, (undocumented). *A. D. Lansot, ca 1850. Louisiana State Museum, New Orleans (1993.105).*

One traveler described the rich jewels worn by a quadroon woman, which included a pair of gold earrings as large as half-dollars, a necklace of gold beads with a carnelian cross and a multitude of plain gold rings.[56] Large gold hoops are still worn today by Creole women of color.[57] Palmyra Philosophy of Cable's *Grandissimes* wore a red coral necklace and a cord and tassel of scarlet silk around her waist. Eliza Potter described a woman attending a Quadroon Ball wearing a headdress of crimson and a full set of coral jewels.[58] It is possible that red-colored jewels were worn as protective charms. Slaves were known for wearing beads, buttons and other notions for their protective powers.[59] Red coral has also been used in the Mediterranean to ward off the evil eye. The wearing of red jewels may have served an apotropaic purpose associated with voodoo.

It is unclear how effective Miro's law

was in restricting the dress of free women of color because their extraordinary dress seems to have continued despite the mandate.[60] While many women of color wore *tignons*, contemporary descriptions and portraits also depict free women of color who do not wear these head wraps (Figure 8). Some of these women consciously chose to have themselves portrayed with *tignons*, although most free people of color made every effort to distance themselves from slavery. Did these women then reclaim the *tignon*? What began as a restriction became somehow reversed.

The *tignon*, it was said, increased the beauty of these women and made them even more appealing.[61] By 1837 we find images of towering head wraps (Figure 9) adorned with jewels and feathers. The forbidden embellishments seemingly migrated from the hair to the head wrap. Similar to perceptions of status displayed through African dress, the increasing

height and abundance of cloth reflected the increased status of the wearer. The *tignon* may have been one of the first emblems of African pride in the New World. Head wraps of the twentieth century commonly have been associated with African American pride. While some women of color attempted to pass for white, it appears that there was a class of women who had no quarrel with their racial heritage. Eliza Potter described some women who were so "independent they will be thought nothing but what they are."[62]

One also finds documented images of white women who wore Madras *tignons* (Figure 10). What could this mean? Was the headdress merely adopted by older women who were experiencing hair loss, or were there other reasons? During this time, plenty of women wore turban-like headdresses in the colonies and in

Figure 9. Portrait of Betsey, a woman of color. *François Fleischbein, 1837. Historic New Orleans Collection (1985.212).*

Figure 10. Mrs. Leonard Wiltz. *L. Sotta, 1841. Louisiana State Museum, New Orleans (8415).*

Figure 11. Fashion Plate, *undated.*
Historic New Orleans Collection (1976.138.8).

Europe (Figure 11). At the turn of the nineteenth century, the style "A la Creole" was all the rage in France, thanks to Empress Josephine, a native of Martinique.

Evidence points to the fact that women of color were indeed important fashion setters during this period. It is probable that they made a significant contribution to the style of women both in the New World and in Europe. Just as Creoles of color made significant contributions to the language and cuisine of the area, they also impacted style.

During the late eighteenth and nineteenth centuries, all women were at the mercy of the white patriarchy, albeit at differing degrees to which they experienced bondage, marginality, and lack of empowerment. Free women of color occupied a precarious position in New Orleans society, unprotected by the law and culture at large. They had close ties with upper-class whites, but they did not enjoy the status or opportunities of the ruling majority. Women of color had two avenues to financial security. While some chose to enter into *plaçage*, others worked hard to accumulate substantial wealth. In some respects the "un-married" free women of color had more liberty than white women of the period because of opportunities for economic independence, social and geographic mobility, and access to education.

> Such women fashioned identities and lives in response to, but outside the dominant model. More powerless than white women in some ways, but with more power over their own lives in others, free women of color dismissed the dominant ideology that counterposed virtue with seduction, white with black. Free women of color resisted the definition of their own lives by others.[63]

Women of color worked in occupations that involved dress since the beginning of slavery. Free women of color inherited the skills to improvise from their slave ancestors, whether it was through their lifestyle, economic livelihood, love life or their dress. Limitations sometimes lead to the most unique and creative inventions. These women were noted for their style and grace, and it is no wonder that white women appropriated elements of their dress.

The exploration of the meaning of the *tignon* in particular proves to be significant for many reasons. It shows how a hegemonic society has used dress restrictions both to limit and to identify a marginalized group of people. Through this investigation, we gain an increased understanding of a highly complex system of race relations and how dress serves as a racial and cultural signifier. We are also forced to question the roots of myths surrounding the sexuality of women of color and how these images shaped their lives. Most importantly, we learn that free women of color felt at liberty to express their physical and cultural beauty through dress, a freedom slaves generally did not have. It seems that for some, what began as a restriction culminated in a statement of cultural identity embodied in the *tignon*. In closing, we are left to contemplate the words of an old Creole proverb: "Bel *tignon* pas fait bel negress." (It isn't the fine headdress that makes the fine woman of color).[64]

Acknowledgements

I would like to thank the Costume Society of America for awarding me the Stella Blum Research Grant. The grant enabled me to spend a month in New Orleans conducting primary research in several different institutions. I would like to thank the following institutions and people for assisting me in my research: Historic New Orleans Collection, Louisiana State Museum, City Archives at New Orleans Public Library, Amistad Research Center, Howard Tilton Memorial Library at Tulane University, Special Collections Unit at the University of New Orleans, Xavier University Archives and Special Collections, and oral historian Barbara Trevigne. I would also like to express my gratitude to my thesis advisor, Dr. Lourdes Font, for the continuing support she has shown throughout this project, and to Professor Pilar Blanco for helping me with Spanish translation. In addition, I would like to thank the Pittsburgh Foundation for awarding me the Walter Read Hovey Memorial Scholarship to conduct research related to this subject. This research was used to write a graduate thesis paper for my Master's Degree in Museum Studies at the Fashion Institute of Technology. My subject is a story I am honored to tell.

1 A profusion of terms to denote every possible racial tincture from negro to mulatto to octoroon was in use at this time. The term *quadroon* derives from the Spanish *cuarteron*, which dates from 1640/50. It was applied to people of one-quarter African and three-quarters Euro/American ancestry. It is important to consider that these terms were often inaccurately applied by the dominant white culture. This term became associated with concubinage in the nineteenth century. Virginia Meacham Gould, *In Full Enjoyment of Their Liberty: The Free Women of Color of the Gulf Ports of New Orleans, Mobile and Pensacola, 1769 to 1860* (Atlanta: Emory University, 1991), 1.

2 In many instances, racial terms were used to describe complexion rather than genotype. Lillian Crété, *Daily Life in Louisiana, 1815 to 1830* (Baton Rouge: Louisiana State University Press, 1978), 76.

3 The word *Creole* derives from the Portuguese word *crioulo*, which denoted slaves of African descent born in the Americas. The term was later used to describe both Europeans and people of color of the New World. In the late nineteenth century the word defined racially mixed people of French, African, and/or Spanish descent who populated the Gulf Coast of North America. Gould, *In Full Enjoyment of Their Liberty*, 47-48.

4 Kimberly S. Hanger, *Bounded Lives, Bounded Places: Free Black Society in Colonial New Orleans, 1769 to 1803* (Durham, N.C.: Duke University Press, 1997), 138.

5 A vivid description of the highly diverse population of New Orleans is found in G. W. Featherstonhaugh, *Excursions through the Slave States* (New York: Harpers and Brothers, 1844), 140.

6 Gwendolyn Midlow Hall, *Africans in Colonial Louisiana* (Baton Rouge: Louisiana State University Press, 1992),

31.

7 Gould, *In Full Enjoyment of Their Liberty*, 90.

8 Marcus Christian, "Slave Clothing." Transcript in the Marcus Christian Collection, Special Collections, University of New Orleans, 2. Benjamin Latrobe noted a particular slave who was valued for her skills as a seamstress.

9 Hall, *Africans in Colonial Louisiana*, 304.

10 Ibid., 24.

11 Ibid., xiii.

12 J. S. Buckingham, *The Slave States of America* (London: Fisher and Son & Co., 1842), 479-88.

13 Bell Hooks, "My style ain't no fashion," *Z Magazine* (May 1992): 27.

14 Hanger, *Bounded Lives, Bounded Places*, 15.

15 Ibid., 57.

16 Ibid.

17 Ibid.

18 Ibid., 70.

19 Gould, *In Full Enjoyment of Their Liberty*, 275.

20 Ibid. This may explain why so few free women of color are identified in city directories by their professions.

21 Hanger, *Bounded Lives, Bounded Places*, 60.

22 Hall, *Africans in Colonial Louisiana*, xxi.

23 Virginia Meacham Gould, *Chained to the Rock of Adversity* (Athens: University of Georgia Press, 1998).

24 Annie Lee West Stahl, "The Free Negro in Antebellum Louisiana," *Louisiana Historical Quarterly* 25, no. 2 (April 1942): 372.

25 A free mulatto woman named Celeste acted as a fashion informant to rich white women in George Washington Cable's "The Adventures of Françoise and Suzanne" in *Strange True Stories of Louisiana* (New York: Scribner and Sons, 1888). Palmyra Philosophy was known for her good taste and skill as a hairdresser is a main character in George Washington Cable's *The*

Grandissimes (New York: C. Scribner, 1899).

26 Sir Charles Lyell, *A Second Visit to the United States of North America* (New York: Harper and Brothers Publisher, 1849), 93.

27 Hanger, *Bounded Lives, Bounded Places*, 66.

28 Crété, *Daily Life in Louisiana, 1815 to 1830*, 83.

29 "Most noteworthy about the practice of *plaçage* is that apparently most free women of color that were placed with white men had white fathers." Gould, *In Full Enjoyment of Their Liberty*, 221.

30 *Daily Picayune*, 17 July 1838, p. 3, col. 4; *New Orleans Daily Delta*, 12 April 1855, p. 2, col. 7; *Le Moniteur*, 22 August 1807, p. 3, col. 2; *Le Moniteur*, 23 February 1811, p. 3, col. 1.

31 *Les Cenelles: A Collection of Poems by Creole Writers of the Early Nineteenth Century* (Boston: G. K. Hall and Company, 1979).

32 Gould, *In Full Enjoyment of Their Liberty*, 249.

33 This song was composed in 1820 by Joseph Beaumont, a free person of color from New Orleans. Rousseve, *The Negro in Louisiana* (New Orleans: Xavier University Press, 1937), 66. The New Orleans opera and theater houses had segregated seating arrangements with specific sections and admission prices for quadroons, who were commonly seated in the balcony.

34 Hanger, *Bounded Lives, Bounded Places*, 92.

35 Ibid., 97.

36 Gould, *In Full Enjoyment of Their Liberty*, 232.

37 Harriet Jacobs, *Incidents in the Life of a Slave Girl* (New York: Oxford University Press, 1988), 46.

38 Gould, *In Full Enjoyment of Their Liberty*, 190.

39 *Cabildo Records*, bk. 3, vol. 1 (2 June 1786): 105-07. Louisiana Division, New Orleans Public Library.

40 "Article 4. I make known that I will punish with all severity of the law all those who live in concubinage of whatever condition or rank they may be, complying exactly with the serious duties the wise laws imposed upon my position.

Article 5. The idleness of the free Negro and Quadroon women is very detrimental, and those who abandon themselves to the same, is because they subsist from the product of their licentious life without abstaining from carnal pleasures, for which I admonish them to drop all communication and intercourse of vice, and go back to work, with the understanding that I will be suspicious of their indecent conduct, by the extravagance of their dressing which is already excessive, and this only circumstance will compel me to investigate the customs of those who will present themselves in this manner." Ibid.

41 Thomas Ashe, *Travels in America* (London: William Sawyer & Co., 1808), 344.

42 *Daily Picayune*, 21 August 1838, p. 2, col. 2.

43 This document is in poor condition and was written in an unusual Spanish dialect that was difficult to translate. Many different translations exist. This translation is a combination of a version by Professor Pilar Blanco of the Fashion Institute of Technology and the one provided by the WPA in the New Orleans Public Library.

44 Gould, *In Full Enjoyment of Their Liberty*, 195-96.

45 Ibid.

46 Helen Bradley Foster, *"New Raiments of Self": African American Clothing in the Antebellum South* (Oxford and New York: Berg, 1997), 249.

47 Ibid., 253.

48 Gould, *In Full Enjoyment of Their Liberty*, 196-97.

49 Ibid.

50 Stephany Ludgiwine Ovide, "La Fille de Couleur: Styles and Perceptions of Women's Fashion in Guadaloupe and Martinique from the 1848 Abolition of Slavery to 1930" (master's thesis, Fashion Institute of Technology, 1997), 36.

51 Joseph Holt Ingraham, ed., *The Sunny South; or the Southerner at Home* (New York: Negro University Press, 1860), 330.

52 Ovide, *La Fille de Couleur*, 36.

53 William H. Russell, *My Diary North and South* (New York: Harpers and Brothers, 1863), 98.

54 New Orleans oral historian Barbara Trevigne, interviewed by author, New Orleans, January 2000.

55 *New Orleans Bee*, 3 March 1856, p. 1, col. 2.

56 Ingraham, *The Sunny South*, 330.

57 New Orleans oral historian Barbara Trevigne, interview by author, New Orleans, January 2000.

58 Eliza Potter, *A Hairdresser's Experience in the High Life* (New York: Oxford Press, 1991), 190-92.

59 Foster, *New Raiments of Self*, 174-75.

60 No legal cases referring to misdemeanors associated with the dress restriction were found in legal indexes or local newspapers.

61 Créte, *Daily Life in Louisiana, 1815 to 1830*, 81.

62 Potter, *A Hairdresser's Experience in the High Life*, 155.

63 Gould, *In Full Enjoyment of Their Liberty*, 232-33.

64 Lafcadio Hearn, *Gombo Zhebes: A Little Dictionary of Creole Proverbs Selected from Six Creole Dialects* (New York: Will H. Coleman, 1885), 8.

BIBLIOGRAPHY

Ashe, Thomas. *Travels in America*. London: William Sawyer & Co., 1808.

Buckingham, J. S. *The Slave States of America*. London: Fisher and Son & Co., 1842.

Cabildo Records. bk. 3, vol. 1. 2 June 1786. New Orleans: Louisiana Division, New Orleans Public Library.

Cable, George Washington. *The Grandissimes*. New York: C. Scribner, 1899.

Cable, George Washington. "The Adventures of Françoise and Suzanne." In *Strange True Stories of Louisiana*. New York: Scribner and Sons, 1888.

Christian, Marcus. "Slave Clothing." Transcript in the Marcus Christian Collection, Special Collections, University of New Orleans.

Créte, Lillian. *Daily Life in Louisiana, 1815 to 1830*. Baton Rouge: Louisiana State University Press, 1978.

Foster, Helen Bradley. *"New Raiments of Self": African American Clothing in the Antebellum South*. Oxford and New York: Berg, 1997.

Gould, Virginia Meacham. *In Full Enjoyment of Their Liberty: The Free Women of Color of the Gulf Ports of New Orleans, Mobile and Pensacola, 1769 to 1860*. Atlanta: Emory University, 1991.

Hall, Gwendolyn Midlow. *Africans in Colonial Louisiana*. Baton Rouge: Louisiana State University Press, 1992.

Hanger, Kimberly S. *Bounded Lives, Bounded Places: Free Black Society in Colonial New Orleans, 1769 to 1803*. Durham, N.C.: Duke University Press, 1997.

Hearn, Lafcadio. *Gombo Zhebes: Little Dictionary of Creole Proverbs Selected from Six Creole Dialects*. New York: Will H. Coleman, 1885.

Hooks, Bell. "My style ain't no fashion." *Z Magazine* (May 1992): 27.

Ingraham, Joseph Holt, ed. *The Sunny South; or the Southerner at Home*. New York: Negro University Press, 1860.

Jacobs, Harriet. *Incidents in the Life of a Slave Girl*. New York: Oxford University Press, 1988.

Les Cenelles: A Collection of Poems by Creole Writers of the Early Nineteenth Century. Boston: G. K. Hall and Company, 1979.

Lyell, Sir Charles. *A Second Visit to the United States of North America.* New York: Harper and Brothers Publishers, 1849.

Ovide, Stephany Ludgiwine. "La Fille de Couleur: Styles and Perceptions of Women's Fashion in Guadaloupe and Martinique from the 1848 Abolition of Slavery to 1930." Master's thesis, Fashion Institute of Technology, 1997.

Potter, Eliza. *A Hairdresser's Experience in the High Life.* New York: Oxford Press, 1991.

Rousseve, Charles. *The Negro in Louisiana.* New Orleans: Xavier University Press, 1937.

Russell, William H. *My Diary North and South.* New York: Harpers and Brothers, 1863.

Stahl, Annie Lee West. "The Free Negro in Antebellum Louisiana." *Louisiana Historical Quarterly* 25, no. 2 (April 1942): 301-96.

CITY DIRECTORIES

City Directory (New Orleans). 1840.

Gibson's Guide and Directory of the State of Louisiana and the Cities of New Orleans and Lafayette. New Orleans: John Gibson, 1838.

Paxton's City Directory. 1830.

Percy's City Directory. 1832.

NEWSPAPERS

Daily Picayune (New Orleans), 17 July 1838.

Daily Picayune (New Orleans), 21 August 1838.

Le Moniteur (New Orleans), 22 August 1807.

Le Moniteur (New Orleans), 23 February 1811.

New Orleans Bee, 3 March 1856.

New Orleans Daily Delta, 12 April 1855.

Joseph H. Hancock II
Jenna Tedrick Kuttruff
Catherine A. Cerny
Beverly Chico
Ruta Saliklis
Cynthia Cooper
Josephine Moreno
Laurann Gilbertson
Merideth Wright

Book Reviews

The Hidden Consumer: Masculinities, Fashion and City Life, 1860–1914

◆ **Christopher Breward**
Manchester and New York:
Manchester University Press, 1999.

While shopping at Saks Fifth Avenue in New York recently, I observed two men admiring each other in wool overcoats. Both commented on how luxurious and soft the cashmere felt and how well it would wear over the years. Yet, each man wondered if his wife would be upset over the expenditure of $600 on such a high-quality garment. I pondered this scene in my mind. While I have always thought fashion to be important, I was led to believe it was because of my lifestyle. However is this really the case? Have men always admired fashion and thought about clothing just as much as women? Have we been so ignorant as to believe that men do not find fashion important because historically it has been thought to be women's domain, thus un-masculine?

Christopher Breward's book *The Hidden Consumer: Masculinities, Fashion and City Life, 1860–1914* answers these questions. The book forces us to take a critical approach and rethink the generalizations about men and their connections to past consumer behavior, especially in the arena of fashion. Breward takes the cultural perspective, drawing from "popular novels, shop catalogues, trade directories, *carte de viste* and street photographs, diaries and vaudeville reminiscences" (17). In the first chapter, he identifies his main purpose as the exploration of the consumption behaviors of young Englishmen in London during the period from 1860 to 1914. He chose this time period because it has been identified as

central to the progression of modern consumer society. The book is not about Veblenian notions of clothing, nor does Breward discuss technological developments and advances in clothing production. This is not a book that re-hashes manufacturing, retailing or consumption. Breward is concerned with male consumers and the development of their desires for fashionable goods. Clothing is examined for its promotion, sale, use and representation among male consumers. Breward challenges historical ideas surrounding men, masculinity and the importance of fashion during the late nineteenth and early twentieth centuries. Issues concerning retail space, customer intimacy, the decision "to buy," and fashionable styles for men of all economic levels during this time period are discussed.

Chapter Two focuses on the importance of revealing masculine individuality through fashion. Breward reveals the important fashion codes and the formations of male personalities and identities through appearance. During this time period, fashion rules and dress etiquette appeared to be just as important for men as they were for women. What is the most remarkable part of this chapter and others to follow is Breward's ability to show that fashion was desired at *all* economic levels, not just by the upper to middle classes.

In Chapter Three, the reader is shown a connection between the individual male and his commitment to fashionable garments and personal style. In one example, Breward presents a brief history of Prince Albert Victor. He also uses household budgets, noting the allocations for men's garments, accessories and various accoutrements. By doing this, the author discovers how men purposely participated in the consumption of fashion goods by allocating portions of their household budget to clothing, thus ensuring their ability to remain fashionable.

Chapters Four and Five investigate the notion of retail space and the importance of atmosphere for male consumption. In Chapter Four, entitled "The Spectacle of the Shop: Provision for the Male Consumer," the reader is given a detailed account of the tailor's shop. Breward discusses the shop space noting the value of creating an atmosphere in which men could purchase fashion items.

Chapter Five denotes the bond between male customer and tailor as well as the importance of customer intimacy for the retailer to acquire clientele. What I found intriguing was Breward's recognition of working-class men employed by retailers who were persuaded by their supervisors to purchase the shop's clothing, which they could not afford, in order to model the store's clothing, thus generating sales for the consumer. By stating this fact, Breward reveals how important it was for shops to compete for male customers. This also demonstrates that men did indeed actively participate in shopping and consumerism. The reader is also shown that fashion advertising became an important tool for presenting the *correct* fashionable image, thus enticing those who viewed the ads to purchase the featured clothing items.

Chapters Six and Seven discuss the various types of men who participated in the consumption of fashion during this time period. As Breward states:

> . . . suburban middle- and lower-middle-class men, alongside the gangs and 'clicks' of the industrial city, constituted a massive market for the fashionable commodity and its imagery, whether appropriating it into rhythms of local fashion systems and assumptions regarding manly style or refuting its expensive connotations for more subversive ends (191).

The author notes the diversity of London during this time period by listing dandies, bodybuilders, female-to-male cross-dressers, middle- and lower-middle-class working men and English upper-class gentlemen. According to Breward, most men consciously identified with some type of group; therefore they dressed for peer recognition as well as for individual style. Some men portrayed themselves to fit the acceptable notions of manliness and masculinity. As queer theorists have also observed, Breward recognizes that dress may have been affected by homosexuality, which the middle classes perceived as threatening to the *normal* lifestyle. In order to be a *real man*, dress choices and styles were narrowed. Therefore it may seem that men's fashion was not as extravagant as women's; however, men still made choices about how best to portray their social standing through personal appearance. They were active participants in the consumption of clothing and other fashion goods.

While this book's text is quite dense and at times difficult to follow, those involved in fashion history, retailing, cultural studies, social history, urban history, gender studies and consumer behavior will the find the book essential reading.

Breward's analysis is thorough. His critique on the culture of men, men's fashion, and men's bodies from 1860 to 1914 allows the reader to see how the influence of fashion, which has been previously ignored, is truly essential for a broader understanding of history.

JOSEPH H. HANCOCK II

Doctoral student, Department of Consumer and Textile Sciences
The Ohio State University, Columbus

The Mummies of Ürümchi

◆ **Elizabeth Wayland Barber**
New York: Norton, 1999.

Elizabeth Barber introduces her book *The Mummies of Ürümchi* with the following make-believe fashion statement from the *Tarim Times* around 1000 B.C. "Calf-length A-line dresses with contrastive piping lead the ladies' fashions, in this year of the great burial. While red and blue with dashes of turmeric yellow continue to dominate the color palette, the stunning effect of bright red trim on maroon suits along with striped leggings remains popular among the gentlemen. . . ." (17). This introduction alone should excite the imagination of the costume historian.

In this book the author extends her vast background and knowledge of early textiles in what is now Europe and the Middle East to an investigation of prehistoric mummies and their clothing recovered in Central Asia. The oldest of the dated mummies are nearly 4,000 years old. Barber presents much more detailed information about the burial dress of mummies from the Tarim Basin than has been previously available in the West. Westerners were first introduced to some of these extraordinary finds along ancient caravan routes through the heart of Asia (now most widely known as the "Silk Road") by an article published in April 1994 in *Discover Magazine*. Many of those spectacular photographs are reprinted in her book.

Following an introduction in Chapter One that points out some of the mysteries involved with the discoveries of early, well-preserved Caucasoid burials in Central Asia, Barber describes the burials and their contents in the following three chapters. With this as a background, she then presents some adventures and findings of late nineteenth- and early twentieth-century Western explorers in the area. As in her two earlier books, *Prehistoric Textiles* and *Women's Work: The First 20,000 Years*,[1] Barber once again combines linguistics with archaeology as a way to expand interpretations of the sometimes meager textile data. In Chapter Six she focuses on linguistics as a means of ferreting out additional information related to the burials. In the remaining chapters, she explores similarities and possible relationships between archaeological discoveries in Central Asia and those in Central Europe, Russian Turkestan, and the Middle East.

Barber's writing style has been previously described as both "glib" and "colloquial"[2] and is geared to the general public who have limited knowledge of textiles and textile production rather than to the serious textile and costume scholar. She goes out of her way to relate information from the burials to everyday contemporary life and this may be appreciated by the lay reader. However, her explanations of weaving and weave structures based on a wolf spider "prowling the grass" become a bit tedious, as do some of her textile terms and fabric descriptions, such as the persistent use of "long-hop twill" rather than 2/3 twill. Even if written for a more general audience, the use of standardized textile terminology is important if the information is to be useful to the scholar. I personally found the metaphorical passage quoted below to be annoying and unnecessary, and it is just one example of many such passages:

> This strange battle between zones of color and weave continues all the way around the baby's head. The broad brown stripe of plain weave that frames the face narrows considerably as it tries to sneak past the checkerboard, until a band of stout tan wefts launched from the opposite selvage forces an uneven halt. Below that a new battalion of heavy pale weft threads in a slightly different weave surges up from the foot end of the mummy, only to be stopped cold at a second patch of red-brown checkerboard behind the ear, and so on. Finally everything gives way to plain weave as the center of the cloth disappears under the little mummy bundle, reemerging on the other side with a new battlefront at the level of the child's neck (80).

The fact that researchers had only limited access to many of the textiles directly associated with the mummies is indeed unfortunate, as some descriptions are based on viewing the textiles through a glass case. As an analyst of prehistoric textiles from North America, I believe that the book would have benefited from contributions and collaboration from Irene Good, "a specialist at the University of Pennsylvania in the laboratory analysis of ancient fibers and textile fabrics," who was also part of the research team (21).

The subject of this book is extremely engaging, and individuals interested in costume and textiles will find it valuable because so little information is available from these early times in Central Asia. Fully clothed burials provide so much more comprehensive knowledge of the dress of past cultures than fragmentary textile evidence, which is more commonly preserved. The possibility of direct cultural ties between the West and the East at such early dates is indeed intriguing and worthy of further investigation. When compared with Barber's earlier books, however, this book fell short of my expectations.

[1] E. J. W. Barber, *Prehistoric Textiles: The Development of Cloth in the Neolithic and Bronze Ages with Special Reference to the Aegean* (Princeton: Princeton University Press, 1991), and Elizabeth Wayland Barber, *Women's Work: The First 20,000 Years, Women, Cloth, and Society in Early Times* (New York: W. W. Norton & Co., 1994).

[2] Jean L. Dreusedow, review of *Prehistoric Textiles: The Development of Cloth in the Neolithic and Bronze Ages with Special Reference to the Aegean*, by E.J.W Barber *Dress* 18 (1991): 81.

JENNA TEDRICK KUTTRUFF

Professor and Curator of the Textile and Costume Museum
School of Human Ecology, Louisiana State University, Baton Rouge

Religion, Dress and the Body

◆ **Linda B. Arthur, ed.**
Oxford and New York: Berg, 1999.

We may be ambivalent in our appraisal of ethno-religious dress, appreciating standardized dress as testament of female spirituality while simultaneously condemning it as a barrier to individual agency. In *Religion, Dress and the Body*, Linda B. Arthur persuades us to examine these conflicting sentiments more closely. The book's ten essays engage us in a commentary on the tensions and complexities of social location.

Within the tradition of Mary Douglas, Michel Foucault, and Pierre Bourdieu, Arthur proposes a sociology of the body that establishes a connection between ethnicity, dress, and the expression of religiosity and is applicable to issues related to dress codes and social control. Employing Bryan Turner's sociology of the body and drawing from her own long-term research on conservative Mennonite appearance, she asserts that by controlling the re/presentation of female identity through dress, religious subcultures can moderate expression of desire and affirm control of women. Regulated appearance potentially underscores the normative values and morality of a community and hence strengthens the linkage of members to each other and their separation from outsiders. However, the brevity of her introduction to the essays does not allow Arthur to develop this theoretical perspective adequately; neither does she demonstrate how the specific phenomena detailed in the essays relate ethno-religious dress to social control of the body. I encourage her to further explore the issues introduced in this book in future writings.

In studies of two conservative Mennonite communities, Beth Graybill and Linda Arthur illustrate how Mennonite women become active agents in structuring the informal and formal measures of social control that uphold socio-religious norms. Attending to the boundary between religious subculture and mainstream American society, Susan O. Michelman observes the impact of Vatican II and increased involvement in the lay community on re-shaping the identities of twenty-four women religious. The transition from the closed community of the religious order and the compelling symbolism of the habit necessitated a re-negotiated self, responsive to both continuing religious and emergent secular relationships. At the same time, Gayle Veronica Fischer shows that James Jesses Strang's attempts to gain power over his Latter Day Saint followers by introducing a more uniform style of women's dress only led to failure. The bloomer style he proposed, directed toward suppressing individual (and fashion) impulses among the women members, may have signaled too forcefully the community's separation from mainstream social life.

Fashion's importance in connoting mainstream society may be more vital than commonly assumed. Karen Anijar characterizes the Jewish American female body as a (re)constructed political text, no longer in touch with her religious origins but modernized in keeping with American commodification and consumerism. With consumption being where identity is formed, fashion becomes a means for Jewish immigrants and their descendents to be American.

The apparent uniformity of ethno-religious dress, however, does not preclude individual expression of identity. M. Catherine Daly argues that Afghan women's wearing of the *chaadar* in an American non-Muslim community signifies the woman's choice not only to practice her religion but also to express ethnicity, occasion, and personality. Barbara Goldman Carrel shows how Hasidic women's head coverings manifest a hierarchy of religiosity that serves to legitimize female status within and between specific Hasidic communities and demonstrates the degree of socialization into Hasidic society.

Social control of dress may reflect the ethno-religious subculture's degree of integration in, or seperation from, mainstream society. By contrasting Amish and Mormon sacred everyday dress, Jean A. Hamilton and Jana Hawley suggest that highly recognizable Amish dress serves as a boundary mechanism binding together the community yet setting apart Amish world view. The religious undergarments of Mormon dress, however, facilitate participation in secular society through their invisibility, both reinforcing individual agency yet reminding men and women of their spiritual connectedness. Similarly, while dominant society may assert control over a minority group to maintain political authority, the subculture may become a refuge with positive consequences for expression of group autonomy. Gwendolyn S. O'Neal elaborates on the role of the Black Church in authenticating the culture and humanity of African Americans. While the aesthetics of dominant society may negate the African American body and self, the Black Church, partly expressed through dress, provides liberation from this stigma.

Finally, essays on the negotiated appearances of European Jews (discussed above), Polynesian Hawaiians, and Dakota Native Americans emphasize the politics of immigration and indigenous acculturation among ethno-religious communities in a Euro-American culture. Frank Salamone examines symbolic appearances in performances at the Polynesian Cultural Center, which is Mormon. Although the traditional costumes have been modified to conform to the moral codes of the Mormon church, the students bring an authenticity of a Polynesian self through more sensuous movements of dance. Sandra Lee Evenson and David J. Trayte examine the role of dress in the negotiated relationship between Eastern Dakota and Whites in the Minnesota territory between the arrival of Protestant missionaries in 1834 and the Dakota/ White war of 1862. While the missionaries considered dress to be indicative of the Dakota's conversion to Christianity, the Dakota switched back and forth between Native and Euro-American styles as a means of economic and physical survival within both Dakotan and White worlds.

Qualitative approaches to inquiry with analyses grounded in contemporary religious life or historic circumstance distinguish the collection of essays. Scholarship reflects varied use of archival documents, participant observation, and in-depth interviews. For the most part, authors integrate these strategies and provide complex interpretations of regulated dress. The essays by Anijar and Carrel stand out in this respect and should be read as a pair. However, in the Graybill and Arthur study, the interview commentary that has been so vital in Arthur's earlier works plays a lesser role. At the same time, it is not clear why two conservative Mennonite communities are discussed or what knowledge is gained from doing so. Similarly, Michelman does not sufficiently support her theoretical explanation through empirical evidence from interviews with women religious. Daly's reliance on translators restricts the researcher's ability to grasp subtle meanings in a person's response and vice versa. This limitation is evident as she builds her argument primarily by attending to an ethno-aesthetic of women's head coverings. Finally, O'Neal could enrich her study through more structured participant observation and

in-depth interviews of members within a church congregation. The depth of her explanation about the Black Church and its theology is not matched by her general characterization of dress.

Interestingly, Daly's call for an emic, or insider's, perspective draws attention to differences in how authors position their arguments. While some offer a sympathetic acceptance that substantiates women's experience, others convey a judgmental analysis that exposes the patriarchy, or maintain a politically neutral explanation that positions meaning in the complexity of religious life. Additionally, the diversity of viewpoints in the essays challenges us to consider the extent to which each author's own socialization within the dominant society and/or the ethno-religious culture shapes explanations of regulated appearance. Indeed, the integration of scholarly training and personal experience in the essays by Hamilton, O'Neal, and Anijar lend added authenticity to their explanations.

Linda Arthur's *Religion, Dress and the Body*, part of the Berg series *Dress, Body, Culture*, promises to stimulate readers to pursue more in-depth investigations and penetrating analyses of dress, religious life, gender identity, and agency.

CATHERINE A. CERNY

Instructor, Solano Community College, Suisun, California

Folk Dress in Europe and Anatolia: Beliefs about Protection and Fertility

◆ Linda Welters, ed.
Oxford and New York: Berg, 1999.

This small interdisciplinary volume builds on the seminal works of earlier scholars, beginning with Sir James George Frazer's 1890s multi-volume anthropological study, *The Golden Bough*, which first classified magic rituals, through Bronislaw Malinowski's works on magic, religion and cultural change, to the pioneering archaeological publications by Marija Gimbutas in the 1980s on the Mother Goddess of Eastern Europe. Now comes a new generation of scholars whose expertise in textile studies adds to our understanding of women, clothing and the vestiges of magic in European culture.

Published in the Berg *Dress, Body, Culture* series, it is a credit to both its individual editor, Linda Welters, and series editor, Joanne Eicher. Fusing archaeology, anthropology, history, women's studies, folklore and textile studies, it achieves a difficult task. First, it interprets with scholarly depth and breadth meanings in folk costume which have little, if any, written documentation; and secondly, its unity of theme and structure gives cohesion to the twelve essays by nine authors, all of whom are women.

The work's leitmotif is "fertility and protection" encoded in women's garments over some 7,000 years of time (from the Neolithic Era to the present) and 10,000 miles of land (Europe and Turkey). While generalizations have often been made by historians and others regarding Neolithic "homeopathic" magical rituals related to fertility of the crops (humans copulating in the fields to insure good crops, for example), this work provides form and substance to the notion that pre-Christian magic attitudes continued, even though the corresponding rituals have been discarded.

Fertility in both crops and humans was and still is essential for life; and it is through the universal practice of producing and wearing clothing (and accessories) over millennia that early practices of magic have been preserved through modified cultural traditions. It is fascinating, yet not surprising, to realize that *signs* and *symbols* first devised by Neolithic (even Paleolithic) peoples for decorating stone and ceramic sculptures, clay pots and bronze figures regarding fertility and protection have been handed down over multiple generations and are still found today on wearing apparel, giving testimony to the universality of the ideas they embody.

Various types of folk clothing items discussed here are interpreted within European and other cultures as having apotropaic qualities, some protecting women against evil forces, others ensuring communal well-being, especially through fertility. For this work, garments (most of which are women's) range from the headdress, the shawl or coat, the chemise (shirt), the apron, to belts and sashes. Particularly important are the embellishments given to these items by way of embroideries or attached fringes—both of which have usually been strategically placed at garment edges or openings (necklines, sleeves, hems) to prevent intrusion by "evil spirits."

After Welters' introduction, Elizabeth Barber's essay on East European bridal clothing serves as a kind of flagship.[1] Building on her pioneering studies *Prehistoric Textiles: The Development of Cloth in the Neolithic and Bronze Ages* and *Women's Work: The First 20,000 Years*, Barber demonstrates how the modern *panjóva* or *plákhta* (woolen back-apron or skirt), worn by married women in Russia and the Ukraine for everyday and special

bridal events, and the "string skirt" (made of long, unwoven fringes), also worn by married women in wide geographic areas from the Balkans in the southwest to the Volga River territories of Mordvinia in the northeast, have their roots in prehistoric times. She uses linguistic data, prehistoric artifacts and field studies to reveal the antiquity of modern traditions. According to Barber, folk cultures have associated betrothal and birthing for young women and wearing the string skirt with the belief that the skirt, which covers female genitalia, also protects a woman against harmful spirits and encourages fertility.

While Barber intriguingly stated that fringes and tassels on clothing are the visible manifestation of the female pubic hair that appears on a girl's body at puberty, signaling her ability to mate, she only implies the next step—that the *motion* of fringes and tassels on clothing when worn has the added function of attracting viewers' eyes to women's genital area, and also the belief that the spirit world (like the wind) contains a power invisible to the eyes which becomes visible through an object that moves.

Headdresses, particularly ones with fringes and tassels, are also found to have magical association with women's fecundity for, as Barber points out, the appearance of pubic hair comes at the age and time when young women become capable of procreation. Thus, hair on the head must also be protected and covered, especially after marriage.

Eight of the twelve chapters are based on fieldwork, along with on-site library and museum research. They spin off from Barber's work, stressing string-fringe garments and/or headcoverings with magical associations. Marlene Breu, for example, referred to folk customs of relating headdresses to seven stages of a woman's life (all tied to

marriage and motherhood) in Turkey.

Linda Welters focused on the Peloponnesian "zonari," a twentieth century string skirt, along with fringed and embroidered garments—including headscarves—found during her field studies in various Greek villages. Vesna Mladenovic encountered magical or supernatural qualities in the use of fringes associated with women's clothing (including the apron and headdress) in western Macedonia. In this case, protection was also created by embroidered geometric patterns associated with women's fruitfulness. She found a metaphoric connection of fringes to water, since fringes as they move are like waves of water (source of life). At a time when pre-Christian Slavic goddess figures were connected with nature, the lower part of the female torso (especially genitals) was compared to the earth and underground waters of life, while the upper part—including the breasts—was comparable to the sky and clouds from which rain comes. Again, the importance of headdresses with red fringes was found. Worn by Macedonian brides during the first year of marriage, this was to protect young wives and newborns against devils and evil spirits.

Patricia Williams provided a different dimension for headwear, showing how married Czech and Slovak women were ritually "capped," marking the end of virginity. Besides indicating a changed social status, the woman's cap (*cepec*) was embroidered with numerous protective and fertility symbols, such as *Dice* ("sown field," an ideogram representing agricultural fertility and found on the abdomen of goddess figures of Eastern Europe, c. 4,500 B.C.); stylized *crayfish* (image derived from birthing female with splayed legs); and *ram's horns*.

While Williams referred to ram's horns as a protective and fertility symbol, she did not explain the visual connection. Mary Kelly did in her study of Hutsul and Boyko folk clothing from the Ukrainian Carpathian mountain region. Kelly noted that ram's horns as related to snake coils are found on cult objects associated with Neolithic goddess figures.

The study of Latvian belts by Welters and Ira Kuhn Bolsaitis provides another dimension for the book's focus by tying in traditions from the Baltic area of northeastern Europe. Symbols woven into woolen belts, believed by contemporary Latvians to mean "good luck," are shown to come from the same ancient goddess traditions, particularly in the use of fringes.

Three essays provide a foil for contrast. Elizabeth Barber's "Curious Tale of the Ultra-Long Sleeve" deals with an ancient myth tied to astronomical festivals honoring dancing spirit maidens with loose hair and long-sleeved robes, who, because they died prematurely before marriage, returned to earth to share their unfulfilled fertility. And Laurann Gilbertson presented the pre-nineteenth-century magical beliefs of rural Norwegians in witches, trolls, giants, gnomes and especially *huldrefolk*. *Huldrefolk* were underworld spirit creatures whose harm to humans, particularly infants and brides, could be diverted by wearing large metallic (sometimes filigree) decorative brooches. Finally, Ruta Saliklis posed an overview question as to what really constitutes a "national costume." Her Lithuanian study contends that unlike folk dress (usually interpreted as traditional clothing worn in specific rural areas), "national costume" can be invented and reinvented for dancing and choral groups depending on changing "political events, socio-economic conditions and a people's self image" (212).

This pioneering work's unusual unity is achieved, despite its many authors, by numerous references from one essay to another, indicating shared

pre-publication drafts and good editorial leadership. One minor suggestion would be to have more maps (beyond the two provided by Barber) which would quickly orient readers to locations described by extensive narratives (some of which are not identified by contemporary political boundaries), thereby easing understanding of related traditions throughout wide geographical areas. And for consistency, an editorial decision on dating (B.C.-A.D. or B.C.E.-C.E.) would be beneficial. There is a philosophical difference. Nevertheless, *Folk Dress in Europe and Anatolia* is a credit to its editor and the series, and makes a major contribution to costume and women's history.

1 Elizabeth Barber's essay was reprinted from *Dress* 21 (1994): 17-29, with revised notes and two appendices.

BEVERLY CHICO

Professor of History and Humanities
Regis University, Denver, Colorado

Women Who Become Men: Albanian Sworn Virgins

◆ **Antonia Young**
Oxford and New York: Berg, 2000.

Albanian sworn virgins are women living primarily in the rural regions of northern Albania who choose to become honorary men. Their gender transformation is so complete that some are unrecognizable as biological females. Antonia Young has written a provocative book on this subject, which is the fifteenth installment in Berg's *Dress, Body, Culture* series.

Although much has been written on the sworn virgins of the Balkans from an anthropological/ethnographic perspective, this is the first publication to consider the way that dress demarcates gender in this highly patriarchal society. The marginalized role of women in northern Albania is summarized in a title on the subject—a woman is "a sack for carrying things".1 Antonia Young quotes from Rose Wilder Lane, daughter of Laura Ingalls Wilder, who described the first few days of married life for a new bride in 1922:

> When the bride arrives at her husband's house she takes a humble place in the corner, standing, her hands folded on her breast, her eyes downcast, and for three days and nights she is required to remain in that position, without lifting her eyes, without moving, without eating or drinking (28).

Women's lives revolved around arduous household tasks and childrearing. It is no wonder that some women chose to escape the hardships of married life by becoming men, particularly in a society that holds sworn virgins in high esteem.

A strength of Young's book is that she clearly articulates the primary motivations for becoming a sworn virgin in Albanian society. She provides the necessary background on Albanian history and culture, particularly on household structure, which explains why sworn virgins are a necessity to their families. In the past, a traditional agrarian household consisted of up to seventy individuals, because the extended family (brothers with their wives and children, parents, uncles, aunts, first and second cousins) all lived under one roof. One man served as the household head, making decisions for the entire family. In the absence of a suitable male leader, a sworn virgin could fulfill this role.

Young identifies three types of sworn virgins. The first are those who are proclaimed to be male by their parents from infancy or early childhood. If a family lacks sons, the parents may decide to raise their daughter as a son in order to have a male heir. The second are self-designated males, who made the decision sometime around adolescence. Again the primary motivation may be the lack of a male heir, but it also may be to safely circumvent an arranged marriage. The third type consists of Catholic nuns who served the Franciscan friars in northern Albania until about 1912. I find the third type highly problematic, because they are too unlike the others to be categorized as sworn virgins.

The organization of the book is awkward. The author is constantly referring the reader backwards and forwards, which is especially frustrating because the page numbers are wrong in the text. The eight chapters proceed through Albania's history and culture, a literature review on sworn virgins, case studies, a chapter on Albanian dress, a chapter on gender theory, and speculation about the future. Cross-cultural comparisons are not made, except for brief mentions, until the seventh chapter, which is much too late, in my opinion. I was thinking of Native American, African and Indian (South Asian) examples long before they

were mentioned in the book. If I were using this book for a college course on dress, I would have my students read the chapters on Albanian dress (Chapter Six) and gender theory (Chapter Seven) before reading the case studies (Chapter Five). The case studies (Chapter Five) are informative, but Young does not draw many conclusions from them. In general, she concludes that the older sworn virgins tend to wear traditional men's dress and the younger ones are more likely to dress fashionably. This does not go far enough. Were there discernable changes in dress before and after the fall of Communism? Did these women bind their breasts? Almost all of the sworn virgins were chain smokers, which makes me think that they were trying to mask their female voices, but there is no discussion of vocal intonation (an important consideration for a complete gender transformation).

Dress scholars may be frustrated by the fact that the chapter devoted specifically to Albanian dress (Chapter Six) is only twelve pages long, and it raises many questions in my mind. In a discussion of veiling (101-103), Young never explains how the veil is worn. The photograph of a young village bride (103) shows her wearing a headscarf. Is this what she means by a veil? The next photograph shows "a man dressed in Catholic women's clothing (early twentieth century)" (107). He is wearing traditional clothing, but what identifies him as Catholic?

Young, a researcher in the South East European Studies Unit at the University of Bradford, has published extensively on Albania. After writing and co-editing a book about women travellers to the Balkans, she decided to see for herself the "sworn virgins" in travellers' accounts.[2] She began her fieldwork on sworn virgins in 1989, at first trying to ascertain whether any still existed. She continued to search for them after the fall of

Communism in 1991, interviewing sixteen in all. Young met a few others and speculated that there may be more. The author reveals very little about herself, except to say that she visited Yugoslavia in the 1950s and 1960s. Her own experiences could be an interesting and informative part of the story, yet they remain untold. How did the sworn virgins relate to her? She was travelling freely just as a man would in Albanian society. She alludes to an unpleasant encounter while travelling, but does not go into detail "for the honour of Albania" (46). She spends more time describing her experience of writing an article on the sworn virgins for *Cosmopolitan* magazine and having them sensationalize it by emphasizing that these women renounce sex.[3] Why else would *Cosmopolitan* run such an article?

My strongest objection is to the cover of this book. Antonia Young's purpose is to give a positive, sympathetic portrayal of sworn virgins. The cover is a close-up of a sworn virgin's face, printed in lime green and black. The color green for a skin tone carries connotations of freaks, aliens or illness, which is not the author's intention. The full photograph in black and white is a very dignified portrait (10), as are all of the other photographs of sworn virgins in the book. The photographs alone are reason enough to buy this book.

Despite its shortcomings, I see this book as the beginning of a discussion on gender and dress in the Balkans that is likely to continue. Now is the time to document the dress of the sworn virgins before the last one disappears, and I applaud Antonia Young for making the attempt.

[1] Ian Whitaker, "A Sack for Carrying Things: The Traditional Role of Women in Northern Albanian Society," *Anthropological Quarterly* 54 (1981): 146-56.

[2] John B. Allcock and Antonia Young,

eds., *Black Lambs & Grey Falcons: Women Travellers in the Balkans* (Bradford, England: Bradford University Press, 1991).

[3] Antonia Young, "The Sworn Virgins of Albania," *Cosmopolitan* (December 1995): 44-48.

RUTA SALIKLIS

The Kate Fowler Merle-Smith Curator of Textiles, Allentown Art Museum Visiting Professor, Lafayette College, Easton, Pennsylvania

The Culture of Sewing: Gender, Consumption and Home Dressmaking

◆ **Barbara Burman, ed.**
Oxford and New York: Berg, 2000.

A 1996 conference at the Winchester School of Art entitled *Home Dressmaking Reassessed* spawned this recent addition to Berg's *Dress, Body, Culture* series. This seminal publication contributes to Berg's recent prolific impact on the field of costume studies, and this book will not disappoint those searching for the latest serious academic inquiry into new areas in the field of dress. The conference papers feature authors from the U.K., U.S. and Canada whose common ground is an interest in the role of sewing in women's lives, primarily in the nineteenth to the mid-twentieth century. Beyond the actual activity of sewing itself, the foci of their interests range from the sewing machine to paper patterns, from promotional efforts to sewing instruction and beyond.

The innovative approach of this book is predicated on its topic. Dressmaking and home sewing have traditionally been covert activities for which little documentary or documented material evidence survives. This dearth of primary sources has resulted in the act of sewing long being ignored by academics; this book illustrates a willingness to delve into the topic creatively and extract meaning from elusive sources, including individual reminiscences captured through oral history. Periodical and trade literature and journals also figure prominently among the sources used by authors, with a broad cultural analysis to extract their meaning. The tacit obscurity of home sewing has been shaped by its gendered nature, but also by issues of class: sewing has thrived in milieu and in time periods that fostered an ethic of making the most of one's resources. Its material evidence is thus also scant, "perceived as very low on the hierarchy of material culture," in the words of editor Barbara Burman. And yet, it is this very nature of the practice that makes this collection of papers a valuable addition to the field of dress.

Burman's introduction can be regarded as the salient feature of this book. The editor's incisive synthesis of the issues underpinning this field of study, as well as those brought out by the authors of the various papers, provides a strong contextual framework for any further work that may be undertaken on this topic. Burman identifies the blurring of distinctions which make it difficult to further circumscribe the field: for instance its dual nature as an act of simultaneous production and consumption, and its encompassing of both public and private spheres. Equally problematic to limiting the field of study to the unpaid making of clothes at home is the frequent concomitant dressmaking for others for economic gain. Conversely, several authors acknowledge the importance of considering women's agency in negotiating style and fabric with a dressmaker, albeit one step removed from the performance of the activity of sewing.

The thematic division of the book, in three parts, ties the issues of sewing and home dressmaking to larger cultural history issues. The gender issue referred to in the title receives no special consideration within the three divisions of the contents; rather it is implicitly dealt with in all areas of the book. The consumption issue alluded to in the book's title is the theme of its second part. The other two sections address firstly class and identity, and lastly dissemination and technology. The reader senses the artificialities of neatly categorizing the varied contributions and establishing a coherent thematic division.

It should nonetheless be considered a strength of the papers that its individual authors encompassed a broad spectrum of current cultural issues, despite encumbering rigid thematic categorization.

The pivotal importance of the sewing machine defines the scope of the book. Indeed, the universality of home sewing prior to the machine's widespread use is acknowledged as being outside the scope of this publication. Instead, the sewing machine provides a starting point for the book's time frame, and provides compelling material for analysis by four authors. Their often overlapping but sometimes divergent interpretations, arrived at from different disciplinary and methodological points of view, provide depth for understanding the impact of this invention and its redefinition of the activity of home sewing. Collectively their analysis encompasses the cultural ramifications of the design of the machine itself, the trade literature which used a gendered discourse of personal relationships to encourage new models of consumption, the class issues which surrounded its integration into the private sphere and its dissociation from the industrial realm, and the economic issues which led to its dual use for waged and unwaged work. The extent of the complementary coverage of this topic from different standpoints adds to the strength of this publication.

The book will also interest scholars who seek methodological models that incorporate individual recollections colored by strong personal connectedness. Several papers take the standpoint of linking constructions of femininity and class to clothing strategy, viewing the activity of sewing as a means to a much greater end. Also worthy of special mention is a contribution by Janet Arnold completed prior to her death in 1998.

Content aside, the scholarly apparatus of endnotes is uniform for each chapter and the index is very comprehensive, avoiding two frequent pitfalls of collections of conference papers. As a final note, costume historians and non-initiates alike of both sexes inquired about the book on the basis of its cover alone while this review was being prepared, indicating that the image seems worthy of more commentary than the brief photo credit provides. The cover's provocative photograph of a nude woman, surrounded by sheer fabric, intently threading a sewing machine counters any possible hint of academic aridity.

CYNTHIA COOPER

Curator, Costume and Textiles
McCord Museum, Montreal

Chimayó Weaving: The Transformation of a Tradition

◆ **Helen R. Lucero and**
Suzanne Baizerman
Albuquerque, NM: University of New Mexico Press, 1999.

Although southwestern textile arts have been addressed extensively by others, Helen Lucero and Suzanne Baizerman's *Chimayó Weaving: The Transformation of a Tradition* fills a void in the history of textiles. The authors' goal is not to reiterate the extensive history of Rió Grande textiles, but to explore the social milieu in which Hispanic weavers operated as they interpreted tradition with influence from mediators, consumers, and others. Chimayó is a town located twenty-three miles north of Santa Fe, New Mexico, that became the center for the production of a unique style of Hispanic weavings known by the same name. The Chimayó style is characterized by a textile that employs plain weave and tapestry techniques with transverse bands at either end and primary and secondary central motifs, often diamond shapes on a solid background. Contemporary Chimayó artisans employ a vast array of influences in their weavings that include elements from Rió Grande blankets and Saltillo sarapes (a rectangular outer garment worn draped over the shoulder or slid over the head through a center slit, poncho-like), as well as unique interpretations of historic styles, ikat yarns and pictorial images. Chimayó weavings were originally worn as sarapes or used as functional, durable blankets able to withstand the harsh conditions of the frontier. Today, Chimayó weavings are woven for non-Hispanic consumers who use them as wall hangings, rugs, pillow covers, and coasters, as well as material for jackets, coats, and vests.

Lucero and Baizerman's *Chimayó Weaving* is based upon extensive fieldwork, and the professional and personal experiences of the two authors whose knowledge, skills, and talents coalesce to provide readers with a text that is insightful from a variety of viewpoints. Lucero draws upon both her dissertation research and personal experience as a Chimayó weaver with "insider" knowledge, networks, and understanding of the region, history, and processes involved. Baizerman, as the "outsider," brings to the subject extensive scholarly experience and analysis of southwestern textile traditions, weaving skills, museum experience, and an Anglo perspective. Data are drawn from primary and secondary sources and extensive fieldwork undertaken by both authors.

The book begins with a preface that provides an outline. A historical chronology follows in which the reader can place developments in Chimayó textiles. The book is comprised of seven chapters, two appendices identifying historic and contemporary Hispanic weavers, chapter notes, Spanish glossary, bibliography, and index. The New Mexican Spanish glossary is helpful since some Spanish terms do not translate to English directly and definitions unique to New Mexican Spanish are delineated. In Chapter One, "Setting," geographic, industrial, and cultural settings are provided and complemented with black-and-white photos of the Rió Grande area. A line drawing of the region is also presented, but would be more helpful with the addition of the natural features of the region to fully understand the interactions between towns, geography, and weaving advancements.

Chapter Two, "The Classic Period: Before 1870" also introduces Chimayó weaving by tracing settlement of the region, social structure, trade, and weaving developments. Particularly noteworthy is the blending and borrowing of textile techniques and aesthetics among Native American, Mexican, and Spanish artisans and settlers. The introduction of color plates highlights the complex interplay of color in textiles during the Classic Period in the Southwest.

In Chapter Three, "The Transitional Period: 1870-1920," Lucero and Baizerman detail the transition of functional Chimayó weavings to trade goods made for an external non-Hispanic consumer. The notes used to document or elaborate a concept are positioned at the end of the text, providing important details and references while not cluttering the layout of the text and images in the body of the book. The color plates continue to highlight aesthetic changes in Chimayó textiles during the transitional period.

The authors discuss the major changes in Chimayó weaving in Chapter Four, "The Modern Period: 1920-1995." A revival in Hispanic weaving and Santa Fe arts led by Anglos that parallels the Arts and Crafts movement in the U.S. is addressed. Art societies and government sponsorship of craft production also fostered interest among Hispanics and Anglos alike that resulted in improved weaving quality and innovation. Chapter four describes key design transformations associated with Chimayó-style weavings during the twentieth century and the growth of Hispanic entrepreneurial efforts and relationships with traders of Chimayó textile products. Finally, Lucero and Baizerman address other markets and efforts that have fostered Hispanic textile production, including art organizations, events, and museums in Santa Fe and the Southwest.

Chapter Four concludes with dazzling color plates illustrating design development and innovation in Chimayó textiles through 1995.

Especially fascinating is the focus in Chapter Five on three weaving families. Their histories and contemporary situations illustrate the inter-connectedness of textile production, family, heritage, and trade that has occurred not only among these three families, but are also representative of other Hispanic families in the Chimayó area.

For the textile aficionado, student, or novice weaver, Chapter Six, "The Technology of The Art Form," provides both a historical and contemporary foundation of the weaving process illustrated by black-and-white plates, color plates, and diagrams. My only regret is that this chapter appears towards the end of *Chimayó Weaving*.

It is in Chapter Seven, "The Transformation of a Tradition," that students, scholars, and other readers interested in the theoretical discussion and application of textile traditions will benefit from a thorough reading. Lucero and Baizerman make the case that contemporary Chimayó textiles have been interpreted from early Spanish and Mexican forms to an ethnic art that represents Hispanic culture in northern New Mexico today. The analysis of "tradition" is solidly supported by scholarship that upholds that craft traditions have always been characterized by change influenced by the historic and contemporary repertoires available and circumstances surrounding artisans.

Lucero and Baizerman have addressed Chimayó textiles as distinct from other southwestern textiles drawing upon extensive primary sources without overly burdening the reader. The text is well organized, although the first two chapters serve as a long introduction to the main topic. This book would be a valuable addition to any university or college library, reference for the scholar and student of costume and textiles, and enjoyable to a casual reader. It is apparent that Lucero and Baizerm an have "interwoven" their skills and experiences to bring costume and textile enthusiasts a scholarly and insightful book.

JOSEPHINE MORENO

Assistant Professor, Textiles, Fashion Merchandising and Design University of Rhode Island, Kingston

The Shining Cloth: Dress and Adornment that Glitter

◆ **Victoria Z. Rivers**
New York: Thames & Hudson, 1999.

With an artist's eye and a scholar's breadth, Victoria Z. Rivers has produced a beautiful and fascinating book in *The Shining Cloth: Dress and Adornment that Glitter*. Rivers' interest in the topic was sparked after she began using light-reflecting materials in her own textile art. She spent the next fourteen years preparing the book by first finding and photographing many different kinds of light-reflective surfaces in textiles and then researching them as expressions of culture. She draws on her own research in India, reports of anthropological fieldwork, and publications on ethnographic textiles and art.

The desire to ornament with shiny materials is universal, Rivers believes. She cites the work of Coss and Moore who found that infants and children were drawn to lick and mouth mirrored surfaces probably because of the mirrors' similarity to the reflective surface of water. Therefore, Rivers says, the "appeal of light-reflecting substances may lie deep within the human psyche" (8).

When first examining the book, the richly colored and elaborately decorated textiles stand out. The 287 color photographs are outstanding. Most of the textiles are presented on pages with black backgrounds, which is dramatic and flattering. Some of the images were provided by the museums that own the artifacts, but many of the photos were taken by Rivers and photographers Barbara Robin Molloy, Thomas Moore, and Larry Kirkland. Fascinating detail shots are interspersed with photographs of garments in full view and in context as worn. Some of the objects have appeared in other publications, but the crisp close-ups in *The Shining Cloth*

provide the viewer with a fresh new perspective on the textiles. The book calls out for a leisurely and close examination. Another artistic touch is that each chapter of text is printed on a different color paper.

Rivers divides light-reflecting materials into three sections: "Silks and Surfaces," including dyes and fabric treatments; "Materials from the Earth" such as metal, minerals, mirrors, and beads; and the shells, seeds, feathers, and beetle elytra (hard, outer wing covers) that are "Gifts from Nature." A strength of the book is that Rivers uses an emic definition of shining objects. At first glance it seems odd to compare cowrie shells and seeds to mica and coins, but the various cultures perceive and use these light-reflecting materials in similar ways.

Rivers includes not only a wide range of shiny materials used on textiles, but also a variety of different reasons for wearing them. Metal and other reflective ornamentation function in cultures to transport wealth, display wealth, power and leadership; channel spiritual expressions; protect through reflection, sound, and the properties of the materials themselves; reinforce hierarchical or gender distinctions; enhance fertility; aid in healing; provide an economically important trade item; give pleasure to the wearer and viewer; suitably reward meritorious service; and serve practical purposes (such as the Bedouins wind-stopping pounded indigo fabric).

The title suggests that Rivers would speak only of textiles worn on the hum an body, so it was interesting to see several household textiles in the book. The sampling of doorway hangings, wall hangings, altar cloths, cradle cloths, and ceremonial mattress edgings illustrate how humans often ornament their physical surroundings with light-reflecting surfaces for some of the same reasons they adorn their bodies. On the other hand, the inclusion of domestic textiles was somewhat disappointing because I would have preferred to see more of the clothing described in the text, like the shirt of netted red coral beads worn by the king (Oba) of the Yoruba people in Benin.

Beads are where adornment and jewelry merge. Rivers wisely limited her book to garments and textile-based adornment because so many types of jewelry (archaeological, historical, contemporary, ethnic/ethnographic) have been well covered in the literature. Readers wishing to branch off toward jewelry will find several fine publications listed in the bibliography. I would add to that list *Metal Techniques for Craftsmen* by Oppi Untracht (New York: Doubleday & Co., 1968), which describes and illustrates many of the decorative techniques used by metal artists in non-western cultures.

Rivers limits the scope of her book to non-western cultures, giving examples from nearly every part of the globe. However, in selecting photographs she summarily excludes the more developed countries in western and northern Europe despite the many so-called "traditional" cultural groups that have lived there. Fish scale sequins are mentioned in the text, but unfortunately the book has no images of them in use. The National Czech and Slovak Museum and Library in Cedar Rapids, Iowa, has a spectacular *kroj* (festival dress) from the Trebon region of Bohemia embellished with carp scales that were cut into small, delicate designs. Another welcome addition would have been the pewter-thread embroidery done by indigenous northern Scandinavian Sami people.

Rivers includes some of the expected, like textiles embroidered with mirrors (*abhala bharat*), and lots of the unexpected. She celebrates the textiles of less well-known cultures, such as the Bagobo

and Bilaan people of the Philippines. Another visual treat was the work of the Aleut and Koniag people of Alaska who apply ground hematite to the surface of hunting bags and caps. Filmy tufts of caribou hair and sinew sewn into the seams add luminescence. There are occasional surprises in the photographs, for example *asu-gutsu*, the shoes of leather with a positively mirror-like lacquered finish worn by Shinto priests in Japan.

One of the most fascinating portions of the text concerns treatments to fabric to make it more reflective. Of course burnishing the fabric by polishing, pounding or ironing is an option, as is adding substances to enhance the process. Gentian violet, an antiseptic, is used by the Miao of southwestern China to transform already lustrous silk damask into what looks like bronze foil. Other additive materials include starches such as rice flour; bird and spider eggs; gum arabic; sap and lacquer; and blood. Sometimes a single product or procedure is used and other times the process follows numerous steps. Rivers refers to the Miao and Dong people of China who follow up to 100 steps.

For the textile scholar, the accompanying text is not nearly as satisfying as the images. At times the text is quite general, as this book is intended to be a survey. Rivers must cover a broad range of years, cultures, and materials and does so quite effectively. She provides a thorough bibliography for further research. Fiber artists will find this book particularly inspirational, and I hope they will be drawn to continue to explore on their own.

A valuable "Glossary and Index of Terms" allows the reader to understand quickly the many native and scientific terms. The captions are particularly well done because they are more like exhibition text labels. Rivers does not just

identify an item; she creates a cultural context for the textile. Unfortunately the choice of typeface in the index makes it difficult to distinguish between the page numbers in regular type and the illustration numbers in italics, but the information is useful none-the-less.

Rivers concludes the book, appropriately, with comments about the evolution of the historical customs of shining cloth. Substitutions of polyester for silk and the widespread use of Lurex, the democratic gold, show that the global tradition of light-reflecting materials has a changing, but bright future.

LAURANN GILBERTSON

Textile Curator, Vesterheim Norwegian-American Museum, Decorah, Iowa

Fitting & Proper

◆ **Sharon Ann Burnston**
Texarkana, TX: Scurlock Publishing,
1999.

The costume world is familiar with costume books providing general surveys from particular historic periods, and equally familiar with gorgeous exhibit catalogues from art museums of the highest of high fashion. It is far rarer, and in some ways more important and useful, to have a book rooted in a particular collection from a particular locality, as well as from a specific time period. Sharon Ann Burnston's *Fitting & Proper*, based on original garments from the Chester County Historical Society in Pennsylvania, is just such a book. It is carefully researched and has a strong sense of place, as well as a sense of the time period from which the garments come. Its clear pictorial format makes that information available to the general reader, theatrical costumer, and historical re-enactor, as well as to the world of costume museums and academic scholarship. Like the work of Janet Arnold, Dorothy K. Burnham, Norah Waugh and Blanche Payne, Burnston has succeeded in salvaging important information from the depths of museum collections and making it accessible by producing pattern diagrams of actual garments.

In *Fitting & Proper*, Burnston provides examples of the full range of late eighteenth-century garments and clothing accessories, allowing the reader an understanding of the relationship of undergarments to the robes, petticoats, breeches and coats that would have been seen in daily life. For the more important or unusual pieces, such as the women's gowns and the men's banyans, she provides examples ranging from the modest to the spectacular. Burnston includes meticulously researched diagrams of thirty-eight of the forty-one pieces, allowing a person familiar with the sewing and construction techniques of the period to make exact reproductions. The photographs are clear and provide details of the significant construction details. To assist in choice of fabric for making reproduction clothing, it would have been helpful to have had a page or two of color photographs of the fabrics themselves, especially of the multicolored fabrics such as the cotton chintz of the wonderful man's banyan, and the printed linen woman's pocket. The color photographs on the front and back covers are well chosen, but leave one wishing for more, especially for those items for which photographs are not available in another listed book or article.

Students of costume with a social history perspective may be disappointed that more information is not given about the social context of the selected pieces, since they are from a known community and often have specific individual or family provenance. While more information on the people who wore the known garments seems beyond the scope of this book, Burnston has provided their names and dates, which is sufficient to allow researchers interested in following up specific individuals or events to gain access to other sources of Chester County information.

Burnston also provides, in an appendix, a review of Chester County estate inventories from 1760 to 1775. The appendix raises interesting questions, and provides a starting place for further research into the size and value of selected wardrobes of the period. For that future research, it may be helpful to enlist the viewpoint of a legal scholar regarding eighteenth-century colonial estate inventories. An estate inventory generally only needs to be taken when the estate must be valued for the purpose of dividing it among the heirs, for selling it and dividing the proceeds, or for estate taxes or "death duties" as they were then known. The estate inventories studied for this project may be missing many households in which the deceased knew that death was imminent, and divided the useful clothing items among the family members as gifts prior to death.

In *Fitting & Proper*, Sharon Ann Burnston has produced a well-researched and accessible body of work, particularly useful for people who want to make reproductions of specific pieces of real clothing rather than settling for generic costumes from the late eighteenth-century period. It is a valuable contribution to the field.

MERIDETH WRIGHT

Independent Scholar (and state court judge)
East Montpelier, Vermont

Jane Farrell-Beck
Claudia Brush Kidwell

The Costume Society of America

presents

The Class Of 2000 Fellows

First awarded in 1991, the designation of Fellow of the Costume Society of America is an honor bestowed on CSA members who have demonstrated exceptional participation and outstanding service to CSA and have made significant contributions to the field of costume. Selection as Fellow of the Costume Society of America is the highest award the Society can bestow on its members. All members of the Society may submit names of members they wish to nominate for this honor.

Jane Farrell-Beck

The Costume Society of America sets high standards of excellence when it considers an individual for the honor of CSA Fellow. Jane Farrell-Beck not only meets those standards, but she far exceeds them. Her career shows an individual committed to teaching, study and presentation of numerous connections between dress, technology and health. Scholars appreciate her ability to document every detail prior to publishing and her use of a wide variety of resources, including patent records, to document innovation and adaptation of technology to costume.

Currently a Professor in the Department of Textiles and Clothing in the College of Family and Consumer Sciences at Iowa State University, Jane has supervised more than thirty graduate students who recognize her as a mentor in their careers. In addition to her numerous presentations at meetings of the Costume Society of America and the International Textiles and Apparel Association (ITAA), Jane has published over twenty refereed articles in a variety of journals including *The Home Economics Research Journal*, *Annals of Iowa*, *Clothing and Textiles Research Journal* and *Dress*. Since she began studying the relationships between dress and health, she has established scholarly interactions with medical historians and has published in such journals as *Caduceus*, the *Journal of the History of Medicine and Allied Sciences*, and the *International Journal of Dermatology*. She has also been asked to present her research to groups such as The Francis Clark Wood Foundation (affiliated with the College of Physicians of Philadelphia) and the Mayo Foundation. Jane also co-edited the second edition of Blanche Payne's *History of Costume From Ancient Mesopotamia Through the Twentieth Century*, a classic textbook widely recognized for its excellent scholarship.

Jane has been recognized at Iowa State University with the Regents' Faculty Excellence Award (1994) and a University Professor Award (1997). She gave the Distinguished Scholar Lecture at the 1998 ITAA Annual Meeting in Dallas and was recognized as a Fellow of ITAA for her work in the historic costume area.

As an active member of The Costume Society of America since 1983, Jane has served on both regional and national boards, been an active participant in the graduate student research competition, been a reviewer for *Dress* and helped develop the criteria and structure of The Scholars' Roundtable. Her efforts to promote excellence in scholarship within CSA are recognized by many.

It is the words of her many students and colleagues that truly tell the story of Jane Farrell-Beck's achievements. "Her joy and complete involvement in her work are obvious as she interacts with new students or tackles a new facet of her large body of work." "One can hear the excitement in her voice and see the sparkle in her eye when she describes how she tracked down a specific detail." "Never did students complain of the course—within the first few weeks of the semester we all loved it as much as she did. . . . I cannot thank Dr. Jane Farrell-Beck enough for believing in me and encouraging me to set higher goals than I ever thought possible."

Compiled by Marianna Garthwaite Klaiman
Assistant to World Wide Marketing,
Sotheby's, New York

Claudia Brush Kidwell

Claudia Brush Kidwell is Curator, Division of Social History, the Costume Collection, National Museum of American History, The Smithsonian Institution, Washington, D.C. She has been associated with that institution since 1961, often serving as a supervisor or department head.

She has enthusiastically shared her expertise and ideas with others—international scholars, colleagues from museums large and small, professors, students, interns, and the general public. The best measure of this contribution is the sincere appreciation and gratitude expressed by those she has helped, those she has nudged and urged, and those with whom she has worked.

A member of the Costume Society of America since 1974, she has been involved from the start. She has served on the National Board of Directors, planned and hosted two National Symposia in Washington, D.C., and has served the society in various capacities at the regional level.

We can be glad that Claudia has put effort into publishing her research because her work became available to a broader audience through the printed word. As one of her supporters said: "Her pioneering insights have repeatedly affected all costume research." Another stated: "What is significant about Claudia's contribution to costume scholarship is not only the thoroughness of her work, but also the importance of the questions she undertakes to answer. Her work never perches in trivial isolation, but rests as a great cornerstone for the rest of us to build on." Another colleague mentioned the difficulty of the subjects she investigates. Two studies immediately come to mind: *Suiting Everyone: The Democratization of Clothing in America* and *Men and Women: Dressing the Part*. Both were exhibitions and publications. *Dress* has also published Claudia's work: "Short Gowns" in 1978 and "Are Those Clothes Real? Transforming the Way Eighteenth-Century Portraits are Studied" in 1997.

A colleague sums up Claudia Brush Kidwell's contributions in this way: "It is probably impossible to measure Claudia's impact on the field of costume study, whether through her writing, her exhibitions, her public presentations, or the mentoring and guidance she has given hundreds of students at every level who have come knocking at her door at the Smithsonian." As impossible as that task may be, we have attempted it, and we have found her excelling at every turn.

In addition to her many professional contributions through exhibitions, publications and lectures, she has a congenial and accessible way of "doing business" with dignity, kindness, courtesy and grace.

Compiled by Inez Brooks-Myers
The Oakland Museum

Mission Statement

The mission of **The Costume Society of America** is to advance the global understanding of all aspects of dress and appearance. The society provides a center of study and information for individuals and institutions in this rapidly growing sphere of interest. Information on activities and membership may be obtained by writing The Costume Society of America, 55 Edgewater Drive, PO Box 73, Earleville, MD 21919.

Dress is the refereed journal published by The Costume Society of America. It represents the highest level of scholarship and addresses the diverse interests of the membership. The entire contents are copyrighted and may not be reproduced in any form without written permission. The Costume Society of America invites contributions to *Dress*.

Dress is indexed by the *Art Index, Clothing and Textile Index and CD Rom, Bibliography of the History of Art (formerly RILA), Artbibliographies, Design and Applied Art Index, IBZ International Bibliography of Public Literature, Historical Abstracts, America: History and Life, Sociological Abstracts,* and appears in the *Uncover database* on the internet.

Requirements for the Submission of Manuscripts to *Dress*

Dress, the journal of the Costume Society of America, includes articles, book reviews, exhibition reviews, letters to the editor and short reports. Articles may be biographies, conservation reports, theoretical discussions or analytical and interpretive papers that describe and place costume in historical or cultural context. Essays should reflect original scholarship based on appropriate primary and secondary sources. Manuscripts undergo blind review and are accepted throughout the year. Contributors must be members of the Costume Society of America. Manuscripts should be sent to: Editor, *Dress*, Costume Society of America, 55 Edgewater Drive, PO Box 73, Earleville, MD 21919.

All manuscripts must be written according to *The Chicago Manual of Style* (14th ed.) with Endnotes and Bibliography as described in Chapter 15, "Documentation 1. Notes and Bilbliography," pp. 487-635. Only double spaced, typewritten or letter-quality printed manuscripts will be considered. (Articles may be 15-25 pages in length, short reports up to 10 pages.) Submission of an article must include one original and five copies of the manuscript, artwork, and figure captions. Authors should consult with the editor if there are problems in doing this. Upon acceptance, and following final editing, authors will be asked to provide the editor with a finalized draft on computer disk indicating type of computer and software used.

One cover sheet with author's name, address, phone number, title of the manuscript and a brief biographical statement should be included with the submission. Begin Endnotes, Bibliography, and the List of Figure Captions at the top of a page. All illustrations for publication must be labeled on the back with the figure number, author's name, and caption. Black and white photographs must be good quality 4x5 or 8x10 inch prints. The author is responsible for obtaining permission to reproduce all artwork. While the Society will exercise reasonable precautions in handling submissions, all manuscripts and artwork offered are the sole responsibility of the contributor.

Publication in *Dress* does not imply endorsement by the Costume Society of America of ideas or opinions expressed by the authors.

The Costume Society of America Regional Divisions

REGION I: New England and the Eastern Provinces
Connecticut, Maine, Massachusetts, Newfoundland, New Hampshire, Nova Scotia, Quebec, Rhode Island, Vermont, New Brunswick, Prince Edward Island

REGION II: Eastern
Delaware, Washington, D.C., Maryland, New Jersey, New York, Pennsylvania

REGION III: Midwest
Illinois, Indiana, Iowa, Michigan, Minnesota, Missouri, Ohio, Ontario, Wisconsin

REGION IV: Northern Mountains, Plains
Alberta, Idaho, Manitoba, Montana, Nebraska, North Dakota, Saskatchewan, South Dakota, Wyoming

REGION V: Western
Alaska, British Columbia, California, Hawaii, Nevada, Northwest Territories, Oregon, Washington, Yukon Territories

REGION VI: Southeastern
Alabama, Arkansas, Florida, Georgia, Kentucky, Louisiana, Mississippi, North Carolina, South Carolina, Tennessee, Virginia, West Virginia, Puerto Rico

REGION VII: Southwestern
Arizona, Colorado, Kansas, New Mexico, Oklahoma, Texas, Utah

REGION VIII: Abroad